Culture and Customs of Germany

Germany

Culture and Customs of Germany

ECKHARD BERNSTEIN

Culture and Customs of Europe

GREENWOOD PRESS
Westport, Connecticut • London

Library of Congress Cataloging-in-Publication Data

Bernstein, Eckhard.
    Culture and customs of Germany / Eckhard Bernstein.
        p. cm. — (Culture and customs of Europe)
    Includes bibliographical references and index.
    ISBN 0–313–32203–1 (alk. paper)
    1. Germany—Civilization—20th century. 2. Germany—Intellectual life—20th century.
3. Germany—Cultural policy—History—20th century. 4. Germany—Social life and customs—20th
century. I. Title. II. Series.
    DD290.26.B47 2004
    306'.0943'09045—dc22   2003055491

British Library Cataloguing in Publication Data is available.

Library of Congress Catalog Card Number: 2003055491
ISBN: 0–313–32203–1

First published in 2004

Greenwood Press, 88 Post Road West, Westport, CT 06881
An imprint of Greenwood Publishing Group, Inc.
www.greenwood.com

Printed in the United States of America

The paper used in this book complies with the
Permanent Paper Standard issued by the National
Information Standards Organization (Z39.48–1984).

10   9   8   7   6   5   4   3   2   1

To Jutta, naturally

Contents

Series Foreword

THE OLD WORLD and the New World have maintained a fluid exchange of people, ideas, innovations, and styles. Even though the United States became the de facto leader and economic superpower in the wake of a devastated Europe after World War II, Europe has remained for many the standard bearer of Western culture.

Millions of Americans can trace their ancestors to Europe. The United States as we know it was built on waves of European immigration, starting with the English who braved the seas to found the Jamestown Colony in 1607. Bosnian and Albanian immigrants are some of the latest new Americans.

In the Gilded Age of one of our great expatriates, the novelist Henry James, the Grand Tour of Europe was de rigueur for young American men of means, to prepare them for a life of refinement and taste. In a more recent democratic age, scores of American college students have Eurailed their way across Great Britain and the Continent, sampling the fabled capitals and bergs in a mad, great adventure, or have benefited from a semester abroad. For other American vacationers and culture vultures, Europe is the prime destination.

What is the New Europe post–Cold War, post–Berlin Wall in the new millennium? Even with the different languages, rhythms, and rituals, Europeans have much in common: they are largely well educated, prosperous, and worldly. They also have similar goals and face common threats and form alliances. With the advent of the European Union, the open borders, and the euro and considering globalization and the prospect of a homogenized Europe, an updated survey of the region is warranted.

Culture and Customs of Europe features individual volumes on the countries most studied and for which fresh information is in demand from students and other readers. The Series casts a wide net, inclusive of not only the expected countries, such as Spain, France, England, and Germany, but also countries such as Poland and Greece that lie outside Western Europe proper. Each volume is written by a country specialist, with intimate knowledge of the contemporary dynamics of a people and culture. Sustained narrative chapters cover the land, people, and brief history; religion; social customs; gender roles, family, and marriage; literature and media; performing arts and cinema; and art and architecture. The national character and ongoing popular traditions of each country are framed in an historical context and celebrated along with the latest trends and major cultural figures. A country map, chronology, glossary, and evocative photos enhance the text.

The historied and enlightened Europeans will continue to fascinate Americans. Our futures are strongly linked politically, economically, and culturally.

Preface

GERMANY is a land of contradictions. On the one hand, it is the country that produced some of the world's greatest musicians such as Bach, Beethoven, Brahms, and Wagner, as well as seminal philosophers like Kant, Hegel, Schopenhauer, and Nietzsche. It is also the country that gave birth to revolutionaries such as Karl Marx and Albert Einstein and eminent writers like Goethe and Schiller, Thomas Mann and Hermann Hesse, Günter Grass and Bertolt Brecht. This then is one side of Germany, the land of "Dichter und Denker" (poets and thinkers), as the French woman of letters Madame de Staël called it early in the nineteenth century. But there is also the other Germany, the country that between 1933 and 1945 surrendered itself to the ideology of National Socialism; the Germany that under Adolf Hitler engulfed the world in a devastating war and embarked on a murderous campaign against Europe's Jews, the Holocaust. To concentrate solely on Germany's magnificent cultural contributions and ignore the darker side of its history would present a wrong picture. But it would be equally incorrect to reduce 2,000 years of German history and culture to the 12 years of the Hitler dictatorship.

This book deals with the customs and culture of *modern* Germany, that is, the country that has emerged from the ruins of the Second World War and has developed into an affluent and stable democracy. Today it is firmly embedded in such international institutions as NATO, the United Nations, and the European Union; indeed, together with its erstwhile enemy, France, Germany has become the motor of European integration, creating, together with other European countries, this remarkable association of 25 states.

The book, however, is not concerned with governmental institutions and Germany's foreign and security policies, fascinating as these might be. Nor can the economy be discussed, the third largest in the world after the United States and Japan, and Germany's largely successful model of a "social market economy." As the title suggests, this book deals with the customs and culture of Germany. But even here painful choices had to be made. Because of space limitations, areas such as philosophy and technology, which, arguably, are part of a broader definition of culture, had to be omitted. For that reason, the substantial contributions of German philosophers such as Immanuel Kant, G. W. F. Hegel, Arthur Schopenhauer, and Friedrich Nietzsche cannot be discussed; nor is there space to explore the important inventions and discoveries of German scientists and engineers such as Wilhelm Röntgen, the discoverer of X-rays, Heinrich Hertz, the discoverer of radio waves, Karl Benz and Gottlieb Daimler, the builders of the first gas-powered car, Robert Koch, the discoverer of the tuberculosis bacillus, and Otto Hahn and Lisa Meitner, the discoverers of nuclear fission, to name only a few.

After a brief chapter on Germany's geography, population, and language, an overview of modern German history with its ruptures and continuities will set the stage for subsequent chapters on various aspects of Germany's culture. The emphasis is on *contemporary* Germany. But the present is always affected by the past. That is true for any country but especially for Germany, where the dozen years of the Third Reich still cast a long shadow. The story of modern culture will therefore always be told before the background of Germany's complex history.

The book attempts to go beyond the well-worn cliches and stereotypes, many of which have been shaped either by the Second World War and Holocaust or, alternatively, by a naive admiration for a Romantic Germany with its cuckoo clocks, castles, and beer-drinking Oktoberfest revelers. It tries to present a fair and accurate account of the remarkable cultural achievements of modern Germany.

I dedicate this book to Jutta Arend, my wife and companion of many years. Without her help and constructive criticism, the book would not have been possible.

Chronology

GERMANIC AND FRANKISH PERIOD

A.D. 9   Attempt by Romans to conquer Germanic tribes fails. Three Roman legions are defeated in Teutoburg Forest by Germanic tribes led by Hermann (Arminius). Romans limit themselves to colonize area west of the Rhine.

4th and 5th centuries   Germanic tribes overrun most of Roman Empire.

800   Charlemagne crowned emperor by pope.

814   Charlemagne dies. His empire breaks apart into an eastern and a western part.

843   Treaty of Verdun: Franks secede from Empire.

962–1806   Holy Roman Empire (patchwork of numerous temporal and ecclesiastical territories).

HIGH MIDDLE AGES

1024–1255   Salian dynasty.

1138–1254   Hohenstaufen dynasty. Frederick I (Barbarossa) leads empire to new flowering.

1348   Founding of first German university in Prague.

REFORMATION AND CONFESSIONAL WARS (1517–1648)

c. 1450   Invention of printing with movable types by Johann Guten-
               berg in Mainz.

1517   Martin Luther posts 95 theses against the sale of indulgences
               in Wittenberg. Beginning of Protestant Reformation.

1546–1547   War between Catholic and Protestant princes.

1555   Peace of Augsburg. Princes determine religion of their territo-
               ries.

1618–1648   Thirty Years' War devastates Germany.

THE TIME OF ABSOLUTISM (1648–1789)

1740–1786   Frederick the Great King of Prussia. Prussia emerges as a
               European power.

AGE OF FRENCH REVOLUTION

1789   Beginning of French Revolution.

1806–1807   Napoleon conquers large parts of Germany.

1814–1815   Wars of Liberation.

RESTORATION AND REVOLUTION (1815–1848)

1848   Revolutions in several German states. First German parlia-
               ment meets in Frankfurt. Failure to establish a united Ger-
               many.

IMPERIAL GERMANY (1871–1918)

1871   Foundation of the Second German Reich at Versailles, after
               defeat of France in Franco-Prussian War.

1871–1890   Otto von Bismarck in office as Chancellor of Reich.

1878   *Kulturkampf*: anti-Catholic campaign orchestrated by Bis-
               marck.

| 1878–1890 | Anti-Socialist laws against the Social Democratic Party. |
| 1914–1918 | First World War. |

THE WEIMAR REPUBLIC (1918–1933)

1918	November 9, Proclamation of Republic. End of monarchy.
1919	Failed communist uprising in Berlin led by Spartakus; Peace Treaty of Versailles.
1923	Hyperinflation leads to complete collapse of German currency.
1929	World economic crisis, beginning of mass unemployment.

THE THIRD REICH (1933–1945)

1933	January 30	Adolf Hitler appointed Chancellor.
	February	Burning of Reichstag in Berlin. Hitler suspends basic rights.
	April	Concentration camps established. Arrests of political opponents of Nazi regime.
1936		Olympic Games held in Berlin.
1938		*Reichkristallnacht:* Nationwide pogrom against synagogues and Jewish stores.
1939–1945		Second World War.
1945	April 30	Hitler commits suicide in Berlin Bunker.
	May 8	Unconditional surrender of German High Command; end of war.

POSTWAR ERA: DIVISION

1945–1949	Victorious allies divide Germany into four zones of occupation (American, British, Soviet, and French).
1949	Founding of Federal Republic of Germany (West Germany) and German Democratic Republic (East Germany).
1949–1963	Konrad Adenauer, first chancellor of West Germany.

1953   Uprising in East Germany.

1961   Berlin Wall built by East German government to stop mass
                defections to the west.

1969   Willy Brandt (SPD) becomes chancellor, becomes architect of
                the *Ostpolitik*.

1972   Basic Treaty between East and West Germany.

1982–1998   Helmut Kohl (CDU) becomes chancellor.

1989   November 9: Opening of the Berlin Wall.

UNITED GERMANY (1990–PRESENT)

1990   October 3: East and West Germany reunited.

1998   Gerhard Schröder elected chancellor of a Red-Green coali-
                tion.

2002   Euro replaces the deutsche mark as legal tender in Germany.

2003   Tensions with the United States over Iraq policies.

1

Geography, Population, Language

GEOGRAPHY

Germany lies at the very heart of Europe. Surrounded by nine neighbors, it shares borders with more nations than any other country in Europe: in the north it is bordered by Denmark, in the east by Poland and the Czech Republic, in the south by Austria and Switzerland, and in the west by France, Luxembourg, Belgium, and the Netherlands. Unlike other European countries, such as Italy, Spain, and the United Kingdom, Germany has few natural borders. Only the North and Baltic Seas in the north and a stretch of the Rhine in the south-west corner of Germany serve as natural boundaries.

With its 137,816 square miles (356,959 square kilometers), Germany is a large country by European standards—the third largest in the European Union. Compared with the United States, however, it is a moderately sized country. Slightly smaller than the state of Montana, it could easily fit 20 times in the area of the continental United States.

Packed into this relatively small country is an extraordinary variety of landscapes. Geographers usually divide Germany into four distinct areas: in the north the North German Plains stretch from the Dutch border in the west to the Polish border in the east. These plains are flat, dotted with small lakes, marshes, heaths, and toward the east, undulating hills. South of that wide belt of flat lands, the Central Mountain Range (*Mittelgebirge*) rises, forming a complicated patchwork of mountains, rivers, and valleys extending from the Rhenish Slate Mountains in the west to the Thuringian and Bavarian Forests in the east. The Alpine Foothills (*Voralpen*) south of the *Mittelgebirge* form a triangle bordered by the Danube in the north, Lake Constance in the west, and the city of Passau in the east. In the very south of Germany, finally, a relatively small section of the Alps forms part of Germany. It is a picture postcard landscape of towering mountains—Germany's highest mountain, die Zugspitze, at 9,718 feet (2,963 meters) is there—onion-domed churches, and lush-green meadows.

All of Germany's rivers flow northwards, except the Danube, which drains in an easterly direction. Among them the majestic Rhine is not only Europe's busiest waterway but also has the reputation of being Germany's most romantic river. Especially, the so-called Middle Rhine between Bingen and Bonn, with its steep hills, numerous castles or castle ruins, and picturesque villages, is a favorite tourist destination.

With its 82 million inhabitants in an area smaller than Montana—that state has a mere 900,000 inhabitants—Germany is a very densely populated country, the third most densely populated one in Europe after the Netherlands and Belgium.[1] Statistically speaking, 589 people jostle each other on every square mile compared with 70 in the United States.[2] Driving through Germany by car or train, however, visitors might ask themselves where do all these people live because what one sees are meadows, fields, green hills, and forests. To be sure, there are fairly large metropolitan areas around Berlin, Hamburg, Cologne, Frankfurt, Munich, and Stuttgart. But surprisingly, this highly industrialized country, with the world's third largest economy, has managed to retain much of its natural environment: 30 percent of Germany is forests, 55 percent of the land is used for crops, meadows, and pasture, and only 14 percent is built up.[3]

In general, Germans are more environmentally conscious than Americans. You can find evidence of this *Umweltbewusstsein* (environmental consciousness) everywhere. For instance, at many street corners, massive color-coded containers are located for different-colored bottles. In a country where recycling is a top priority, separation of waste into paper, organic matter, metal, and so on has become a science. Another sign for a keener concern for a clean environment is that cars are banned from most historic city centers. Instead, thousands of miles of bicycle paths have been built. Cars themselves have become much more fuel efficient than in America. The result of all these measures and many others is that the Germans consume about half of the energy that America does and produces less than half of the annual waste[4] without loss of the high standard of living they enjoy. No wonder that the Green Party was the first party in any industrialized nation to win parliamentary seats. At present it forms a coalition government with the Social Democrats (SPD).

Climate

Germany lies in the same latitude as Northern Maine and Washington State; as a matter of fact, four-fifths of Germany lies north of the 49th parallel that divides the United States and Canada. In spite of its northern location, Germany has a fairly temperate climate. Rarely does it get bitingly cold in the winter or swelteringly hot in the summer, although rain is always to be expected, even in July. Within Germany there are great variations of climate. Whereas the Moselle and Rhine valleys have a relatively mild climate, allowing the growth of vine, the southern and eastern parts as well as the higher elevations have a more continental climate with colder winters. The microclimate of the island of Mainau in Lake Constance even permits the growth of palm trees and lemons.

Destination Germany

Because of its natural beauty, rich cultural and historical landmarks, excellent infrastructure, and central location, Germany has always been a tourist country. But while the romantic Rhine valley, the cobblestoned Old Town (*Altstadt*) of Heidelberg, and the fairytale castles of Ludwig II of Bavaria have for centuries attracted visitors from other countries, Germany has much more to offer, as the growing popularity of Germany as a tourist

The picturesque marketplace of Hildesheim. Photo by Eckhard Bernstein.

destination, by foreigners and Germans alike, shows. In 2000, for instance, 18 million foreigners visited Germany as tourists, while one-third of all Germans spent their vacations in one of the numerous vacation regions of their own country.[5]

There are many reasons why Germany is attractive to vacationers: first, Germany boasts a large number of historic cities, each with its own unique past. There is, for instance, 2,000-year-old Trier, Germany's oldest city, with its well-preserved Roman buildings, gigantic Roman city gate, the Porta Nigra, and amphitheater; there are any number of smaller well-preserved medieval cities like Rothenburg ob der Tauber, Nördlingen, and Dinkelsbühl; there are Baroque jewels like Dresden, which has been rebuilt after the devastating bombing in 1945; there is the small town of Weimar, home of German literary classicism, or modern cities like Frankfurt, Cologne, Hamburg, or Berlin with their vibrant cultural and economic life. Secondly, having been settled for thousands of years, Germany has what in German is called a *Kulturlandschaft* (a cultural landscape), that is, on every square mile there are witnesses of stone of the Germanic, Roman, and Christian pasts. This rich cultural heritage is acknowledged by the Unesco. No fewer than 29 sites in Germany are included in the Unesco World Heritage Sites (see Table 1.1). Germany offers thousands of churches, ranging from the mighty Romanesque cathedrals in Speyer, Worms, and Mainz and the towering Gothic cathedrals in Cologne, Ulm, and Freiburg to simple Romanesque, Baroque, and Rococo churches in small villages. It also offers monasteries galore, either still in use or converted into museums. There are also hundreds of castles of all ages, each with its own history. Some of them have been turned into modern hotels, and 43 of them have been transformed into youth hostels. And it is not only Neuschwanstein, the castle that served as a model for Disneyland's Magic Kingdom and the three other castles that King Ludwig II of Bavaria had built in the nineteenth century, but hundreds of others from various periods that form part of Germany's rich patrimony. There is, for instance, the Wartburg perched high on a mountain in the Thuringian Forest, where the reformer Martin Luther began the Herculean task of translating the Bible into German. More than 200 years later, King Frederick the Great of Prussia relaxed from his royal duties in the Rococo castle Sanssouci near Berlin, philosophizing with the Frenchman Voltaire and entertaining his friends with flute concertos. But Germany does not only have numerous churches, monasteries, and castles but also has retained a remarkable amount of its natural environment—and that is the third reason why visitors choose Germany as a vacation land. Germany offers the vacationer an array of extremely diverse landscapes, ranging from the windswept Frisian islands in the north,

Table 1.1 Unesco World Heritage Sites in Germany

- Aachen Cathedral
- Speyer Cathedral
- Würzburg Residence with Court Gardens
- Pilgrimage Church at Wies
- The Castles of Augustusburg and Falkenlust at Brühl
- St. Mary's Cathedral and St. Michael Church in Hildesheim
- Roman Monuments, Cathedral St. Peter, Church of Our Lady at Trier
- Hanseatic City of Lübeck
- Palaces and Parks of Potsdam
- Abbey and Altenmünster of Lorsch
- Mines of Rammelsberg and Historic Town of Goslar
- Town of Bamberg
- Maulbronn Monastery
- Collegiate Church, Castle and Old Town of Quedlinburg
- Völklingen Ironworks
- Messel Pit Fossil Site
- Cologne Cathedral
- Bauhaus and its Sites in Weimar and Dessau
- Luther Memorials in Eisleben and Wittenberg
- Classical Weimar
- Wartburg Castle
- Museumsinsel Berlin
- Garden Kingdom of Deassau Wörlitz
- Monastic Island of Reichenau
- The Zollverein Coal Mine Industrial Complex in Essen
- Upper Middle Rhine Valley
- Historic Centers of Stralsund and Wismar

Source: http://whc.unesco/whc/pages/sites/maplist/euramer.htm.

the sunny valleys of the Moselle and Rhine in the west, the mist-shrouded mountains of the Harz Mountains and the bizarre sandstone formations of the Elbsandsteingebirge in the east, to the hiker's paradises of the Black Forest and the Alps in the south.

As avid sport enthusiasts, Germans have developed an excellent infrastructure of bicycle paths (about 25,000 miles) and thousands of miles of hiking trails. Fourthly, for those interested in music, theater, and art, Germany offers 180 state-supported theaters, 80 opera houses, 141 professional symphony orchestras, and more than 5,000 museums (see chapters 8 and 9). Finally, Germany is well-known as a venue for international fairs and exhibitions. Each year hundreds of thousands of exhibitors and millions of visitors flock to one of the 180 international fairs to present and look at products and services.[6] Among them, the Centrum der Büro- und Informations Technik (CeBIT [Center for Office and Information Technology]), the world's largest computer fair, and the Frankfurt Book Fair, again the world's largest one in its sector, are perhaps the two most famous ones. So established is Germany's tradition of fairs and exhibitions that two-thirds of all fairs in the world are held in Germany.

THE POPULATION

With approximately 82 million inhabitants, Germany is the second most populous country in Europe. Only Russia has a greater population. Not all of these 82 million, however, are German citizens. As a matter of fact, with 7.3 million foreigners living in the Federal Republic, Germany has one of the largest foreign populations in Europe. And the Germans themselves are far from being a homogeneous group. On the contrary, Germany consists of a variety of distinct regions, and because its political unification occurred late in comparison with other nations—in 1871 under the direction of Otto von Bismarck—regions and people living in them have retained much of their unique characteristic traits. The Rhinelanders, for instance, having a sunny disposition, are said to enjoy life more than others; Swabians have the reputation of being hardworking, they are born tinkerers, ingenious and parsimonious; Bavarians have the image of being fun-loving and beer-guzzling; Thuringians and Saxons, on the other hand, are said to be music-loving, and they have Bach, Handel, Schumann, and Wagner to prove it; the Frisians are supposed to be taciturn; Hamburgers are considered Anglophiles and cosmopolitan; and Berliners are famed for their quick wit. Although generalizations about large groups of people, whether from a country or a region, are always problematic if not downright dangerous, there is always some small core of truth to them. But no matter whether these stereotypes are true or not, most Germans feel a strong attachment to the *Heimat* (home region) they grow up in and, when asked where they come from, will frequently answer "from Bavaria" or "from Saxony" rather than "from Germany." Among the Germans no other group is prouder of its regional identity than the Bavarians. Franz Xaver Kroetz, Germany's most successful playwright, famously declared: "I am not a German; I am a Bavarian." Upon entering Germany from Switzerland or Austria, visitors are greeted by a large sign "Willkommen im Freistaat Bayern" (Welcome to the Free State of Bavaria). A much smaller sign underneath will tell you that you are about to step onto the territory of the Federal Republic of Germany.

East and West Germans

These traditional regional differences have been overshadowed by another divide, that between East and West Germans, following the reunification of the former communist East Germany and the democratic West Germany in 1990. Forcefully separated by a wall and strong border fortifications and exposed for more than 40 years to diametrically opposed ideological, political, and social systems, the citizens of the two German states had developed their own identities. These differences seemed to evaporate when in November 1989 the Berlin Wall came down and East Germans went into the streets chanting "Wir sind ein Volk!" (We are one people!). After the remarkably speedy reunification of Germany in 1990, however, this spirit of euphoria and brotherhood soon disappeared, and differences broke out as soon as the mind-boggling difficulties and costs of the reunification became obvious. Resentments on both sides emerged. The East Germans, or *Ossis,* viewed the West Germans, or *Wessis,* who were taking over their country as arrogant know-alls (*Besserwessies*), while the West Germans looked down on their East German brothers and sisters often as lazy and stubborn and resented the hefty "solidarity tax" that was imposed on top of their income tax to pay for the reconstruction of the East German economy and infrastructure. The physical Berlin Wall had been replaced by a "wall in the head." In the meantime, almost 15 years after the reunification of the East-West divide, this mutual resentment is slowly disappearing, as East and West Germans are getting to know each other better, and many of their prejudices are being revised through personal encounters and cooperation.

Ethnic Minorities

Within the boundaries of the Federal Republic live a number of indigenous ethnic minorities that, though assimilated into the German surroundings, have retained their language and cultural distinctness. Among them the Sorbs, or Sorbians as they are sometimes called,[7] are the largest with 120,000 members.[8] They are a Slavic minority that has lived since the sixth century in what is now the eastern part of Brandenburg and Saxony. They have their own newspapers, literature, television stations, and folk festivals. Elementary and middle schools are bilingual. Recognizing their importance for a culturally diverse country, the German government financially supports their efforts to retain their identity. The same is true for the Danish minority in northern Schleswig-Holstein (around 60,000) and the Frisian minority in western Schleswig-Holstein (10,000).

Germany: A Land of Immigrants?

Distinct from these indigenous minorities who have lived in Germany for centuries are the minorities created by the relatively recent influx of foreigners. As of the beginning of this century, 9 percent of the population, or 7.3 million, were foreigners.[9] Germany has become, whether the Germans like it or not, a *Einwanderungsland* (land of immigrants). And since these immigrants tend to settle in large cities, the proportion of foreigners in cities tends to be high: in Frankfurt every fourth inhabitant is a foreigner; in Stuttgart every third; Hamburg has more mosques than any other city in Europe; and in some schools in metropolitan areas German children are a distinct minority.[10]

The arrival of foreigners is a relatively new phenomenon, profoundly changing Germany from a relatively homogeneous society a mere four or five decades ago to an ethnically diverse country. The foreigners are composed of three distinct groups: the "guest laborers" (*Gastarbeiter*), the asylum seekers, and the ethnic Germans. In the mid-1950s the German government began recruiting laborers, mostly from Mediterranean countries, to counter an acute labor shortage. Though the recruitment stopped in the early 1970s, when the German labor market was saturated, millions of these *Gastarbeiter* and their families have settled in Germany. The largest group, with about 2 million, are Turks, followed by citizens of former Yugoslavia, Italy, and Greece. The second group of foreigners are the so-called asylum seekers (*Asylbewerber*). Aware that many of its own citizens sought, found, or were denied political asylum by other countries during the Third Reich, West Germany inserted into its 1949 constitution an ultraliberal asylum provision, one of the most generous in the world. The wave of asylum seekers reached record levels in the early 1990s. In 1992 alone, 440,000 men and women sought asylum in Germany, placing a tremendous burden on the finances of the Federal Republic because asylum seekers were fed, housed, and supported. A more stringent law passed in 1992 considerably reduced the number of applicants in subsequent years, but with an annual average of 70,000 still represents a sizable number. The third group that have entered Germany in large numbers in the last decades are ethnic Germans. According to a law going back to 1913, Germany considers Germans those who are of German descent and not necessarily those sons and daughters of immigrants who live and sometimes have lived for a long time in Germany. Thus anybody whose ancestors emigrated from Germany is considered a German. This has led to the paradoxical situation that children of, let us say, a Turkish *Gastarbeiter* who have been born, educated, and socialized in Germany and speak with impeccable Swabian accents, are not considered German, while somebody from Kazakhstan whose ancestors emigrated 200 years ago and who has only a smattering of German, is regarded a German and immediately receives German citizenship. Following the collapse of communism in Eastern Europe and the Soviet Union, hundreds of thousands of these ethnic Germans have remembered their German heritage and, taking advantage of the German law, have come to the country of their ancestors. Because immediately upon their arrival they receive financial and social assistance as well as training, they represent a considerable burden on the German taxpayer. At the height of this immigration in the early 1990s, annually 400,000 *Spätaussiedler* (late resettlers) arrived in Germany. Since then the law has been tightened and the number has been limited to 200,000 per year. Social integration has been much more difficult than anticipated.

THE LANGUAGE

Germany's official language is German. It is also spoken in Austria, Switzerland, Liechtenstein, Luxembourg, the eastern parts of Belgium, and the northern parts of Italy in Southern Tyrolia. Being spoken by approximately 100 million, it is the most widely spoken language in the European Union.

German consists of a variety of dialects reflecting the variety of historical regions. A Frisian fisherman speaking in his native *Plattdeutsch* (German spoken in the Flat [platt] Lands) will hardly understand a Bavarian farmer and vice versa. And *Schwyzerdütsch,* spoken by approximately 65 percent of the Swiss population, is incomprehensible to most Germans no matter where they come from. This does not mean that Germans are unable to communicate with each other. Over the centuries a standardized language has evolved that is used in writing and speaking by all educated Germans; it is called *Hochdeutsch,* a term that is derived from the fact that it was spoken in the High (upper = *hoch*) lands of Germany. Although radio and television have contributed significantly toward a standardization of spoken German, there are very few Germans whose German is not colored by a regional dialect. In addition, in recent decades, a modest revival of dialects has taken place reflecting the trend toward regional loyalty.

As a language, German belongs to what linguists call the Indo-European group of languages, that is, languages spoken in the huge land mass stretching from India to western Ireland. All these languages are more or less related. Within that vast extended family, English and German are not only cousins but siblings because they both belong to the Germanic branch, together with Dutch, Danish, Swedish, Norwegian, Afrikaans, and Yiddish. As a matter of fact, it can be claimed that English is derived from German because two German tribes, the Angles and Saxons, sailed from northern

Germany circa A.D. 400 to England where they settled on the British Isles. For that reason there are thousands of cognates in English and German whose common heritage is obvious. A few examples: *haus*—house; *apfel*—apple; *ring*—ring; *gras*—grass; *katze*—cat; *sonne*—sun; *freund*—friend; *haar*—hair; *schule*—school. Add to these the thousands of words that are derived from Latin, such as *situation, kondition, studieren* (to study), *orientierung* (orientation), and it becomes clear that any English speaker has a considerable head start when learning German. Nor is the pronunciation of German very difficult. Being largely a phonetic language, it is spoken the way it is written. That, then, is the good news. The not-so-good news for foreigners learning German is the German grammar. As one critic observed: "English and Danish have shorn grammar to a minimum; German has complicated it."[11] For example, whereas English has one definite article, *the*, German has eight for the three genders, masculine, feminine, and neuter, and various cases: *der, die, das, dem, den, deren, dessen, denen,* used depending on the case and gender. A further complication is that adjectives are declined, meaning that they take on different endings depending on the case and gender and whether they are preceded by a definite, indefinite, or no article at all. For learners of German whose native language, such as English, is less inflected, this presents countless headaches, prompting American humorist Mark Twain to remark that he would rather decline two drinks than one German adjective.[12]

In spite of these apparent difficulties, millions of people from all over the world study German. They learn it because of its usefulness in commerce, its inherent beauty and its ability to open doors to a magnificent literature and to an unmatched array of philosophers. In eastern Europe alone, 12 million students learn German; 68 percent of all Japanese students study German and altogether there are about 20 million people in the world who are currently learning German as a foreign language.[13] Although German, which at the beginning of the twentieth century was the universal language of science, has long been replaced by English as the lingua franca of science, 40 percent of scientists in the United States still recommend the study of German. In Poland and Hungary the figure is over 70 percent. German is also the most commonly used language on the Internet after English and is still in second place in the field of scholarly publications.

The richness of German is possibly due to two facts: first, its remarkable ability to constantly coin new words to denote new ideas and phenomena and, second, its hospitality toward the import of words from other languages. In the sixteenth century, for instance, thousands of Latin words entered German; the eighteenth century saw the import of a large number of French words; and the present, since the end of the Second World War, has witnessed the influx of English words. English has permeated the German language in all areas, none more so than in advertising, especially in commercials targeted at younger audiences, since English is associated with youth, progress, and modernity. In some cases the preponderance of English is so pronounced that it has evolved into the horrible mixture of English and German, called "Denglish" (Deutsch and English). In their enthusiasm for English, the Germans occasionally go so far as to invent English-sounding words that either do not exist in English or that have an entirely different meanings in the original language. A cell or mobile phone, for instance, is called "ein Handy"; young people in their twenties are referred to as "Twens," in analogy to "teens"; a talk show will be hosted by "ein Talkmaster" or "eine Talkmasterin," the "-in" being the female form.

In contrast to the deluge of English words that have flooded contemporary German, German's contribution to English is relatively modest, but apparently greater than that of many other languages, as the British author Richard Hill observes, "It is extraordinary how much the language [i.e., German] has contributed to the English, French and other vocabularies of philosophy and perception, through lack of suitable alternatives."[14] Here are a few examples: In philosophy we talk about *weltanschaung* (a world view),[15] *zeitgeist* (the spirit of the age), and *weltschmerz* (world weariness); in literature *bildungsroman* (novel describing personal development), *leitmotif* (a recurring theme), *sturm und drang* (storm and stress; late 18th century Romantic style), and *urtext* (original text) have been adopted by educated English speakers; in psychology *angst* (inner fear or torment), *gestalt* (the shape or pattern of something), and *schadenfreude* (the malicious pleasure in the misfortune of others) have found a place in the specialists' vocabulary; in politics *blitzkrieg* (a quick, lightning war), *lebensraum* (living space), and *realpolitik* (real-life, often cynical politics) are often used. There are of course also numerous terms that have to do with food, such as *schnitzel, sauerkraut, pretzel, frankfurter, hamburger, apple strudel, weiss beer,* and *bock beer.* And all of us began our education by going to the *kindergarten,* another German import.

NOTES

1. Eric Solsten, ed., *Germany. A Country Guide* (Washington, D.C.: Library of Congress, 1996), 155.

2. Federal Republic of Germany, ed., *Questions and Answers* (New York: German Information Center, 1996), 4.

3. All figures according to Solsten, *Germany. A Country Guide,* 135, and Federal Republic of Germany, *Questions and Answers,* 1f.

4. Richard Lord, *Culture Shock. A Guide to Customs and Etiquette. Germany* (Portland, Ore.: Graphic Arts Center Publishing Co., 1999), 41, 43.

5. Bodo Harenberg, *Aktuell 2002* (Dortmund: Harenberg Lexikon Verlag, 2001), 218.

6. The Federal Government of Germany, *Facts about Germany* (Frankfurt am Main: Societäts-Verlag, 2000), 357.

7. For instance, Gregory H. Wolf. "The Sorbians: A Slavic Minority in Germany," *German Life* (August/September 2002): 25–27.

8. According to Solsten, *Germany. A Country Guide,* 162.

9. Heinz P. Lohfeldt, ed., *Spiegel-Almanach 2002* (Hamburg: SPIEGEL-Buchverlag, 2001), 90; Jürgen Gros and Manuela Glaab, *Faktenlexikon Deutschland. Geschichte, Gesellschaft, Politik, Wirtschaft, Kultur* (Munich: Heyne, 1999), 41.

10. *Eyewitness Travel Guides. Germany* (London, et al.: Dorling Kindersley Publishing, 2001), 15.

11. Jethro Bithell, *Germany. A Companion to German Studies* (London: Methuen & Co., 1955), 18.

12. In Charles Neider, ed., *The Comic Mark Twain Reader* (Garden City, New York: Doubleday & Co., 1977), 282.

13. All these and the following figures according to two brochures distributed by the Goethe Institute, the German organization whose mission it is to cultivate German. *Go Global.... Select German* and *Why German is 4U* (n.d.).

14. Richard Hill, *We Europeans* (Brussels: Europublications, 1992), 79.

15. All definitions are taken from Ben Schott, *Schott's Original Miscellany* (London: Bloomsbury, 2002), 94.

2

Modern German History: Ruptures and Continuities

FOR THOSE WHO EXPERIENCED it personally or witnessed it on television, November 9, 1989, is forever etched in their memories: the day when the Berlin Wall, that infamous structure that for almost 30 years separated East from West Berlin, was opened. Only if one remembers the pain and anguish the Wall had inflicted on millions of people, does one understand the indescribable joy of the Berliners. Tears of joy flowed freely. The small, smoke-belching East German cars, the two-stroke Trabants, were welcomed in the west like heroes. Total strangers embraced each other; champagne flowed. In front of Berlin's Brandenburger Gate, young people danced on the Wall. On that day, one of the most memorable days in German postwar history, Walter Momper, West Berlin's mayor, told a large crowd of West and East Berliners: "Today the Germans are the happiest people on earth!" The unthinkable had happened. The Wall, meant to stand for another 100 years, as Erich Honecker, the powerful leader of Communist East Germany at that time, had warned as late as June 1989, had crumbled.

The fall of the Berlin Wall and the subsequent unification of East and West Germany a year later represent the "happy ending" to a century that was marked by two bloody wars, the short-lived experiment of the Weimar Republic, the 12 years of the Nazi dictatorship, and the painful separation of Germany into a democratic West Germany and a communist East Germany.

The following sketch of modern German history is meant to provide a context for subsequent discussions of various aspects of German culture. Culture does not develop in a vacuum but is profoundly shaped by historical forces. This is especially true for Germany where the state always played a much larger role as a patron of the arts than in the Anglo-Saxon countries.

Political events had therefore a greater impact on cultural institutions than elsewhere. In addition, for many German artists the turbulent history of their country, especially the 12 years of the Nazi dictatorship, remains an obsessive preoccupation in their works.

As a nation, Germany is a young country; younger than France, England, and the United States. It was only in 1871 when, for the first time in its history, a unified German national state was established. To be sure, for more than 800 centuries, from 962–1806, the Holy Roman Empire of the German Nation had existed in central Europe, but this political entity lacked any internal cohesion despite its impressive name. Although the emperor was the titular head, his power was limited. There was no imperial army, no central administration, and no system of tax collection. Nor was there any capital. Although located in the center of Europe, the empire itself lacked a center. The German king was elected in Frankfurt am Main, and crowned in Aachen; his imperial regalia, scepter and crown, were kept in Nuremberg; and the permanent assembly of the representatives of the various members convened in Regensburg. In reality, as the French philosopher Voltaire is reputed to have said, this unwieldy realm in the center of Europe was neither Holy nor Roman nor an Empire. Instead it was a loose association of hundreds of principalities, dukedoms, imperial cities, secular and ecclesiastical territories.

In this highly fragmented political entity (a map of which resembled a colorful American quilt), the real power had shifted to the territorial princes who jealously saw to it that their influence remained undiminished. Culturally, this lack of a central authority proved more a boon than a liability. Because the princes competed with each other not only politically but also culturally, a number of centers of art emerged, giving Germany the literary and cultural diversity that a French observer at the beginning of the nineteenth century half-admiringly called "sweet anarchy."[1] And even today, after more than 130 years as a unified nation state, the former historical fragmentation is reflected in its federal structure and the rich variety of cultural centers. Unlike France and Great Britain, where cultural activities tend to be concentrated in their capitals, Paris and London, Germany has Munich, Düsseldorf, Stuttgart, Hamburg, Dresden, Hanover, and Cologne in addition to Berlin—each with a thriving cultural scene.

The Holy Roman Empire ended in 1806 and for 65 years Germany consisted of 37 separate and distinct territories. An attempt in 1848 to establish a German national state failed and Germany as a national unit came about only thanks to the diplomatic skill of Otto von Bismarck, since 1862 prime minister of Prussia, the most powerful state in German lands. Starting with that important date, modern German history can be divided into five distinct periods, each of them representing a break with the previous period:

- Imperial Germany (1871–1918)
- The Weimar Republic (1919–1933)
- The Third Reich (1933–1945)
- The Two German States (1949–1990)
- Reunited Germany (1990–present)

IMPERIAL GERMANY (1871–1918)

For the first 20 years, imperial Germany was dominated by Otto von Bismarck, chancellor of the German Reich. In his domestic policies he made serious errors. His fight against the Catholic Church, for example, the so-called *Kulturkampf*, as well as his neurotic persecution of the Socialists were misguided struggles. In both cases, the opponents came out strengthened rather than weakened. These errors, however, are compensated by his progressive social policies, resulting in real accomplishments by any measure, no matter whether they were inspired by humanitarian motives or intended to cut the ground from under the feet of the Socialists. These measures gave Germany the most advanced social welfare system in Europe. Autocratic and controversial in his domestic policies, Bismarck was a master diplomat in foreign affairs. With consummate skill he forged an elaborate system of alliances, while assuring Germany's neighbors that it was a "satiated" nation without any expansionist ambitions in Europe. This only changed with the ascension to the throne of Wilhelm II, the grandson of Wilhelm I, the first emperor. Not satisfied to be in the shadow of Bismarck, he assumed an increasingly important role and in the process destroyed the finely woven net of alliances of the chancellor. While his ambitious navy-building program angered England, which concluded a treaty with France, Wilhelm also failed to renew the Reinsurance Treaty with Russia, so that on the eve of the First World War, Germany's only ally was the Austrian-Hungarian double-monarchy. Bismarck's nightmare of Germany's encirclement had become true.

The First World War (1914–1918)

On June 28, 1914, the Archduke of Austria, Franz Ferdinand, was assassinated by a Serbian nationalist in Sarajevo. How this event sparked a world-wide conflict that killed millions of soldiers and obliterated four empires (the German, Austrian-Hungarian, Russian, and Ottoman empires) will be discussed forever by historians, as will be the question of the responsibility for the outbreak of that war. The war pitted France, England, and Russia on the one hand against Germany, Austria-Hungary, and the Ottoman Empire on the other. For Germany it meant a two-front war, in the east and the west. In the west Germany invaded France by violating Belgium's neutrality, which brought England into the war. German troops advanced quickly toward Paris until the German offensive was brought to a halt on the river Marne. Henceforth, for four years, the war in the west bogged down and was fought in the trenches where bitter and fierce battles were fought over yards. Millions died. In the east, meanwhile, the central powers were more successful so that Russia, by 1917, shaken by the Russian Revolution, sought and obtained an armistice. With the entry of the United States in 1917, the scales were clearly tipped in the allies' favor. Outflanked and outgunned in the field, threatened at home by a sailors' mutiny that had evolved into revolutionary uprisings in major German cities, the supreme command of the German army sought an armistice, which was concluded on November 11, 1918, a day still celebrated in the United States as Veterans Day. Two days earlier, the emperor had abdicated and fled to neutral Holland and a democratic republic had been proclaimed.

THE WEIMAR REPUBLIC (1918–1933)

While the war with the external enemy was thus brought to a halt, fighting continued in Germany itself, especially in Berlin where communists, well-supplied with money from the Soviet embassy, fought against government troops. This state of civil war was one of the reasons why the small central German town of Weimar and not Berlin was chosen as the seat of the Constituent Assembly, whose main task was to draft a constitution. Yet there was another reason for the choice of Weimar: at the beginning of the nineteenth century, the two major German poets Johann Wolfgang von Goethe and Friedrich von Schiller had turned this provincial town into a great cultural center. And it was this period of a better, humanistic Germany, the country of the "poets and thinkers," that the well-intentioned politicians wanted to evoke—after the Germany of an aggressive militarism had led to the disastrous war. Although the Constituent Assembly returned to Berlin in the spring of 1919, once the civil war had been ended, the name "Weimar Republic" remained and is now used to denote the time between the end of the First World War and the appointment of Adolf Hitler as chancellor in January 1933.

For the first time in their history, Germans enjoyed a democracy with an excellent constitution, modeled on the constitutions of West European countries and the United States. It granted, among other basic rights, for the first time full suffrage to women, one year before the United Sates extended the same privilege to them. But instead of embracing this new democracy, Germans remained skeptical and the new republic remained an unloved state, lacked broad support, and eventually died because of that lack of backing. Responsible for that were primarily two events: the Treaty of Versailles and the hyperinflation of 1923.

The Treaty of Versailles was not only harsh but also unnecessarily punitive. Forgotten were U.S. President Woodrow Wilson's statement contained in his Fourteen Points that "open covenants should be openly arrived." The Germans were not admitted to the negotiations. Forgotten was another demand by Wilson, namely the right of self-determination, at least as far as the Germans and Austrians were concerned. The latter were explicitly forbidden to join the German Reich, as they wanted. Sudeten Germans were integrated into the newly created Czechoslovakia, against their will. Large areas in the east and west, approximately one-sixth of the area of the former Reich, were given to Poland and France. Germany also lost all its colonies.

Since the chief aim of the allies was to crush German militarism, the once mighty army was reduced to 100,000 men, the navy to 15,000. Germany was further prohibited from having an air force, heavy artillery, and tanks. Huge amounts of reparations—in 1920 the Allied Reparations Commissions set the amount at 132 billion gold mark to be paid until 1950 to France and Belgium—were imposed. Although a large majority of the Germans rejected the treaty, the Social-Democratic-led government signed it—a painful but responsible act in view of the alternatives—threat of renewed bloodshed and blockade, serious unrest, communist revolutions, and further annexations.

The second event that undermined the foundations of German society and their trust in the new republic was the crippling hyperinflation of 1923. Between January 1923 and November of that same year, the value of the German currency, the mark, dropped so precipitously that a loaf of bread that had cost less than a mark in 1918, sold for 201 trillion marks in November of 1923. The effect on the average German was devastating. Pensions, annuities, and government bonds were wiped out. Savings accounts became worthless overnight. Especially the middle class, which stood for stability and hard work, was hard hit. As the American historian Henry Cord Meyer observed: "Thus the nascent German Republic came to life as an economic cripple and with the psychologically deforming birth scar of the Versailles treaty."[2]

After the stabilization of the currency, relative stability returned to German politics. Considerable reductions in reparations were negotiated. With the signing of treaties with its former enemies and its admission to the League of Nations, the precursor organization of the United Nations, Germany's international isolation ended. However, with the stock market crash of October 1929, the so-called golden twenties, the time between 1924 and 1929 came to a sudden halt. Although the Great Depression was worldwide, it especially affected Germany because the large American loans pumped into the country were hastily withdrawn or not renewed. By 1932 the number of unemployed jumped to six million, or 44 percent of the workforce. The constitutional parties, that is, those parties who believed in the Weimar constitution, proved unable to cope with this crisis. In this situation it was the extremist parties on the left and the right, with their promises of radical solutions, that showed huge electoral gains. In the parliamentary elections of November 1932, the communists received 5.9 million votes. But the real winners were the National Socialists led by Adolf Hitler. Under his leadership they jumped from a few hundred thousand votes in 1928 to 11.9 million. Exploiting the bitterness of the Germans against the Treaty of Versailles and the reparations, denouncing the so-called November criminals, that is those Social Democratic politicians who had signed the Treaty of Versailles, and playing on fears of communism, anti-Semitism, and anticapitalism depending on his audience, Hitler presented himself as the last hope for Germany to lead his country out of its misery, promising not only work but also law and order and liberation from the hated "Weimar system," as the Nazis contemptuously called the Weimar Republic.

THE THIRD REICH (1933–1945)

On January 30, 1933, Adolf Hitler was appointed chancellor by the aging president of the republic, Paul von Hindenburg. The "seizure of power" (*Machtergreifung*) was celebrated by jubilant crowds and endless torchlight parades. Within a few months of Hitler's appointment, Germany was transformed from a parliamentary democracy to a one-party dictatorship. Using the Reichstag fire on February 27, for which he blamed the Communists, as a pretext to suspend most of the basic rights, he began a campaign of persecution against Social Democrats and Communists, his principal domestic enemies. Special concentration camps were established as early as February 1933. After his party won 43.9 percent of the votes in the last free elections on March 5, Hitler pushed through parliament the so-called Enabling Act (*Ermächtigungsgesetz*), which allowed him to govern without parliament. Political parties were either banned or dissolved themselves; political opponents and Jews were dismissed from their civil service jobs. Most youth organizations were merged into the Hitler Youth. In the following years, Hitler systematically and ruthlessly consolidated his power. In 1934, for instance, he combined the functions of the president and chancellor in his person and called himself "Führer." The Third Reich (*Reich* = empire), so called because it followed the Holy Roman Empire and the Empire of Bismarck and Wilhelm, was firmly established.

But the Third Reich was not solely based on terror. It sought and won the approval of large segments of the German population. Many measures taken by the National Socialists up to 1938 met with broad public approval. Hitler had ended the chaos of the Weimar Republic with its constant street fights between Communists and his own followers. Most Germans, even those not sympathetic to the Nazis, shared his rejection of the Treaty of Versailles, which he systematically repealed. Few objected to the persecution of Communists.

What really boosted Hitler's popularity, however, were his undeniable domestic and foreign policy successes and achievements. His greatest achievement in domestic policies was the reduction and eventual elimination of unemployment. While there had been six million unemployed in 1932, by 1938 there was virtual full employment. Having found a job after years of unemployment might not have necessarily transformed workers into ardent National Socialists, but it might have made them less skeptical toward the regime.

Hitler's broad approval also resulted from his undisputed successes (from the German point of view) in foreign policy. Step by step, he succeeded in revising the Treaty of Versailles: the creation of the German air force in 1935; the introduction of the draft; the occupation of the demilitarized Rhineland in 1936; the so-called *Anschluss* of Austria in the spring of 1938, that is the bloodless invasion and annexation of his homeland prohibited by the Treaty of Versailles—all these moves were in violation of that treaty. The European powers protested only meekly. Indeed, his next move and greatest prewar foreign policy triumph, the annexation of the Sudetenland in September 1938 was achieved with the express approval of the Western powers and was the result of the Munich Conference in which the British Prime Minister Neville Chamberlain, the French Prime Minister Edouard Daladier, and the Italian Duce Benito Mussolini ("Il Duce"), in their "appeasement policy," ceded the German-speaking part of Czechoslovakia to the Third Reich. Hitler's popularity soared. Many Germans (as well as many foreign observers) looked at him with genuine admiration, some with near religious veneration.

The Second World War

Although Britain and France sought to preserve peace by giving in on the question of the Sudetenland, they pledged their military assistance to Poland in case of a German attack. Hitler was duly warned. So, when the German army invaded Poland on September 1, 1939, Great Britain and France declared war on Germany without, however, opening a second front in the west. Swift victories of the German armed forces against Poland in the fall of

1939 were followed by the defeat of Denmark and Norway in the spring of the following year as well as the unexpectedly quick victory over France in June 1940.

However, since from the very beginning Hitler's main objective had been the creation of living space (*Lebensraum*) in the east, the invasion of the Soviet Union in June 1941 was, from Hitler's point of view, the next logical step. At the beginning, the German armed forces managed to penetrate deeply into the vast Soviet territory, but soon what was envisioned as a blitzkrieg turned into a protracted and long struggle in which the German troops were confronted with the harsh Russian winter and a front that extended over 3,000 miles. In December 1941, the German offensive ground to a halt. Despite renewed advances in the summer of 1942, it became clear by the winter of that same year that the war was not winnable by Germany. At Stalingrad, the German Sixth Army was completely defeated. Most historians therefore regard this battle as the turning point of the war.

The invasion of American and British troops in Normandy in June 1944 and the large-scale Soviet offensive in the east marked the final phase of the war. British and American troops reached German soil in September 1944, Soviet troops in October. At the same time, with German air defenses virtually all eliminated, a relentless bombing campaign by the allies reduced most German cities to rubble. With every square mile of Germany occupied and Hitler having committed suicide on April 30, the German Reich surrendered unconditionally on May 8, 1945. The Third Reich ceased to exist.

The Holocaust

Anti-Semitism was a central element of the National Socialist ideology. Absorbing century-old Anti-Semitic European prejudices in European societies, Hitler put into practice policies that became increasingly radicalized and finally culminated in the Holocaust, the murder of millions of Jews.

Hitler's campaign against Jewish citizens began almost immediately after his seizure of power in January 1933 with a one-day boycott of Jewish stores on April 1 and was followed, a few days later, by a law dismissing all Jews or "non-Aryans" from the civil service, including universities. Other exclusionary, anti-Jewish legislation followed. These measures were systematized in the Nuremberg laws of September 1935. They radically curbed the rights of Jewish citizens, prohibited marriages and sexual relations between Jews and non-Jews. The relentless campaign culminated in the *Reichskristallnacht* (night of the broken glass) on November 9, 1938. Allegedly a spontaneous outbreak of the people's rage against the murder of a German diplomat in Paris by a 17-year-old Jew, in reality a state-sponsored, well-organized pogrom, it resulted in the burning of 190 synagogues and the destruction of thousands of Jewish businesses. A flood of new laws and decrees further degraded and marginalized those German Jews who had not yet been able to emigrate (of the 500,000 Jews in Germany, about half had left Germany by 1939).

The war brought a further radicalization of Hitler's racial policies. For the millions of East European Jews in the German-occupied territories, emigration was no longer possible. National Socialist Germany embarked on the last and most sinister phase of its anti-Jewish policies: the genocide of the Jewish people. Although the policy of the "final solution," as this policy was called euphemistically, was only decided upon in January 1942 in a top secret conference in a villa on the Wannsee in Berlin, mass killings of Jews in the conquered East European territories had been going on earlier. But to the barbaric thinking of the Schutzstaffel (SS), the organization responsible for the liquidations, the mass shootings, and poisoning through diesel fumes in closed trucks proved to be too inefficient. Special camps were established with the express purpose of liquidating as many human beings as possible. Of these death camps, Auschwitz, Poland, has come to symbolize the most evil aspect of the Third Reich. All in all, an estimated five to six million Jews from all over Europe perished in these camps. In addition, hundreds of thousand Romany, homosexuals, and Jehovah's Witnesses were incarcerated and died.

Resistance to Hitler

After the war, a British newspaper called the German resistance the "non-event" of the twentieth century. This was not only unfair but blatantly false. The German resistance was more widespread than could have been expected under the conditions of terror prevailing in the Nazi dictatorship. It included a broad spectrum of people ranging from Protestant pastors such as Dietrich Bonhoeffer and Martin Niemöller to communists and socialists; from former Nazis, Jesuits, conservatives, adolescents to the military, and the intelligence services. Acts of resistance ranged from distributing leaflets, hiding fellow citizens who happened to be Jewish, and sabotage to establishing contacts with foreign governments and assassination attempts. It is true, however, that the German resistance did not topple the Nazi dictatorship. In the end, it was American and Soviet tanks that brought down the Third Reich. But the same could be said about the other, much vaunted resistance movements in Nazi-occupied Europe. None of these was able by itself to bring an end to the Nazi regime.

The difficulties German dissidents faced were twofold. For one thing, the Third Reich was a state based on terror. Its leaders persecuted their own citizens with great brutality. Up to 1938, its concentration camps were filled exclusively with hundreds of thousands of German citizens. The second difficulty, paradoxically, stemmed from the broad public support Hitler enjoyed during much of his regime. Acting against the government basically lacked popular support and meant swimming against the current. During the war, resistance became even more difficult, not only because the Gestapo tightened the grip on dissenters and intensified its persecutions, but also because resistance against one's own country was viewed by many as high treason.

In spite of these difficulties, there were thousands who dissented in a country where there was little room for dissent; thousands who engaged in dangerous actions—well aware of the risks to themselves and their families—and thousands did pay with their lives for these acts of courage. Among those who paid with their lives, the members of the *White Rose* (*Weisse Rose*) are probably best known. This group of students at the University of Munich wrote, duplicated, and distributed a number of leaflets between June 1942 and February 1943. In these leaflets, they indicted Hitler's policies, revealed the mass killings of Jews in Nazi-occupied Poland, and called for passive resistance. The principal figures, brother and sister Hans and Sophie Scholl, were arrested in February at the university while distributing leaflets. With terrifying speed they were tried and executed five days later. Their accomplices suffered the same fate a few months later.

While the intention of the members of the *White Rose* was to rouse their fellow countrymen out of their indifference, conformity, and apathy, others tried to end the reign of terror by killing its head, Adolf Hitler. Indeed, there were 15 assassination attempts—all of them failed, however, strengthening the Führer's conviction that Providence was holding a protective hand over him.

The most promising attempt to kill Hitler was initiated by Colonel Claus von Stauffenberg in 1944. It involved an elaborate plot and a surprisingly large number of participants. It, too, failed. The bomb Stauffenberg had placed under the sturdy oak table in Hitler's East Prussian headquarters, the Wolf's Lair, exploded, killing a number of people but not Hitler, who sustained only slight injuries. The planned coup d'etat collapsed on the very same day. The punishment was swift and cruel. Stauffenberg and other fellow conspirators were shot the very same day of July 20, 1944. Others were tried before the "People's Court." Hundreds were arrested and executed.

The Two German States (1949–1990)

Postwar Germany

In 1945 Germany lay in ruins. Most of the major cities were reduced to rubble. Roads and railway lines were damaged; the German economy had collapsed. Every square mile of Germany was occupied. Germany had lost 6.5 million soldiers; half a million civilians, including 80,000 children, had died as the result of Allied air raids. In Berlin alone, 50,000 people had perished in the bombings. But no other city suffered more than Dresden, "the Florence on the river Elbe," as it was called, a city without any significant industry. In a series of air raids on February 14 and 15, 1945, it was leveled by Allied bombers. The number of casualties has never been exactly determined but estimates range between 35,000 and 135,000 dead. In other German cities, millions of people had lost their homes. To the physical destruction came the shame and guilt of having served a regime that was ultimately responsible for that catastrophe. No wonder that people thought of that year as the lowest point in German history and spoke of the *Stunde Null* (Zero Hour).

In a number of conferences before and after the war, the victors divided Germany into four zones: an American, a British, a French, and a Soviet zone. The capital, Berlin, located in the midst of the Soviet zone, was split into four sectors, one for each of the occupying powers. Large areas east of rivers Oder and Neisse were detached from Germany and given to Poland and the Soviet Union. Twelve million Germans who had been living there for centuries were expelled in one of the largest resettlement actions in history. It is estimated that on these treks in the cold winters of 1945 and 1946 two to three million lost their lives due to starvation, hypothermia, typhoid, and other diseases.

The Cold War, Marshall Plan, and Berlin Airlift

The division of Germany into two states had not been the original intention of the Allies but was the result of the Cold War between the Soviet and American blocs that began in 1946–47 and ended only with the collapse of the Soviet Union in the early 1990s. During the height of the Cold War, no country was more affected by this global confrontation than Germany. When the Iron Curtain was dropped, it went right through Germany. And nowhere was it felt more directly than in Berlin.

Against the background of the evolving Cold War, a number of decisions made by the United States can be explained. These included the so-called Marshall Plan and the Berlin Airlift. Faced with the prospect of having to feed millions of starving Europeans and fearing at the same time that these same people, if not fed, would be an easy prey for Soviet expansionism, George Marshall, then U.S. secretary of state, announced a plan in 1947 to help Europeans get on their feet. The Germans especially remember with great gratitude the Americans' gesture of extending a helping hand to their defeated country. The second event that profoundly affected the German-American relationship was the Berlin Airlift. In a move designed to force West Berlin, that is the three combined Western sectors, to become part of Communist East Berlin, the Soviets in June 1948 blocked all access roads, railroad lines, and shipping canals to and from Berlin, thus cutting it off from its lifeline to the Western zones. In response to the Soviet blockade, the United States and Great Britain organized one of the greatest airlifts in history, supplying a city of 2.5 million people for 11 months with food, fuel, coal, building materials, and everything else a city of this size cut off from its hinterland needed for survival. During the peak of the airlift, a plane landed every two to three minutes at one of West Berlin's two airports. The blockade was only lifted in May of 1949, after the Soviets had realized the futility of their efforts. For German-American relations, the Berlin Airlift proved to be a turning point. The victors of the Second World War were now seen as protectors and allies. The same pilots who four years ago had dropped bombs on Berlin, now dropped small packages of raisins for starving and grateful children from Berlin. The "raisin bombers," as the quick-witted Berliners dubbed them, became a familiar and welcome sight—and a symbol for the new relations between the two countries.

The Founding of the Two Germanys

As the tensions increased between the Soviets and Americans in the course of the Cold War, the Western allies eventually agreed to establish a state consisting of the three western zones. Under their watchful eyes, political parties had begun to be formed as early as the fall of 1945. By 1948 they were represented on the regional and national levels. A constitution, the Basic Law (*das Grundgesetz*), was drafted, and on May 23, the Federal Republic of Germany (or West Germany) was founded. Bonn was chosen as the provisional capital. In October of the same year, the Soviets responded by creating the German Democratic Republic (GDR) or East Germany. For 40 years, two German states, each tied to a different global power bloc, existed side by side.

West Germany

For the first decade and a half, politics in West Germany's parliamentary democracy was shaped by one man, Konrad Adenauer, the chairman of the conservative Christian Democratic Union (CDU).

Acquainted in his youth with Bismarck, a dynamic mayor of Cologne during the Weimar Republic, and dismissed by the Nazis in 1933, Adenauer was already 73 when he was elected chancellor in 1949. His principal foreign policy goal was to integrate West Germany firmly in the Western alliance, even if that meant putting off Germany's unification indefinitely. During his 14

Konrad Adenauer called "Der Alte" (The Old Man).
Reprinted by permission of *Der Spiegel.*

years in office—two years more than Hitler's Third Reich—he succeeded in binding West Germany into the political, economic, and military alliances of the West, so that by the beginning of the 1960s, West Germany was securely anchored in the European Union and NATO. Remembering the three wars France and Germany had fought against each other since 1870, Adenauer and the French President Charles de Gaulle made the reconciliation and friendship of the two countries a cornerstone of their policies.

West Germany's gradual return into the family of nations was accompanied by an extraordinary sustained economic boom in the 1950s. Exports skyrocketed and Germany, which only 15 years ago had lain in ruins, by 1960 had become the third largest economy in the world, after the United States and Japan. The reasons for this "economic miracle," as it became known, were many, among them the introduction of a free market economy, the traditional German work ethic, good labor-management relations with very few strikes, the availability of a large workforce, and certainly also the Marshall Plan.

East Germany

At the end of the war, the Soviet dictator Joseph Stalin had foisted upon the Soviet zone a group of East German Communists who followed a different policy. Instead of a parliamentary democracy, a Soviet-style semi-dictatorship headed by Walter Ulbricht was established that could only be maintained by repressive measures, a sizable secret police, the Stasi, and the presence of half a million Soviet soldiers.

The economy was radically transformed after the model of the Soviet Union. Privately owned factories were expropriated and turned into "people-owned," that is, state-owned plants; farms were collectivized. The economic difficulties resulting from these measures were exacerbated by the continuing dismantling of entire factories, which were shipped to the Soviet Union as reparations. These difficulties, combined with the repressive political regime, resulted in widespread dissatisfaction, which found expression in an uprising on June 17, 1953. Predictably, it was crushed by Soviet tanks. The brutal repression of any political opposition, the economic difficulties, and the attraction of the more affluent West Germany led to a flood of refugees. Between 1949 and 1961 alone, in little more than a decade, 2.6 million people left the German Democratic Republic, threatening its very existence. When the wave of refugees reached alarming proportions in the summer of 1961, the GDR authorities erected a wall around Berlin on August 13, the sole function of which was to keep East Germans from leaving their country. Since the Wall's object was to prevent East Germans from escaping to the West, it went up all around West Berlin, stretching for more than 100 miles, of which 23 miles cut straight through Berlin itself. The few telephone lines between East and West Berlin were cut, as were the subways and streetcar lines. Buildings on the East German side immediately bordering the Wall were demolished since they had been used by desperate East Germans to escape in the days immediately following the construction of the Wall. Watchdog runs, ditches, electrified fences, patrol roads, and 285 watch towers manned with armed guards with instructions to shoot at anyone trying to escape were built. Similar fortifications were erected along the West German–East German border.

Still, in the following years, hundreds of East Germans managed to flee: they dug tunnels, constructed primitive submarines, air balloons, and light airplanes. Some succeeded, others failed. An estimated 200 were killed while attempting to reach freedom.

Unwilling to risk a world war, the western powers did not intervene. However, in the summer of 1963, five months before his assassination, U.S. President John F. Kennedy came to Berlin to assure the Berliners of his solidarity. The words uttered by him on this occasion have entered the history books: "All free men, wherever they may live, are citizens of Berlin. And therefore, as a free man, I take pride in the words 'Ich bin ein Berliner.'" Kennedy's speech, welcome as it was at the time, could not hide the fact that the building of the Berlin Wall cemented the German partition. Germans on both sides of the Iron Curtain resigned themselves to the existence of two separate states. Any prospect of an eventual reunification seemed remote.

Willy Brandt's *Ostpolitik*

After almost 20 years of conservative governments, Willy Brandt, in 1969, became chancellor of a left-center coalition consisting of his own Social Democrats and the liberal Free Democrats. In addition to initiating a number of long-overdue domestic reforms, Brandt embarked on a new course in foreign policy. His *Ostpolitik,* as it became known, did not replace Adenauer's policies of Western integration—West Germany remained firmly anchored in the Western alliance—but complemented it by negotiating treaties with Eastern and Central European Communist states, including East Germany. Among these treaties, those with Poland and the GDR were the most important. In order to allay Polish fears of German attempts to revise the postwar borders, Germany recognized the Oder-Neisse line as Poland's western border. Brandt's new policy also changed the relations between the two German states. In the Basic Treaty (1972) with the GDR, West Germany recognized East Germany as a sovereign state—something it had adamantly refused to do in the previous 20 years. The two German states exchanged "permanent representations" (but no embassies) and in 1973 both were admitted to the United Nations. Though the Berlin Wall and the border fortifications remained as impenetrable as before, the "policy of small steps," as Willy Brandt called the rapprochement between the two German states, produced marked improvements for the East Germans, such as some relaxation of the travel restrictions. For his contributions to world peace, Willy Brandt was awarded the Nobel Peace Prize in 1971.

The Berlin Wall, however, continued to divide Berlin. When it was breached after 28 years on that memorable day in November 1989, it triggered the indescribable joy sketched at the beginning of this chapter.

The Road to Unification

The fall of the Berlin Wall in November 1989 and the subsequent unification of East and West Germanys less than a year later were the result of a whole bundle of factors, of which the developments in the Soviet Union and the courage of thousands of East Germans were probably the most important.

By the mid-1980s, Mikhail Gorbachev, the new leader of the Soviet Union, embarked on a new policy of reform and democratization in his own country. Erich Honecker, East Germany's aging leader, and his fellow members of the Politburo, however, were in no mood to follow the Soviet Union in its reform course. "If your neighbor put up new wallpaper, would you feel obliged to have your own wallpaper changed too?" asked one of the SED hard-liners dismissively.[3]

Elsewhere in Communist Eastern Europe, the Soviet reforms were welcomed and imitated. For instance, Hungary, encouraged by the developments in the Soviet Union, dismantled the barbed-wire fence to Austria in the spring of 1989. East Germans, watching these events on West German television, rushed to Hungary on the pretext that they were planning to spend their vacations in this Socialist brother country. In the following weeks, thousands of them escaped across the now open border to Austria and from there to West Germany. Others sought refuge in the West German embassies in Prague and Warsaw, hoping to find their way to West Germany. By the fall, thousands of badly needed physicians, engineers, and skilled laborers had left East Germany. The trickle of refugees had become a torrent.

In the meantime in East Germany, in September and October, the Monday prayer services, followed by peaceful demonstrations, had steadily increased in the city of Leipzig. Dissidents lost fear of the all-powerful Stasi, so that by the beginning of October in Leipzig, Dresden, and other cities, the demonstrations attracted hundreds of thousands of people, and in East Berlin over half a million gathered on November 4. The demands were always the same: more democracy and a lift on travel restrictions. Abandoned by the Soviet Union and by their own people, the Communist East German government seemed powerless and the hasty replacement of Honecker by the younger but equally hard-line Egon Krenz could not avert its demise. And nothing shows clearer the confusion prevailing in the East German government than the fact that a harmless announcement by a Politburo member on November 9 sparked a world historical event. At the end of a long press conference, Günther Schabowski had mumbled the words: "Private trips to foreign countries can be applied for without precondition." Interpreting this statement as a license to travel to the West, thousands of people had gathered within hours near the Wall and forced their way into West Berlin. The Wall, hated symbol of oppression and inhumanity, was finally opened.

The fall of the Wall did not mean the end of the GDR or immediate German unification. Fears by some Western allies, especially Great Britain and France, of a strong united Germany had to be allayed as well as the understandable reluctance of the Soviet Union to lose its westernmost military outpost. That the two Germanys were united in a peaceful manner with the full approval of all four World War II allies has been called "one of the greatest triumphs of diplomacy in the twentieth century."[4] A large portion of the credit for the speedy unification must go to the West German Chancellor Helmut Kohl. Though he did not create the international conditions that made this event possible, he seized the opportunity, saying, "We must gather in the hay before the storm," and with great diplomatic skill and single-minded determination shepherded the process to its successful conclusion.

The major steps in this historic process are quickly recounted. By the spring of 1990, it had become clear that a majority of the East Germans did not want a reformed GDR but a merger with West Germany. The chant "We are *the* people" heard in the fall of 1989 had been replaced by "We are *one* people." In the March elections of 1990, for East Germans the first free elections in almost 60 years, an alliance of conservative parties favoring unification won a majority and formed a government. At the same time it became obvious that the GDR economy was crumbling. Against the advice of economists, Helmut Kohl pushed through a monetary union with the GDR effective July 1, 1990, whereby West Germany in a generous gesture exchanged the almost worthless East German mark for the mighty deutsche mark at the rate of one to one. Meanwhile, delicate negotiations were conducted between the four allies and the two German states, the so-called four-plus-two talks. While the United States under President George H. W. Bush unreservedly supported German unification, the Soviet Union was feared to object to it. But in a year that was filled with unexpected events, there was another sensation. In a meeting with Chancellor Helmut Kohl, Mikhail Gorbachev agreed not only to the unification but also to the full membership of a united Germany in NATO. Subsequent negotiations between the two German states in August and September produced a 900-page Unification Treaty. On October 3, 1990, this treaty was signed. The GDR ceased to exist and Germany was one united country again. The successful West German model was transferred to the erstwhile Communist East Germany.

UNITED GERMANY (1990–PRESENT)

Euphoria over the successful unification soon made way for the sober realization of the immense cost of the undertaking. Although always praised as one of the strongest economies in the eastern bloc, the East German economy turned out to be hopelessly outmoded and grossly overstaffed. Most of the state-owned factories had to be privatized; large toxic waste sites had to be cleaned up; the telephone system had to be completely rebuilt; and pensioners who never had paid a penny into the West German system had to be taken care of. Annual transfers of $100 billion to what has become known as the new states represent a tremendous drain on the German economy. In spite of these huge infusions former East Germany continues to lag behind the states in Western Germany in all economic aspects: unemployment is almost twice as high, the productivity considerably lower. It has also become clear that the Wall in the heads, that is, the mental differences between East and West caused by living for 40 years under different political and social systems, is harder to overcome than the physical wall in Berlin that had disappeared with surprising speed.

NOTES

1. Madame de Staël in her book *De l'Allemagne* (On Germany) (1813).

2. Henry Cord Meyer, *The Long Generation. Germany from Empire to Ruin, 1913–1945* (New York: Walker and Company 1973), 8.

3. Henry Ashby Turner, Jr., *Germany from Partition to Reunification*, rev. ed. of *The Two Germanies since 1945* (New Haven, London: Yale University Press, 1992), 223.

4. Lothar Kettenacker, *Germany since 1945* (New York: Oxford University Press, 1997), 198.

3

Holidays, Customs, Leisure

"HEIDELBERG, SAUERKRAUT, OKTOBERFEST. What else does Germany have to offer?" The answer to this magazine ad of the *Deutsche Welle,* the worldwide German radio and television service, might be: "Scores of holidays and festivals."

In general, Germans have more holidays than Americans. In some of the states (*Länder*) as many as 15 legal holidays are celebrated, compared to the 11 in the United States. In addition, there are numerous local and regional festivals. No other aspect of a country allows such deep insights into the character of a people and their shared values than a look at how they observe their holidays, celebrate their customs, and spend their leisure time. What follows is a sketch of some of the major holidays and festivals, arranged roughly in the sequence in which they are observed throughout the year, beginning with New Year's Eve and ending with Christmas, as well as a discussion of how Germans, one of the most affluent people in the world, spend the considerable free time they have at their disposal.

HOLIDAYS AND CUSTOMS

New Year's Eve

The new year is ushered in with a lot of noise in Germany. Loud fireworks are set off, church bells are rung, and champagne corks are popped. Everybody wishes everybody else *"Ein frohes neues Jahr!"*—"A happy new year!" Before that, however, on New Year's Eve, called Silvester in Germany after Pope Silvester I (314–35), whose day is commemorated on December 31, family and friends gather for drinking, eating, or watching the Johann Strauss operetta *Die Fledermaus* on television. Some families might play games, among them one that involves dropping molten lead into cold water. The resulting figures are then interpreted as an indication of future events. If a figure looks like a ring, an engagement or marriage cannot be far off; if the shape resembles vaguely an airplane or ship, travels seem in the future. A heart-shaped figure indicates love. If your leaden figure remotely looks like a pig or a four-leafed clover, consider yourself fortunate, because pigs and four-leafed clovers are traditionally regarded as harbingers of luck. For that reason they are also often featured on New Year greeting cards and decorations. Beware, however, of patterns that look like crosses and broken rings: they might augur death and separation. One of the strangest and very popular traditions is watching a 15-minute film on television, shot in black and white in 1963 and called "Dinner for One or the 90th Birthday." It has achieved cult status. It is in English, but every German seems to know by heart the dialogue exchanged by the increasingly tipsy Miss Sophie and her butler James: "Same procedure as last year, Madam?"—"Same procedure as every year, James." Finally, for many Germans, Silvester without a *Feuerzangenbowle* (literally, fire prongs punch) does not feel right. Red wine spiced with orange and lemon juice, cinnamon and cloves is heated in a fireproof bowl; stainless steel prongs holding a large sugar cone are placed across the top of the bowl. Then the cone is soaked in 150 proof rum and lit. The wonderful glow of a burning sugar cone combined with the smell of the spiced wine creates an unforgettable Silvester atmosphere.

Epiphany or Holy Three Kings (Heilige Drei Könige), on January 6, commemorating the journey of the three Magi to Bethlehem, is observed as a legal holiday only in Catholic areas. For Cologne, the day has special significance. In 1164 supposed relics of the three kings were brought to the city. The priceless relics were housed in a magnificent golden shrine that today remains one of the greatest treasures of the Cologne cathedral.

Carnival

Karneval (carnival) or *Fasching*, as it is called in southern Germany, the pre-Lenten celebration that for weeks holds Cologne, Mainz, Düsseldorf, and other cities along the Rhine and in southern Germany in its grips, is often called the fifth season. It begins on the 11th day of the 11th month at 11 minutes after 11. Interrupted by the Christmas season, it gathers momentum in January and culminates in the noisy crescendo of the "three crazy days" (*drei tolle Tage*) before Ash Wednesday in February or March. (The exact day depends on Easter.) Things get serious on women's carnival (*Weiberfastnacht*),

Table 3.1 German Holidays

New Year's Day	January 1	Neujahrstag
Epiphany*	January 6	Heilige Drei Könige
Good Friday	March/April	Karfreitag
Easter Sunday	March/April	Ostersonntag
Easter Monday	March/April	Ostermontag
Labor Day	May 1	Tag der Arbeit
Ascension Day	May/June	Christi Himmelfahrt
Whitsun Sunday	May/June	Pfingstsonntag
Whitsun Monday	May/June	Pfingstmontag
Corpus Christi*	May/June	Fronleichnam
Assumption Day*	August 15	Mariä Himmelfahrt
Day of German Unity	October 3	Tag der deutschen Einheit
All Saints Day*	November 1	Allerheiligen
Christmas Day	December 25	1. Weihnachtsfeiertag
Second Day of Christmas	December 26	2. Weihnachtsfeiertag

*Legal holidays in some states only.

on the Thursday before Ash Wednesday, when women take over the regime in city halls and offices. Men should not wear expensive, $60 silk ties on that day, because one of the traditions of *Weiberfastnacht* is that women are free to cut off with impunity the ties of any males they can get their hands and scissors on. The following weekend, innumerable balls, parties, and meetings of the carnival societies (*Karnivalsvereine*) take place. On *Rosenmontag*—Rose Monday—(which incidentally has nothing to do with roses but the word *rasen*—to get wild), the cities of Cologne, Mainz, and Düsseldorf are turned upside town; business comes to a standstill. In Cologne, for instance, a five-mile-long parade featuring huge floats that often lampoon politicians winds its way through the narrow streets, accompanied by bands playing the latest carnival hits (*Karnevalsschlager*). The streets are lined with millions of onlookers, dressed in funny costumes. They are drinking, cheering, swaying, and trying to catch some of the candies thrown down from the floats. Munich's *Fasching* does not feature huge parades but is famous for its numerous masked balls. In the southwest area of Germany, in the Black Forest, *Fasnet* has retained some of its folkloristic and pagan character. In the town of Elzach, fools dressed in red-fringed clothes, with wooden masks and large hats covered with snail shells, beat bystanders with blown-up hogs' bladders.

Although carnival is a regional celebration restricted to those predominantly Catholic areas along the Rhine and Bavaria, the huge Rose Monday parades, as well as the often witty carnival meetings, are televised nationally. This has prompted other regions to celebrate their own versions of carnival.

Revellers at the *Alemannic Fasnet,* or carnival, with masks. Photo by Ingo Schneider.

In any case, *"Am Aschermittwoch ist alles vorbei"*—"On Ash Wednesday every-thing is over"—as a well-known *Karnevalsschlager* proclaims. The Lent season has begun.

Easter, Ascension Day, Whitsuntide, and Corpus Christi

The lent season ends at Easter. For Christians Easter is of course an impor-tant holiday commemorating Christ's passion and resurrection, and many Christians will attend church on Good Friday. Since both Good Friday and Easter Monday are legal holidays in all states, many families use this long weekend for travel or relaxation. On Easter Sunday, families often go for a walk. As in the United States, the Easter rabbit and eggs have been tradition-ally associated with that holiday. If there are children in the family, these eggs are carefully hidden in the house or garden and must be hunted.

Another legal holiday in all federal states is Ascension Day (*Himmelfahrts-tag*), commemorating Christ's ascent to heaven. It takes place 40 days after Easter and 10 days before Whitsun or Pentecost (*Pfingsten*) and thus always falls on a Thursday. Like so many religious holidays, it has been largely secu-larized. Since the nineteenth century, it has been celebrated as a day when men, and only men, go on outings. Amidst singing and drinking, men could be among themselves and let their hair down. The custom is no longer as popular as it used to be. Nowadays, at least married men are likely to prefer to spend time with their families. The association, however, with its nineteenth-century tradition remains. Today, *Himmelfahrt* has become Father's Day in Germany, while Mother's Day is observed, as it is in the United States, on the second Sunday in May. *Pfingsten* itself, the seventh Sunday after Easter, is another religious holiday that has lost much of its original significance. Originally commemorating the descent of the Holy Spirit upon the apostles, this holiday—Whitsun Monday is also a legal holiday in Germany—is often used for mini-vacations, especially since most schools are off for a week. Churches and houses are often decorated with green twigs. Corpus Christi (*Fronleichnam*) in May or June and St. Mary's Assumption (*Mariä Himmelfahrt*) in August are legal holidays only in federal states with a predominantly Catholic population. The Corpus Christi processions, at which the consecrated host is carried in a monstrance, are colorful events, celebrated especially in rural areas, with men and women participating in their local costumes (see p. 83).

May 1—Labor Day and Day of German Unification

Amidst all these religious holidays, falls a genuinely secular holiday: The international day of labor. It is observed in most countries of the world on May 1, except the United States, where Labor Day is celebrated on the first Monday in September. In Germany, where labor-management relations are in general quite good, most workers seem to honor this international day of work by simply not working or by listening to trade union leaders demanding yet another pay raise. The other purely secular holiday is October 3. It was introduced in 1992 to mark the reunification of the two Germanys in 1990. Reflecting the federal nature of Germany, its central celebration is always held in a different German state. No particular traditions have developed yet.

Otherwise, the summer months are remarkably free of legal holidays. It is the time for festivals.

German Festivals

There are more than 100 music festivals held in Germany annually between the spring and fall. Among the best known are the Munich Opera Festival, the Contemporary Music Festival in Donaueschingen, the Dresden Music Festival, the Berlin Jazz days, the Schleswig-Holstein Music Festival, and the Bach Week in Ansbach. But none attracts more visitors than the Richard Wagner Festspiele in Bayreuth. In July of every year, fans of the German composer Richard Wagner descend on the Bavarian city of Bayreuth to attend one or several of this composer's operas. For politicians and other celebrities, putting in an appearance at Bayreuth is a must; for Wagner aficionados, it is the highlight of the summer season, and patiently they sit through the composer's operas, which are not known for their brevity.

Patience is also required for the other world-renowned festival, the Passion Play at Oberammergau. It is performed every 10 years and goes back to an event more than 370 years ago. In 1633 the citizens of that Bavarian village vowed to reenact Christ's suffering every 10 years if their community was spared from the plague, which was raging through southern Germany at the time. The dreadful epidemic subsided and the Oberammergauers kept their promise. The reenactment of the passion, death, and resurrection of Christ performed by a huge cast of 1,500 lay players with 17 leading roles, tests the patience of the most hardiest spectators. It begins at 8:15 in the morning and ends only at 5:30 in the evening, with a two-hour break for lunch. Still, tickets are sold out years in advance. The next festival is scheduled for 2010.

The summer months are also the season for numerous pageants, such as the *Meistertrunk* (Master Drink) performed around Whitsun time in the old and romantic city of Rothenburg ob der Tauber. The play commemorates an incident that took place in the middle of the Thirty Years' War (1618–1648) when the Catholic General Johann Tserclaes, Count of Tilly, and his 60,000 troops besieged the city. To pacify the general the town council presented the general with a huge mug of wine. Tilly took a sip or two but then challenged the mayor to drink the mug in one gulp. The mayor succeeded and the city was spared. Scholars have dismissed the story as pure legend; it is more likely, they say, that the Rothenburgers made peace with Tilly by handing over a huge amount of ransom money; but who wants to spoil a good story? Plus, the *Meistertrunk* has become an irresistible tourist attraction. In addition to the annual Whitsun reenactment, the brave mayor's drinking feat is remembered several times daily by the clock figures on the town's city hall.

An incident from the Thirty Years' War is also commemorated in the nearby town of Dinkelsbühl, like Rothenburg ob der Tauber a well-preserved medieval town, but with fewer tourists. Beleaguered by Protestant Swedish troops, the children of the town successfully begged the commander of the besieging troops to spare the town. The soldiers took pity and left. Though the story is legend, the people of Dinkelsbühl celebrate the historic episode with a 10-day festival complete with reenactments of the event, music, fairs, and other entertainments.

Landshuter Fürstenhochzeit

No other festival, however, compares in splendor with the *Landshuter Fürstenhochzeit* (The Landshut Wedding of the Princes). It commemorates

Landshuter wedding of 1475 reenacted. Courtesy of Gemein-
nütziger Verein "Die Förderer" e. V. Landshut.

the wedding of the Bavarian prince, later duke Georg with the Polish princess
Jadwiga in 1475 in the Bavarian town of Landshut. At a cost of 60,700 florins
(in today's money, approximately $13 million), the wedding was the late
Middle Ages' most expensive and largest feast. Since 1903 it has been reenacted every three years in all its splendor, complete with historical wedding
processions and medieval tournaments.

Knightly tournaments are made fun of, it seems, in the annual *Fischer-
stechen* (Fishermen's Jousting Competition) in Ulm. Strong, skilled young
men standing on the bow of flat boats try to push their opponents with a
pole into the water. The competition has developed into a real Volksfest
with traditional costumes, brass bands, and a nightly parade of illuminated
boats.

Berlin's Love Parade

Finally mention must be made of the so-called love parade, a modern folk festival that has taken place in the German capital on the second Saturday in July every year since 1989. It is a celebration for the fans of techno music. Hundreds of thousands of young people dance to the throbbing beat of that music in all discos, and in the streets and parks where the music is beamed from trucks with powerful amplification systems. Berlin's senate approved the love parade as a "political demonstration," thus guaranteeing the huge cleanup costs, although for the outsider, it is hard to understand what is political about the love parade, whose official motto is "*Friede, Freude, Eierkuchen*" (Peace, Joy, Pancakes). Pancakes are the last things consumed during this mega-event. It is more likely that beer and the drug "Ecstasy" provide the stimulus and nourishment for the hundreds of thousands of techno freaks. The love parade has become an export hit: love parades are now celebrated in Vienna, Tel Aviv, and Mexico City.

Wine and Beer Festivals

The fall is the season for innumerable wine festivals—at least in those wine-growing regions along the rivers Rhine, Mosel, Main, and Saar, as well as in Baden in the southwest corner of Germany. Every community seems to have its festival with parades, wine tastings, street shows, concerts, fireworks, and the coronation of a wine-queen. Bernkastel-Kues on the river Mosel has a special attraction: from the town's fountains spews forth the famous Mosel wine. The largest wine festival in the world, however, is in Bad Dürkheim in the Palatinate. Incongruously called *Wurstmarkt* (Sausage Market), this wine festival attracts half a million people each year.

In terms of size, popularity with foreigners and alcohol consumption, no wine festival can compete with Munich's Oktoberfest. It all started almost 200 years ago, in October of 1810, when the Bavarian crown prince Ludwig (later King Ludwig I) married Princess Therese of Saxony-Hildburghausen. Outside the city gates a large party was held. The people of Munich liked the festival and have repeated it ever since. Celebrated for 16 days in the last two weeks of September and ending on the first Sunday in October (hence the justification for calling it Oktoberfest), it has become the largest beer festival of the world, attracting over seven million people a year.

The Oktoberfest begins with the traditional tapping of the first keg of beer by the mayor of Munich, followed by a parade of men and women in local folk costumes, the *Trachtenparade,* complete with beer wagons drawn by stout brewery horses. But the real action takes place on the *Theresienwiese*

Oktoberfest, Munich. Courtesy of Munich City Tourist Office. Photo by Christl Reiter.

(Therese's meadow), named after that Saxon princess, or just *Wies'n* (meadow). Gigantic beer tents are erected, beer flows by the gallons, total strangers sing and sway, arms linked, to the music of numerous brass bands, while athletic waitresses continuously haul the heavy one-liter glass tankards. Since each of these "steins," as they are only called in the United States—the Germans simply refer to them as "*Maß*" (literally, measure)—weighs about five pounds, one can imagine what athletic prowess is required by the waitresses who can lug up to 10 of these tankards to their thirsty customers. With the beer, incredible amounts of sausages, roasted chicken, and oxen on the spit are served. On the *Wies'n,* you will also find amusement rides, including

Waitress serving beer at Munich's Oktoberfest. Courtesy of Munich City Tourist Office. Photo by Heinz Gebhardt.

a gigantic Ferris wheel and a scary roller coaster, just the thing you need after you have eaten a couple sausages and downed a few *Maß*.

Munich's Oktoberfest is the largest and economically most important tourist attraction. Guests, including many foreigners, leave behind $800 million annually. The Oktoberfest has become such a success that it is copied throughout the world, in 3,000 cities, "from Tokyo to Cincinnati."[1]

After the joyful wine festivals and the exuberant Oktoberfest, November is a month for somber reflections. Usually a month of overcast skies, fog, and rain, November is an appropriate time to remember the dead. This is done on All Saints Day, a legal holiday in predominantly Catholic states, while Protestants honor their dead on *Totensonntag* (Sunday of the Dead), observed on the last Sunday before Advent. There is also the common *Volkstrauertag* (National Day of Mourning), corresponding to the American Memorial Day, when families and friends decorate their deceased relatives' and friends' graves with flowers and plants. In addition, Protestants observe Buß-und Bettag (Day of Repentance and Praying). Since 1995, however, it is no longer a legal holiday.

Amidst all this preoccupation with death and repenting, if that is what is done, a delightful custom for children has survived: on the evening of November 11, that is Saint Martin's Day, small children, accompanied by their parents, wander through the streets with homemade lanterns, singing appropriate songs like "Ich geh' mit meiner Laterne" ("I go with my lantern").

The custom is observed in both Catholic and Protestant regions. But since Protestants do not venerate saints, they commemorate Martin Luther's baptism day and thus can also participate with a clear Lutheran conscience in that custom that brings light into an otherwise dreary November night. In the Thuringian town of Erfurt, Protestant and Catholic children, in ecumenical harmony, wander together through the streets of that ancient city: Catholics in memory of the saintly bishop of Tours who famously shared his coat with a beggar and Protestants in memory of Martin Luther, the founder of the Lutheran confession, who for many years lived in a monastery in that town.

Christmas

Christmas is the biggest and most important German holiday. It has survived unscathed through the Nazi dictatorship and the atheistic East German Communism. Of course, many countries celebrate Christmas but none, it seems, with such intensity as the Germans. Is it then surprising that many German traditions have been adopted by other countries? The American custom of putting up a Christmas tree is such a German import, as is the more recent appearance of Advent calendars and gingerbread houses. Santa Claus, at least in the form we know him in his fur-lined, albeit brown, and not red, coat and white beard, was first drawn and popularized in a painting by the Austrian Romantic painter Moritz von Schwind (1804–71). Nor should we forget that many Christmas carols, such as the ever popular "Stille Nacht, Heilige Nacht" (Silent Night, Holy Night) came to this country from the German-speaking world. And although the Nutcracker Suite, that perennial Christmas favorite, was composed by the Russian Tchaikovsky, it is based on a story by the German Romantic poet E. T. A. Hoffmann. Finally, what American Christmas would be complete without the "Messiah"? It was composed by Georg Friedrich Händel, a German composer. (Incidentally, in Germany it is Johann Sebastian Bach's "Christmas Oratorio" that is performed every Christmas.)

The Christmas season starts with the first Sunday of Advent. Unlike Americans, who put up and decorate their Christmas tree weeks before Christmas, Germans generally wait until Christmas Eve with that ritual. Instead they prepare a simple wreath with four candles. Every Sunday before Christmas, one candle is lit, until on the fourth Sunday of Advent (which can coincide with Christmas Eve) all four candles are burning. Another Advent custom is that of the Advent calendar, a cardboard with a colorful picture depicting a Christmas scene and 23 small windows, each for one of the 23 days of December preceding Christmas Day plus a slightly larger one for that magical day itself, Christmas Eve. Each day children are allowed to open one window revealing a picture with a Christmas motif. Predictably, in affluent Germany, the images of apples and angles, candles and cookies have recently been replaced by real chocolate and candies. The upper Frankish town of Forchheim has gone one step further: it transforms its city hall facade into a gigantic Advent calendar. Behind wooden shutters, especially built for that purpose, Christmas gifts donated by local businesses are hidden. Every day at 6 P.M., a shutter is opened revealing a present, which is then raffled off.[2]

But for children, 24 days is a long time, even if they can count down the days until Christmas with the help of an *Adventskalendar.* Luckily, they do not have to wait until Christmas to be given some presents. On the eve of December 6, on St. Nicholas Day, they place their shoes outside their rooms. In the morning, the saint—or more likely their parents—has left candy in their boots or shoes, or if they have not behaved, a switch for future punishment.

Parents will buy at least some of their gifts at an outdoor Christmas markets (*Weihnachtsmarkt*). Today, almost every German town seems to have a Christmas market, although Stuttgart claims to have the largest, Nuremberg the most romantic, and Dresden the oldest (it was founded in 1434). Strolling between brightly lit stalls, surrounded by the smell of roasted almonds and warmed by the hot red-wine punch, the *Glühwein,* you can buy everything that is needed for Christmas: ornaments and candles for the Christmas tree, hand-carved nutcrackers and figures for nativity scenes, spicy gingerbread cookies (*Lebkuchen*), or the famous *Stollen* (sweet bread). The German *Weihnachtsmärkte* are so popular and have become such a tourist attraction that American tourist operators have arranged special trips to visit them. For those unable to fly to Germany, there is the Chicago Christmas market, featuring many items you would find on a German *Weihnachtsmärkt,* however minus the *Glühwein.* Because of America's strict alcohol laws, only a non-alcoholic punch is sold. The British, too, though usually skeptical toward whatever comes from across the channel and especially from Germany, seem to have taken a liking to the German custom. In Manchester, Leeds, Birmingham, and Edinburgh (Scotland), "Whynacktsmarkets" as they are phonetically spelled, complete with *Glühwein* stalls and sausage stands, enjoy increasing popularity.[3] In Germany, the Advent time is also a good time to send off Christmas cards, although Germans do not seem to be as enthusiastic collectors of these cards as Americans, who display them on their mantelpieces like trophies.

The Christmas season culminates in the three days of December 24, *Heiligabend* (Holy Night, Christmas Eve), and the two Christmas holidays of December 25 and 26, both legal holidays. Although Christmas Eve is not a

Christmas market (Christkindlesmarkt), Nürnberg. Courtesy of the Congress-und-Tourismus-Zentrale, Nuremberg.

legal holiday, stores will close at midday to give families time to make last-minute preparations because it is *Heiligabend,* not Christmas Day, that is the highlight of the entire Christmas season. And in the center of that celebration is the Christmas tree, the *Tannenbaum.* It knows no confessions, no parties, and no ideologies. It can be found in public places and private homes. For Germans, Christmas without a tree is no Christmas at all. Even today, most Germans still use real wax candles on the tree, feeling that the wonderful glow of real wax candles far outweighs the minimal fire hazard a candle-lit *Tannenbaum* poses in their stone-built houses or apartments. Decorating the Christmas tree is a matter of individual taste: some like it with tinsel, others without. Some prefer only straw ornaments, others glass balls.

Where does the custom of the Christmas tree come from? Legend has it that Martin Luther introduced the tree as a Christmas tradition. That is not true. The illustration showing the Protestant reformer and his family sitting around a candlelit tree comes from a later century. In fact, the tree can be traced back to seventeenth-century Alsace, at that time part of Germany. From Germany, it was brought to England by Prince Albert, the German-born husband of Queen Victoria, who displayed it at Windsor Castle. Quickly Her Majesty's subjects imitated that royal custom. To the United States it was brought either by Hessian soldiers fighting for the British or by German immigrants.

On Christmas Eve, many families, even those whose church attendance during the rest of the year is spotty, will attend church. After that and a meal often consisting either of potato salad and sausages or carp, the *Bescherung*, the exchange of gifts, takes place. For small children, it is either the *Weihnachtsmann*, a secularized Saint Nicholas, or the *Christkind* (Christ child) who has left the gifts. The difference between these two figures has to do with history and geography: the *Weihnachtsmann* brings presents in Northern and Central Germany, while the *Christkind* (a mysterious, angel-like figure who is seldom depicted) bestows presents to children in southern Germany. Under the influence of advertising, Santa Claus, or the *Weihnachtsmann*, is also becoming popular in Bavaria and other southern German states. After the *Bescherung*, adults may also attend a midnight mass or service that both Catholic and Protestant churches offer.

The first day of Christmas (December 25) is usually spent with your family, especially with your most immediate family, while on the second day (the 26th), friends and acquaintances are visited. In recent years, families have often spent their Christmas holidays at ski resorts or on the sunny beaches of a Caribbean island.

LEISURE ACTIVITIES

Germans work hard. Without the traditional work ethic, Germany would never have been able to rise from the ashes of the Second World War and build a country that has the third largest economy, in terms of gross national product, behind the much larger United States and Japan. But is this image of "all work, no play" still true? German critics charge that in the last decades their country has changed from an achievement-oriented society into one interested only in fun and the next vacations: "all play, no work," as it were, and the former chancellor Helmut Kohl (1982–1998) once worried that Germany was in danger of becoming "*a kollektiver Freizeitpark*"—a collective amusement park. The fact is that the average German employees spend significantly less time at work than their American colleagues. While American workers spend 1,904 hours per year on their jobs, their German counterparts work only 1,573 hours.[4] The reason is that German workers not only have a shorter work week but also that they are entitled to more paid vacations than their American colleagues: 31 days per year, whereas workers in the United States have only 12 days. Only the Finns (37.5), Italians (35), and the Dutch (31.8) are entitled to more paid vacation days. Add to these paid vacation days some 12 to 15 legal, religious, and secular holidays—the exact number depends on the state you live in—and you can easily imagine that a German has almost two months of paid vacations per year.

How do Germans spend the time when they are not at their desk, at the assembly line, or behind a counter? How do they organize their free time?

German *Wanderlust*

Polls have shown that in the evening, most Germans watch television, read newspapers and magazines, or listen to music. They also enjoy meeting with friends or dropping in a neighborhood pub (*Stammlokal*) for some beer or wine, or a game of cards, especially *Skat*. On weekends, many Germans enjoy being outdoors. Walking, playing soccer, hiking, swimming—there are some 7,000 public indoor and outdoor swimming pools in the country—are the most popular outdoor activities, as we will see below. Interesting as these statistics may be, they probably do not differ dramatically from those leisure activities of other nations. What really distinguishes the Germans from most other nations is their insatiable wanderlust, that is their obsession with traveling. Germans have become the world champions in visiting foreign countries: they are going abroad in greater numbers than people from any other country in the world. Even tourists from Japan and the United States, both countries with much larger populations, are easily outnumbered by German world travelers.[5] Annually, 40 million visit a foreign country at least once a year, spending at least 40 billion euros (approximately $44 billion) in their host countries. According to another international survey conducted in the summer of 2002 by the Luxembourg Radio and Television Concern RTL, Germans are also considered the most popular tourists by their host countries. The result of the poll even surprised the Germans themselves, who in the past had often been embarrassed by some of their countrymen who with their excessive drinking and crude conduct on the beaches of Spain and Italy occasionally gave rise to the image of the "ugly German." But in this latest survey, foreigners lauded the Germans for their attempts to respect foreign cultures and learn their languages.

What are the favorite countries Germans like to spend their summer vacations in? They are Spain, Italy, Austria, Turkey, and France.[6] It might not be surprising that among the five top vacation destinations, three (four, if we assume that many Germans go to the south of France) are Mediterranean countries with guaranteed sunshine during the summer months. Germans are inveterate sun-worshipers. And so, every summer, dire warnings by dermatologists concerning the danger of skin cancer notwithstanding, millions of them head south to the beaches of Spain and Italy. The annual migration to the south has made it even necessary to stagger the summer school vacations by state, so that students from Hamburg, for instance, will go back to school at a time when Bavarian children just begin their summer holidays. Without that arrangement the German highways (*autobahnen*) would be even more hopelessly clogged than they usually are. The Spanish island of Mallorca is so overrun by German tourists that it is jokingly referred to as the 17th federal state. Even in winter many Germans do not want to be without sunny beaches. In recent years, the Dominican Republic has become the Germans' favorite Caribbean island for winter vacations.

Increasingly, however, many Germans, eschewing the convenience of the "package tours" (which, however, still account for 50 percent of all travels) strike out on their own. One will encounter Germans climbing up Mt. Kilimanjaro in Africa, trekking through Nepal or Tibet, hiking the Inca trail in Peru, visiting tea plantations in Sri Lanka, or exploring pre-Columbian cultures in Central America. In a society that values health and fitness, so-called *Aktivurlaub,* a vacation during which you learn or improve a mental or physical skill, has also become popular. Finally, one should not forget that statistically the country that tops the list of destinations for Germans is Germany itself. Almost a third of the population elects to stay at home. That holidaying in Germany is growing in popularity not only with foreigners but also with Germans themselves should not be surprising. As a tourist country Germany has a lot to offer: an attractive and varied landscape ranging from the flat marshlands on the coasts of the North and Baltic Seas with a coastline of about 2,100 miles and undulating hills and mountains in central Germany to the lovely and sometimes breathtakingly steep vineyards on the Mosel and Rhine and the mountains in the German Alps. Countless castles, palaces, and churches dot the landscape. About 25,000 miles of bicycle trails crisscross the country as well as 62,000 miles of marked hiking trails provide the ideal conditions for an *Aktivurlaub.* There are accommodations for every taste and budget ranging from pricey world class hotels to the simple and very affordable 600 youth hostels. Germany *ist eine Reise wert*—is worth a trip. Even for Germans.

Sports

Germans like all sorts of sports, either as active participants or passive spectators. Soccer, called *Fußball* in Germany, is by far the most popular sport in Germany, especially among men. "*König Fußball*" (King Soccer) reigns supreme. As one observer noted, "No one single U.S. game can compete in popularity—you'd have to roll baseball, football, volleyball and ice hockey together to come close."[7] Every weekend millions of Germans, mostly men since "the football fever attacks the male more than the female population,"[8] are glued to their television sets to watch the games of the first and second federal soccer league (*Bundesliga*). *Fußball* stars, such as Franz Beckenbauer, achieve and retain celebrity status, long after their active careers have ended. But *Fußball* is more than a spectator sport: the German Soccer Association (*Deutscher Fußball Bund*, DFB) has 6.25 million members, with an astonishing 26,700 clubs and 172,716 different soccer teams, mostly amateur clubs.[9] The popularity of soccer on all levels might also be due, at least in part, to the success of the German national team in the European and world championships: it won the European championship in 1972, 1980, and 1996 and the World Cup in 1954, 1974, and 1990. In 1966, 1982, 1986, and 2002, the team made it to the finals, becoming vice world champions. Equally successful is the women's soccer team. In 2001, it won the European championship for the fifth time, and in 2003 it won the world championship.

Soccer, however, is not the only sport Germans are actively engaged in. 26 million Germans, almost a third of the population, belong to one of the 86,000 sport clubs. With a total membership of 3.1 million, the gymnastic clubs (*Turnvereine*) are the second largest sport organizations (after soccer), followed by tennis clubs. The popularity of tennis clubs is due to two successful players, Boris Becker, the three-time Wimbledon champion (1985, 1986, and 1989) and the brilliant Steffi Graf, who ranked number one on the World Tennis Federation's list longer than any other player, man or woman. Though both players have retired from active tennis, they remain popular, and Germany has become one of the biggest tennis markets in the world, hosting numerous tournaments.

How much the success of German athletes can boost the popularity of a sport becomes clear when we look at the accomplishments of two men in very different sports. When Jan Ulrich won the Tour de France in 1997, bicycle road racing caught on in Germany, and Michael Schumacher's repeated wins in the Formula One Racing world championship may not have triggered a boom in car racing, but it certainly provided a tremendous boost for the TV ratings of the stations broadcasting this sport.

Clubs (*Vereine*)

Certainly not all Germans kick a ball, swing a tennis racket, pedal through the German landscape, or jog on one of the many public *Trimm-dich* trails (get-in-shape trails) in their free time. But millions spend their leisure time in the company of others, in clubs. There are 345,000 *Vereine* (clubs) in Germany with 70 million members.[10] There are clubs for every possible interest, ranging from stamp and coin collecting, dog and rabbit breeding, to railroad modeling, sailing, and gliding. Marksmen, carnivalists, and amateur wireless operators pursue their hobbies and socialize in these clubs. There are clubs formed by people with long noses and tattooed bodies. There is even a club consisting of fanatical club-opponents. Predictably, it has only about 100 members.[11]

Have the Germans become too lazy? Can they still keep up in an increasingly competitive global market economy? These are questions that are frequently raised by worried critics. It has been pointed that the issue has to be seen in a postwar perspective.[12] After the war, the Germans worked extremely hard, not only to rebuild their destroyed country but also to forget the war and the shame of having supported the Nazi regime. Today these motivations have disappeared. The country has been splendidly rebuilt and after almost 60 years the Third Reich has receded somewhat into the background. Germans have become less workaholic and more like citizens of other nations.

NOTES

1. According to the newspaper *Die Welt,* 9 July 1999.

2. Barbara Rias-Bucher, *Feste und Bräuche. Eine Einladung zum Feiern* (Munich: Deutscher Taschenbuch Verlag, 1999), 211.

3. http://www.spiegel.de/kultur/gesellschaft/0.1518.22703.00.html (December 20, 2002).

4. According to Gros and Glaab, *Faktenlexikon Deutschland,* 101.

5. *Newsweek,* International Edition, 22–29 July 2002, 36.

6. *Der Spiegel* 12 (2002): 99.

7. Susan Stern, *These Strange German Ways and the Whys of the Ways. A Cultural Guide to the Germans and Their Customs* (Berlin: Arlantik-Brücke, 2000), 218.

8. Ibid.

9. *Deutschland Magazine* 2 (2002): 11.

10. The Federal Government, *Facts About Germany,* 404.

11. Roberto Giardina, *Anleitung, die Deutschen zu lieben* (Munich: Goldmann, 1998), 248.

12. John Ardagh, *Germany and the Germans. An Anatomy of Society Today* (New York: Harper & Row, 1987), 114.

4

Food, Wine, Beer, and Fashion

ONCE UPON A TIME, Germans subsisted on a diet of potatoes, sausages, and sauerkraut. At least that is the stereotype most foreigners had. These times are long gone, if they ever existed, although images of these past Germanic eating habits persist in cartoons showing potbellied Germans devouring heaps of sausages and sauerkraut and washing these down with huge quantities of beer.[1] Today the German cuisine has become more international, more varied, and lighter. Visitors from abroad are often impressed by the variety of food available in restaurants and supermarkets. They may also be surprised that, according to the 2001 Michelin Guide, the restaurant-rating bible for the global gourmet, Germany has more three-star restaurants than any other country in Europe except France and that more than 200 German restaurants have been awarded one, two, or three stars by Michelin.[2] Few Germans, however, eat in Michelin-rated restaurants. What does the average German eat and drink? The question is important because food and drink are significant manifestations of a culture and, as such, are much more accessible even to the casual visitor than, let us say, literature, theater, and the arts. In addition to sketching Germany's culinary landscape and its beer and wine cultures, we will also discuss briefly the world of fashion in this chapter.

GERMAN CUISINE

There are good reasons why in recent decades German cuisine has become much more international and cosmopolitan: first, since the 1960s Germany has attracted a large numbers of immigrants, primarily from countries around the Mediterranean, and these immigrants have opened restaurants all over the country so that Germany today has a plethora of Greek, Italian, Spanish, Turkish, and Yugoslavian restaurants, establishments that are complemented by numerous Chinese, Thai, and Indian eateries. As a British critic observes, "Germany's palate has been globalized."[3] Secondly, the Germans have brought back from their frequent travels abroad recipes and an appetite for exotic dishes. Back at home and with fond memories of their vacations in mind, they will try their hands at Spanish paellas, Greek salads, Turkish gyros, Mexican quesadillas, and Japanese sushi. And thirdly, the abolition of all trade barriers between the countries of the European Union and the free exchange of goods have brought to German supermarkets an unprecedented variety of foods and fruits that a mere 50 years ago might have seemed exotic. International cooking is in. But the German diet has also become lighter. Especially younger Germans have become more health-conscious and have turned to a lighter diet featuring salads, plenty of fruit, multigrain bread, and in general more wholesome food.

There are, however, a few food staples in the traditional German diet that no amount of internationalization are likely to replace. First, there is the German bread, "arguably the best in the world."[4] There are 200 kinds of bread, none of them resembling "those synthetic-tasting Styrofoam textured loaves on super-market shelves in the United States,"[5] as one American food critic put it, although to be fair, there are now in the United States many bakeries which offer many different kinds of bread. German bread styles range from the light and crusty baguette-style French bread, from *Weizenbrot* (wheat bread) and bread with nuts or sunflower seeds to *Roggenbrot* (rye bread made from sourdough), *Vollkornbrot* (bread made from rough ground kernels), *Leinsamenbrot* (a rye bread with linseed) to *Pumpernickel,* a heavy dark Westphalian specialty, which is baked for a long time (16–24 hours) at a low temperature.[6] The German bakery is such an institution and the freshness of its daily bread and rolls (*Brötchen*) of such importance that it has even been exempted from the otherwise unbendably strict laws governing the opening and closing of stores, the so-called *Ladenschlussgesetze:* bakeries (*Bäckereien*) are allowed to open earlier than other stores (at 6:30 A.M.) and are also permitted to open on Sundays during certain hours. The significance of bread is also reflected in the fact that there is a German *Brotmuseum* (bread museum) in Ulm displaying 1,300 items (out of a total collection of 14,000) pertaining to bread. The museum also features a life-size model of a bakery around 1900, displays documenting six millennia of bread-making techniques, rooms devoted to the cultural and social history of bread, and an extensive library of 4,500 books, catalogs, and other items.[7]

But man does not live by bread alone. The second food item Germany is justly famous for is the sausage, the *Wurst.* Just as France has hundreds of

Woman selling pretzels and bread, Oktoberfest, Munich. Courtesy of Munich City Tourist Office. Photo by Christl Reiter.

varieties of cheeses (which prompted Charles de Gaulle to complain, "How can you govern a country that has 345 different kinds of cheese?"), so Germany has hundreds of different kinds of sausages. All in all there are said to exist some 1,500 varieties of sausages. A well-stocked department store such as Berlin's Kadewe might not have all 1,500 varieties in its excellent delicatessen department, but it will have hundreds including 60 different kinds of liverwurst. Not such refinement will be found in the ubiquitous German *Würstchenbude* (sausage stand), a familiar sight in any German city, a fast-food place existing long before McDonald's and Burger King established their restaurants in Germany. The *Würstchenbude* is the home of the bratwurst (a pale smoked sausage made out of finely minced meat), the knackwurst (a short, plump smoked sausage), and the *Curry-Wurst,* a diced bratwurst with ketchup and curry-powder that after the war took the country by storm and still is a national favorite (Chancellor Schröder seems to have a particular weakness for it). The *Weisswurst,* on the other hand, a white veal sausage made with cream and eggs and served in a tureen of warm water between 11 and 12 in the morning, is strictly a Bavarian affair. As a matter of fact, an imaginary east-west line (roughly along the 50th parallel), jokingly referred to as the *Weisswurst*-equator, separates north and central Germany from the south—sausage-wise, that is.

The third staple in the traditional German kitchen is the potato—the *Kartoffel.* The nineteenth-century German poet Heinrich Heine said: "Luther convulsed Germany—but Francis Drake calmed it down again. He gave us the potato."[8] German cooks have developed dozens of creative ways of preparing this lowly vegetable. Potatoes can be served as mashed, fried, baked, boiled, stuffed, steamed, or au gratin. They can also be used in soups, stews, and salads. There are potato croquettes, potato soufflés, and *pommes frites* (french fries). There are even restaurants, the so-called *Kartoffelhäuser,* in which the entire menu revolves around the potato.

Are there typical German dishes? Yes, but given the enormous regional differences, it is virtually impossible to give even a hint of the variety of traditional German cuisine. Here are a few arbitrarily selected dishes. A typical German meal, for instance, is the *Sauerbraten,* a kind of marinated beef potroast served with red cabbage and dumplings. The schnitzel, another popular meat entree, is basically a boneless cutlet pounded very thin and often breaded. There are pork, veal, and even turkey schnitzel. Favorites all over Germany are the *Rinderouladen* (beef rolls), consisting of thin beef slices filled with bacon, chopped onion, pickles, and mustard and then rolled, browned, and stewed. Because of their proximity to the sea, North Germans enjoy many entrees prepared with fresh fish. Hundreds of miles to the south, in Bavaria, one might enjoy the *Schweinshaxn,* a roast pork knuckle served encased in a crispy layer of fat and washed down with a *Maß* (a liter) of beer—definitely not a dish for those anxious about their waistline. Although served all over Bavaria, the most beautiful setting for savoring this hearty dish might be the Benedictine monastery of Andechs near Munich. Every year thousands of guests make their pilgrimage to this monastery, not necessarily to worship the deity in the lovely Rococo church but to partake of *Schweinshaxn* prepared by the monks. A typical dish from the Palatinate, and eaten only in that region, is the *Saumagen* (literally, sow stomach). The former German chancellor Helmut Kohl, a native of that area, invariably took his friend, the French President Francois Mitterand, to the picturesque village of Deidesheim, where he invited him to *Saumagen.* It is unknown how the dainty French palate reacted to this hearty German dish. But the excellent German-French relations seem to have survived even this severe test. Actually, in spite of its unappetizing name, the *Saumagen,* the stomach lining of a sow filled with a spicy mixture of minced meat and potatoes, is reportedly a very tasty entree.

What are the main meals of the day for Germans?

A typical German breakfast (*Frühstück*) is not as hearty as an American one. It does not include brown hash, scrambled eggs, warm sausages, or bacon bits. But it is also far removed from what some American hotels advertise as a "continental" breakfast, generally a poor excuse for a meal, consisting of a cup of coffee and a Danish. For breakfast Germans will have butter, cheese, salami, sliced meats, boiled eggs, tea or coffee, orange juice, cereal, yogurt—and rolls. These crunchy-crusted *Brötchen,* sometimes sprinkled with sesame and poppy seeds and coming in all kinds of styles, always have been an indispensable part of the German breakfast. But while in the good old days the baker would bring them to your house at the crack of dawn, today you will have to fetch them yourself. Incidentally, all hotels in Germany include a generous buffet breakfast in the cost of the overnight stay.

For most German families the midday meal (*Mittagessen*) is still the main meal of the day. It is the time when children come home from school and are served a hot meal. Although sometimes working men and women will go home for that meal, most will have a hot meal in the company cafeteria. Around four o'clock, it is time for *Kaffee und Kuchen* (coffee and cake), that typical German (and Austrian) leisurely coffee break featuring a cup of coffee and a piece of cake. You can enjoy *Kaffee und Kuchen* at home or in a *Konditorei,* a café cum pastry-shop. There you will be faced with the agony of having to choose a piece from the mouth-watering selection of pastries, tortes, and cakes, because, as one British travel author exclaimed, "If you have a sweet tooth, welcome to heaven!"[9] And Mimi Sheraton, an American author of a book on German cooking, wrote: "Here I must begin by admitting defeat. I could never do justice to the variety of German cakes, tortes, pastries, cookies and sweet yeast dough cakes. The Germans, along with their first cousins the Austrians, are unquestionably the world's best bakers."[10] As you are looking at the glass-encased display in a German *Konditorei,* there are scores of cream-filled, fruit-topped, nut- and chocolate-laced tarts, cakes, and cookies. There are yeast cakes and cheesecakes. There is of course the *Apfelstrudel* and the Black Forest Chocolate Cherry torte, the *Scharzwälder Kirschtorte,* that delicious concoction of chocolate, kirsch-soaked cherries, and whipped cream.

After enjoying a substantial lunch and indulging in the calorie-rich *Kaffee and Kuchen* feast, Germans understandably keep their evening meal, the *Abendessen,* relatively light. It consists of various kinds of bread, cheeses, sliced meats, and maybe a salad or some pickled cucumbers.

Eating Out

As the Germans have become more prosperous, they have begun to dine out more frequently. There are plenty of restaurants in every price range, international and German, to satisfy their appetites ranging from the three-star restaurants to humble fast-food eateries. The most expensive dining establishments are usually the restaurants with uniformed waiters and table-cloths. Less formal is normally a *Gaststätte.* In only very few restaurants are there hostesses who will seat you. In most restaurants it is customary that guests find their own seats. Joining strangers sitting already at a table in a crowded restaurant is quite common and accepted. A final practical matter. Since a service charge of 15 percent is included in the bill, the guest is not expected to give another 15 percent tip. It is sufficient to round off the amount. If the bill comes to 78.50 euros—the euro being the official currency of Germany since 2002—give 80.

Guests who are in a hurry or on a tight budget (or do not want to deal with the hassle of slow waiters), might head for a fast-food restaurant, for Germany has not escaped the invasions of McDonald's, Burger King, and Pizza Hut. There was, however, fast food in Germany before the forays of these American chains on the German market. There has always been the venerable *Würstchenbude,* the sausage stand, as we saw above. It is found at railroad stations, marketplaces, and other highly frequented places. Moreover, in the last decades the *döner kebabs* have taken Germany by storm. In spite of its characteristic German umlaut, *döner* is a Turkish word and refers to a vertically rotating roasting spit of lamb or roast beef. Sold in small shops and street stands by Turkish immigrants throughout Germany, the meat sliced off from this spit is packed into a sandwich or a pita with onion, tomatoes, and spices added. According to one source, "by the mid-1990s annual sales of the *döner kebabs* in Germany totaled more than the combined sales of the three major fast food chains there, McDonald's, Burger King, and Wienerwald."[11] And according to another source, "every day 250 tons of döner meat are consumed."[12] Still, the golden arches and the logos of Burger King and Pizza Hut are everywhere, and the homogenized hamburgers and pizzas taste the same way in Chicago as they do in Paris and Munich, with the exception that you can wash down your Big Mac in Germany with a glass of beer—something that is unthinkable in the United States.

BEER

Germany is a beer-lover's paradise. Barely the size of Montana, the Federal Republic has a total of 1,270 breweries with around 5,000 different beer labels, compared with the 375 breweries in the United States, of which 300 are microbreweries and brewpubs.[13] In addition, 80 percent of all breweries in Europe are in Germany. Comprising a tiny 1.3 percent of the world's population, Germany produces 10 percent of the world's beer output. And after the Czechs, the Germans drink the second-largest amount of beer per capita,[14] although if you restrict your statistics to Bavaria, the inhabitants of that state out-drink everybody in the world with a total of 230 liters, or almost 60 gallons, per head annually.

The craft of brewing beer or beer-like beverages was already practiced by the old Germanic tribes, long before the Christian era. In the Middle Ages it was the monks who not only kept the art of beer-brewing alive but also refined it. During the Lenten-fasting season they complemented their meager diet with strong liquid bread, beer. As a matter of fact, the oldest working brewery in the world, the Weihenstephan Brauerei in the Bavarian city of Freising, has been in operation for almost 1,000 years. Founded in A.D. 1040 by Benedictine monks, it still produces one of the finest German beers. Today, however, only 11 monasteries are engaged in this lucrative sideline of monastic life, among them the immensely popular monastery of Andechs near Munich that attracts millions of visitors every year. The rest of the breweries are owned by very secular consortia, families, shareholder companies, or even cities.

Beer is brewed everywhere in Germany: in the north where world-class beers such as Beck's, Holsten, and Jever are brewed; in the west, the home of Bitburger, Warsteiner, and Karlsberger beer; and in the east with Radeberger (from Dresden) and Köstritzer beer. But the undisputed stronghold of brewing for more than 1,000 years has been Bavaria, home of Paulaner, Spatenbräu, and Löwenbräu—names familiar to any beer devotee in the world.

The variety of beer labels is matched by the different styles of beer. Common to all of them, however, is that they are all brewed according to the German *Reinheitsgebot* (purity law), a law that stipulates that only four ingredients, malted barley, hops, yeast, and water, may be used in the brewing process. That law was not promulgated by some health-conscious consumer group in the twentieth century but by the Bavarian duke Wilhelm IV in the year 1516—almost 500 years ago. Considered the oldest consumer protection law in the world, it is usually scrupulously heeded by brewers. When in 1986 a brewer was arrested in Bavaria for adding chemicals to his beer, he apparently considered this revelation of his violating the *Reinheitsgebot* so embarrassing that he committed suicide in his Munich prison cell.[15] Since 1994, April 23, the day when the *Reinheitsgebot* was proclaimed in 1516, is celebrated by German brewers with events and festivities—and lots of beer.

Among the many different kinds of beer, such as *Alt,* an amber-colored beer associated with the city of Düsseldorf; *Lager,* a beer with relatively small amounts of hops, which is stored (to store means *lagern* in German) from six weeks to six months; *Export,* a beer with relatively high alcohol content to survive a long journey; *Weizen* (wheat), *Hefeweisen* (yeast wheat), *Kristall-weizen* (crystal wheat), and *Malzbier* (malt beer); *Pils* is the most popular. In fact, statistically speaking, with approximately two-thirds of all German beers being brewed according to the *Pils* recipe, Germany is a *Pils* land.[16] What is a *Pils* or, to be more exact, a pilsner? It is a bottom-fermented beer with a pronounced hop aroma. Invented in 1846 by the Bavarian brewer Josef Groll in Pilsen (hence the name), a town which is now in the Czech Republic but at that time was part of the Austrian-Hungarian empire, it quickly spread through Germany. Increasingly popular is also *Weizenbier,* which is brewed with wheat instead of the traditional barley, and *Hefeweizen,* a beer with a slightly higher content of yeast. Around the city of Köln or Cologne, as it is referred to in the English-speaking world, *Kölsch* is very popular. It is a top-fermented blonde beer that is served in small 0.2-liter cylindrical glasses, contemptuously referred to as test tubes by the Bavarians, Germany's unchallenged experts on beer drinking, who never touch anything smaller than a *Maß,* a one-liter tankard. While in Berlin, one might want to sample a *Berliner Weisse,* a tart, low-alcohol beer that is often served with a dash of green woodruff or red raspberry syrup to counter its slightly acidic taste. Although refreshing on a hot summer day, it will never be drunk by a true beer purist—except in an emergency. The old city of Bamberg is home of the *Rauchbier,* a delicious beer with a distinct smoky flavor. Finally, those beer drinkers with something stronger in mind might ask for a *Bockbier* or even *Doppelbock,* dark beers with an alcohol content of seven percent or more. Strangely enough, the name has nothing to do with the German word *Bock* (billy goat), although that animal is often featured on labels of *Bockbier,* but is derived from the North German city of Einbeck where this type of beer was first brewed. *Bockbier* is only one of the terms American microbreweries have appropriated from German to market their own products. Other terms such as *lager beer, weissbeer, hefeweizen,*and *Octoberfest beer* testify to the continuing influence of the German beer-brewing craft on America and other nations.

WINE

Is Germany then a country of beer drinkers? Well, according to statistics, in 2002 Germans for the first time spent more money on wine than on beer.[17] This does not, of course, necessarily mean that they consumed more wine than beer because wine is usually more expensive than beer, but it points to an interesting trend. Among the wines Germans imbibed were, of course, many imported wines, especially from France, Spain, and Italy, but also many native wines. In recent years, it seems, German wines have come a long way and according to many experts Germany now produces "the best white wines in the world."[18] This was not always the case. In the 1960s German vintners, in an effort to expand their exports, produced crate after crate of sweet sugary wine, which they sold under the generic labels of *Blue Nun, Liebfrauenmilch,* or *Schwarze Katz*. The sweetness, often enhanced by the addition of sugar, masked the taste or lack of it. The reputation of the German wine was ruined and it took years to repair the damage. But today, German quality wines enjoy a high reputation all over the world and in the United States "the popularity among consumers is making major strides," according to a survey.[19]

Germany's northern location—geographically the center of Germany is on the same latitude as northern Newfoundland and Winnipeg—and its variable climate has both disadvantages and advantages. Since it affects the quality of the wine to a much greater degree than the relatively uniform climates of southern Europe or California, the vintage, that is the year when a particular wine was bottled, is very important. Years with warm summers and abundant sunshine produce better wines than years with rainy summers. But the relatively cool climate also has its advantages. Grapes ripen more slowly and thus can develop a more intensive aroma.

In spite of Germany's northern location there are surprisingly many vineyards. Altogether there are 13 wine-growing regions in Germany, most are situated around the Rhine and its tributaries, the Ahr, the Mosel, the Main, and the Neckar, and range from the small Ahr region in the North to Baden in the south, an area stretching for 240 miles south from Heidelberg to Lake Constance, on the right bank of the Rhine. Since statistically this region receives the most sunshine in Germany, it can boast in its advertising that its wines are "spoilt by the sun"—"*Von der Sonne verwöhnt.*" The largest annual vintage, however, is produced in the Pfalz, Palatinate, a large area of vineyards north of Baden, on the left bank of the Rhine. It is the home of the German *Weinstrasse,* a 53-mile road that winds its way through the 144 picturesque villages that comprise this region. However, as far as the high quality of the wines and spectacular scenery are concerned, few areas in Germany can match the Mosel valley, as Stefan Andres (1906–1970), a German writer and a native of this region, said: "Drinking [wine] is like praying—and my favorite place of worship is on the Mosel."[20] For 150 miles that river meanders through breathtaking landscapes, dotted with small picturesque villages and towns, such as Bernkastel-Kues, Traben-Trabach, Zell, Cochem, and Piesport, to name only a few. Since the vineyards, on many stretches of the river, are precipitously steep, the grape-picking frequently has to be done by hand so that according to an old saying, one leg of a true Mosel vintner is always shorter than the other. Once the backbreaking work is completed in the fall, the vintner and thousands of tourists celebrate the numerous wine festivals.

Whether a wine bottle hails from the Ahr, the Rhine, or the Mosel, it will always have a label telling consumers everything they want to know about the origin, vintage, and quality of the wine. The label is the birth certificate of a wine. But decoding a German wine label can be an intimidating task. In order to understand it, it is therefore helpful to familiarize oneself with some basic viticultural terms. By law, German wine is classified into two broad categories: the very inexpensive *Tafelwein* (table wine), a blend of various wines, and *Qualitätswein* (quality wine). The *Qualitätswein*—and the serious wine drinker will only drink that—is further divided into *Qualitätswein bestimmter Anbaugebiete* (QbA) meaning quality wine of certain designated regions and *Qualitätswein mit Prädikat* (QmP) meaning quality wine with a special attribute. The latter category carries one of the following six *Prädikate* (attributes) that indicate the grape's degree of ripeness at the time of harvest. *Kabinett* means wine made from the fully ripened grapes of the first harvest. It is usually the driest. *Spätlese* (late harvest) is harvested later and therefore somewhat sweeter. *Auslese* (selection) wine is made from very ripe grapes. Grapes that are picked when they are overripe are used for the *Beerenauslese* (berry selection). This is a very sweet wine offered frequently as a dessert wine. The grapes for the *Eiswein* (ice wine) are picked and pressed after the first snap frost of the season. Praised as "liquid gold" or "nectar of the gods," by wine connoisseurs,[21] it is a truly remarkable wine. The crowning achievement of German viticulture, however, is the *Trockenbeerenauslese* (dry berry selection), a wine that is made from individual berries shriveled to raisins. It is obviously harvested very late in the season.

Important for the wine is of course also the type of grape used. The most widely used grape for white wine in Germany is the *Riesling,* followed by *Silvaner, Rivaner* and *Müller-Thurgau,* and *Gewürztraminer.* Popular grapes for red wine are *Spätburgunder* (Pinot Noir) and *Dornfelder.*

WEINGUT

1 HANS WINZER

D-12345 WINZERDORF

2 2000
3 RIESLING KABINETT 4
5 HALBTROCKEN
6 WINZERDORFER REBBERG

7 RHEINGAU

8 GUTSABFÜLLUNG
QUALITÄTSWEIN MIT PRÄDIKAT
9 A.P. NR. 12 345 678 01

alc 11,5% vol   PRODUCE OF GERMANY   e 750ml

Fictitious German wine label. Reprinted by permission of the German Wine Information Bureau, New York.

After that crash course in basic German wine terminology, you might be ready to decipher a German wine label. What first seemed to be nonsensical gobbledygook, turns out to contain indispensable information for a true wine lover: (1) The first item identifies the vintner and his village (here the fictitious village of Winzersdorf). (2) The second line indicates the vintage, that is, the year the grapes for that particular wine were harvested. As mentioned, because of Germany's northern location, weather can be variable. Hence the vintage is very important. (3) This line names the grape, while line (4) denotes the time when a grape was harvested. Line (5) indicates the level of dryness, line (6) specifies the particular vineyard. Line (7) identifies the region of a particular wine and (8) reveals that the wine was bottled by an individual vintner or estate (*Gut)* and not by a cooperative of wine growers.

Line (9), finally, informs the buyer about the official control numbers as well as producers and estates.

Although for the wine connoisseur the labels are easy to decode, the German wine growers association, in an effort to make these labels easier to read, have recently introduced a simplified labeling system. Starting with the vintage of 2000, quality German wines imported into the United States will have two classifications: *CLASSIC* and *SELECTION*. According to the *Deutsches Weininstitut*, the new category of *CLASSIC* denotes "wines that are above average in quality, harmoniously dry in taste and made from one of the classic grape varieties," while the new designation *SELECTION,* targeted at wine connoisseurs and collectors, "identifies top-quality, dry varietal wines that are typical of their vintage and vineyard site—all of which appear on the label—and subject to restricted yields, selective harvesting by hand and additional sensory testing."[22]

As anyone who has ever glanced at a wine magazine knows, wine enthusiasts have developed their own jargon in describing wines. Thus a typical appraisal of a Mosel wine might go like this: "Mosel rieslings at their best combine delicacy and intensity, an ability to concentrate fruit and mineral flavors into a seemingly weightless essence and a knack of combining profound complexity with endlessly thirst-quenching drinkability."[23] Cheers! Or as the Germans say, "*Prost!*"

FASHION

For decades German fashion designers have stood in the shadow of Paris and Rome. For some time now things have been changing. Today names like Jil Sander, Wolfgang Joop, and Helmut Lang are as familiar in Paris and London as they are in Tokyo and Berlin. In the United States, Jil Sander's name is reportedly better known than that of Chanel and Armani.[24] Her elegant, somewhat austere clothes made from expensive textiles are sold all over the world as are those of her compatriot Wolfgang Joop, who has reigned as Germany's best known fashion king. And German-born Karl Lagerfeld for decades has been a presence on the haute couture scene in Paris, where he designed for the fashion house of Chanel. Among the younger designers, Bernhard Wilhelm and Markus Lupfer have won international acclaim for their creative designs. Berlin-born Helmut Newton revolutionized fashion photography in the 1970s by placing his models in outdoor settings.

Fashions have to be modeled. There have been a number of German models who have walked down the catwalks of international fashion shows. Probably best known is Claudia Schiffer. Discovered at age 17 in a German disco by a French modeling agent, this top model worked, like Lagerfeld, for years for the fashion house of Chanel and has been featured regularly in fashion magazines like *Elle* and *Vogue*. Nadja Auermann and Heidi Klum are two slightly younger models. The latter was recently voted Germany's most erotic woman[25] and was featured on a series of stamps issued by the independent nation of Grenada, a small island in the Caribbean. Avid readers of Victoria's Secret catalogs and *Sports Illustrated* swimsuit issues and calendars might also recognize her.

If Jil Sander and Wolfgang Joop are Germany's top fashion designers and Claudia Schiffer and Heidi Klum the country's top models, Düsseldorf has developed into Germany's fashion capital. To this cosmopolitan city on the Rhine international designers are drawn and it is in Düsseldorf where the annual CPD (Collections Premieren Düsseldorf) fair takes place. With its 60,000 annual visitors and 2,000 exhibitors, it is still the largest fashion show in the world. Since German reunification in 1990, however, Berlin has also become a center for avant-garde clothing and design, and the annual fashion fair "Moda Berlin" attracts thousands of visitors.

However, in spite of the emergence of these prominent names in the world of fashion, German fashion design does not enjoy the same status in Germany as it does in France and Italy. While it is viewed in those countries as an creative cultural activity almost on the same level as painting, music, and theater, in Germany, on the other hand, fashion has always ranged fairly low on the totem pole of cultural achievements. This explains the fact that German designers and models are often better known abroad. But while fashion might not be viewed as highly as in France as a cultural activity, it is certainly taken seriously as an economic issue. As a matter of fact, with 40 billion euros in turnover sales, the fashion sector is not only one of the largest consumer sectors in the German economy but also represents an important export factor. Apparently Germans not only export Porsches and BMWs but clothing as well. With 64 percent of its dresses sold abroad, Germany by 1999 occupied an astonishing fourth place after China, Hong Kong, and Italy,[26] and in Europe has become the second-largest exporter of textiles after Italy. Firms like Hugo Boss (Germany's largest manufacturer of men's clothing), Escada, Steilmann, Strenesse, and Bogner are familiar in many countries, as is Adidas, definitely not in the business of haute couture, but by far the largest company selling (mostly sports) clothing.

In caricatures German men are often depicted wearing lederhosen and sporting a Bavarian hat adorned with a large brush pin, while women are wearing dirndls, those colorful full-skirted dresses with tight bodices. To be sure, in Bavaria you might occasionally run into a man with lederhosen and women dressed in these florid costumes. Outside of Bavaria, however, the chances of encountering lederhosen or dirndl-clad Germans are slim. And if you should see someone sporting a Bavarian hat in Hamburg or Frankfurt you can be sure that you are looking at a Japanese or American tourist who bought this item in a souvenir shop in Heidelberg or Munich. Today, traditional costumes—and they are as varied as there are different German regions—are worn only on festive occasions, in parades or processions, especially in rural areas. *Trachten* (traditional costumes) have become a thing of folklore.

NOTES

1. The other remaining vestige of the image of the sauerkraut-devouring Germans is the disparaging name *Kraut* going back to the First World War and used even now by the British tabloid press for the modern Germans.

2. Sharon Hudgins, "New (and Old) Trends in German Cuisine," *German Life* (February/March 2002): 51.

3. Simon Richter, "Food and Drink: Hegelian Encounters with the Culinary Other," in *Contemporary German Cultural Studies,* edited by Alison Phipps (London: Arnold, 2002), 182.

4. Andrea Schulte-Peevers, et al., *Lonely Planet. Germany* (Melbourne, Oakland, London, and Paris: Lonely Planet Publications, 2002), 130.

5. Leah Larkin, "Brot from the Backhaus," in *German Life* (February/March 2003), 30.

6. The name is said to go back to the time of Napoleonic wars. When the French general was offered a piece of that heavy bread by a Westphalian farmer he is reported to have said "Pour mon Nickel!" [For my Nickel], Nickel being the name of his horse. In the course of time "pour mon Nickel" evolved into Pumpernickel. Or so the story goes. Cf. Phyllis Meras, "How German Dishes Got Their Names. The Origins of German Foods," *German Life* (February/March 2003), 34.

7. Sharon Hudgins, "Our Daily Bread," *German Life* (February/March 2003), 33.

8. Quoted in Lord, *Culture Shock,* 171.

9. Schulte-Peevers, et al., *Lonely Planet. Germany,* 131.

10. Mimi Sheraton, *The German Cookbook. A Complete Guide to Mastering Authentic German Cooking* (New York: Random House, 1968), 409.

11. Hudgins, "New Trends," 48.

12. Richter, "Food and Drink," 185.

13. Gregg Smith, *The Beer Enthusiast's Guide* (Pownal, Vt.: Storey Communications, Inc., 1994), 7.

14. All these fact are from Schulte-Peevers, et al., *Lonely Planet. Germany,* 113.

15. *Terramedia kommunikation & werbung gmbh,* http://www.bier.de/d08-etiketten/reinheit.html.

16. *Terramedia kommunikation & werbung gmbh,* http://www.bier.de/d01-wasistbier/pilsgegen.html.

17. *Journal,* Deutsche Welle, television broadcast, 1 January 2003.

18. Peter Hénault, "Eiswein: Liquid Gold," *German Life* (October/November 2001), 32.

19. *German Wine Information Bureau USA,* http://www.germanwineusa.org (May 2002).

20. Quoted in Sharon Hudgins, "Motoring Along the Mosel Wine Route," *German Life* (August/September 2002), 17.

21. Hénault, "Eiswein," 32.

22. Quoted from "German Wines at a Glance," an English brochure of the Deutsches Weininstitut in Mainz, 2001.

23. David Schieldknecht, "Slate Soul: The Mosel's Essential Rieslings—Where Soil and Style Converge," *Wine and Spirits Magazine,* April 2002. Quoted in German Wine Information Bureau USA, http://www.germanwineusa.org.

24. http://www.vogue.de/vogue/personalities/whoiswho/old/00279.

25. http://www.orange-today.co.uk/news/story/htm.

26. All these figures are taken from an article in *Die Badische Zeitung* of 24 August 2002 and Harenberg, *Aktuell 2002,* 215.

5

Women, Marriage, and Education

WHATEVER HAPPENED TO THE German housewife (hausfrau)—allegedly so typical for Germany that English had to borrow the word from German? Is she still confined to *Kinder, Küche, Kirche* (children, kitchen, church), the famous three *K*'s that were supposed to circumscribe her world? Or is she the self-confident, totally emancipated woman conquering one male bastion after the other, as portrayed in some accounts? What is the situation of women in Germany at the beginning of the twenty-first century? Inextricably linked to that question is the changing role of the family in contemporary Germany. Is it true that we find a "pluralization of family forms,"[1] that is, in addition to the traditional form of parents and their children we find "continually changing combinations of one parent and changing partners, same-sex couples and single-parent fathers and mothers."[2] The third topic that will be explored in this chapter is education—a key issue to which Germans traditionally have attached great importance, and central to any analysis of German culture since cultural attitudes are shaped and formed by the educational system. What, then, are the aspects of the German educational system that are excellent and worthy of imitation, and what are aspects that seem to be in dire need of reform?

WOMEN

The Basic Law (*Grundgesetz*), Germany's constitution of 1949, is quite clear about it: men and women have equal rights. But as so often, there is a gap between the noble sentiments expressed in the law and the reality and even today, more than 50 years after the Basic Law was promulgated, there are major inequalities between the genders. In spite of decades of struggle, women are, on average, paid less than men; their number in the professions and businesses is relatively small, especially in the upper echelons; and they are still expected to juggle the double duties of working outside the house and raising children. True, today's typical woman is self-confident and has little semblance to the submissive Gretchen-type of yesterday, but as Susan Stern, a British-born, American-educated academic and keen observer of the German scene says: "they [women] are an important part of the work force; they are the backbone of the family. They are also overworked, underpaid, and generally discriminated against."[3] To understand the position of today's women in Germany, a brief look back might be useful.

As in other countries, women in Germany were given the right to vote and to be elected to public office rather late. It was in 1919, a few months after the end of the First World War and the "November Revolution," when women received voting rights, one year before their sisters in the United States. Women used the new opportunities so long denied to them eagerly. In the first parliament of 1919, 10 percent of the deputies were women. Women were also able to make their mark in the professions, in the arts, and in literature. But also socially the Weimar Republic transformed women's life, "Women sported short haircuts and skirts as fashion spearheaded and reflected the new opportunities."[4] In retrospect, though, the cigarette-smoking, sexually liberated, and Charleston-dancing woman so glamorized in film and novels of the Weimar Republic was always an exception. For the vast majority of women, not that much had changed. The modest progress, however, that had been made on the road to women's emancipation was reversed when the National Socialists came to power in 1933. In the view of the new rulers, a woman's place was at home: she was meant to be a mother and helpmate of her husband. Women were discouraged to attend universities; working outside the house was frowned upon. Indeed we find not a single woman of note in politics, although we find prominent women in the arts as actors, dancers, and film directors, such as the irrepressible Leni Riefenstahl, the director of such films as *Triumph des Willens* (*Triumph of the Will*, 1935) and official films of the 1936 Berlin Olympic Games.

In order to encourage women to devote themselves exclusively to home and hearth, generous social legislation was passed and mothers with many children were honored. The German Mother's Cross, the equivalent of the Iron Cross, was bestowed on mothers who had four or more children; those with eight or more children received the Golden Mother's Cross and a coveted personal letter from the Führer. Perhaps surprisingly from today's point of view, making a woman's world "her husband, her family, her children and her house," as Hitler said in a speech in 1934,[5] was welcomed by most women who voted in large numbers for the National Socialists. After all, these were good, old-fashioned Christian and bourgeois values sanctioned by centuries of tradition.

During the Second World War (1939–1945), however, women increasingly were required to work as factory or office workers, teachers and in professions from which they had been displaced a few years ago. Although this obviously ran counter to the ideological convictions of the National Socialists, it had been made necessary by the acute labor shortage caused by the fact that men were at the front or had been killed. The achievements of women during the war and the immediate postwar period were enormous. With over 4 million men killed in the war and over 10 million held prisoners by the Allies, women had to fend for themselves and their children. The women of the ruins (*Trümmerfrauen*)—in Berlin alone there were 60,000 of them—who doggedly cleaned away the millions of cubic feet of rubble in the destroyed German cities, are the best known symbol for these brave women.

Once the men had returned from the war, however, they were able to reassert their authority and women, by and large, meekly resigned themselves to their traditional role as mothers and housewives. That this loss of freedom and independence was a difficult one and often led to severe traumatic experiences was thematized by Helma Sanders-Brahms in her film *Deutschland, bleiche Mutter* (Germany, Pale Mother, 1979; see chapter 9). Moreover, the fact that a law placing the primary responsibility for the household on a woman and requiring a husband's permission if the woman was to take on an outside job was only repealed in 1977 tells much about the persistence of traditional role models in conservative West Germany.

Against this background the feminist movement arose in the 1960s and early 1970s. It challenged the traditional division of gender roles, demanded the right of a woman to pursue a career and pressed for the legalization of abortions. The feminist movement in many ways prompted a rethinking and an examination of long-held assumptions and must be credited with some of the advances women have made in the last decades. Its effectiveness, however, was severely hampered by its fragmentation. At one point there were more than 140 groups,[6] including those that preached hatred against all men and elevated lesbianism as the only valid ideal for a woman. Today, feminists seem more pragmatic, working patiently on the numerous issues facing women in contemporary Germany.

What, then, is the situation of women in Germany at the beginning of the twenty-first century?

Great strides in the struggle for women's equality have been made, but clearly a lot remains to be done to reach the goal of equality mandated in the constitution. The most obvious advances were made in politics. Whereas in the first postwar German parliament of 1949 women were represented with only 9.8 percent, in the parliament of the 1998–2002 legislature the number had risen to 31 percent.[7] In addition, in the cabinet of Chancellor Gerhard Schröder, 5 of the 14 federal ministries are headed by women. Even the conservative CDU is currently chaired by a woman. The relative progress in this area has not been an easy one and a good deal of male resistance had to be overcome. Some semblance of gender equality has been made possible by the introduction of quotas by political parties. The Green Party, for instance, has a 50–50 quota, while the other parties have less stringent quotas.

In the economy, women represent 43 percent of all employees. But not only do women earn less money—on average 64 percent to 74 percent of what men earn[8]—but there also are very few who make it to the top. In response to "hitting the glass ceiling," many enterprising women have decided to found their own companies, and indeed one-third of all new company start-ups are established by women. Like most industrialized countries, let alone some developing countries where discrimination of women is the rule, Germany is still very much a male-dominated society in business.

In academia the situation is not much better. Although 44 percent of all students are women, they are clearly underrepresented on the teaching staffs, where only 23.5 percent are female. And even this figure is misleading because it includes all ranks. The higher the qualification, the smaller the percentage of women. A mere 9 percent of all professors are women and only an embarrassingly 5 percent of women are found among the highest rank, the so called C-4 professorships.[9]

The reasons for these inequalities are complex and depend on whom one talks to. Many women place the blame squarely on men who are, in their opinion, reluctant to give up any of the power and influence they have traditionally been accorded. Employers, on the other hand, maintain that women often are not dedicated to their careers, which they interrupt to have children, thus making an investment in their career development is not a worthwhile proposition. The fact is that Germany makes it very difficult for women to balance motherhood and career. There are, for one thing, not enough daycare centers, nurseries, and kindergartens. Once children are older and attend school, they are released at noon or at one o'clock so that they can have lunch at home. This means that mothers (or fathers if they choose to be responsible for the care of their children) can only work half days. But even that is problematic because school schedules may differ from day to day and children might be released at 11 o'clock because the teacher is sick or absent for some other reason. There are virtually no substitute teachers in the German school system. Realizing what difficulties the system creates for the working parent, some *Länder* have introduced a limited number of *verlässliche* (dependable)

Grundschulen (primary schools). This is a curious and revealing term suggesting that most schools are not dependable in their tasks of taking care of the children—which is of course true.

In view of this situation, many women opt for the so-called three-phase model: they start a career, interrupt it to have and raise children, and then, once their children are out of school, return to their profession. Clearly this model, in which a woman spends her most productive years at home, is not exactly career-furthering and helps to explain why so few women are found in top positions. The government means well. It has introduced generous provisions such as the educational leave (*Erziehungsurlaub*) whereby a woman *or* a man can stay at home for up to three years during which time the employer has to guarantee her or his return to her or his previous position. Only a tiny fraction of men elect to take the *Erziehungsurlaub*—an indication of how deeply ingrained the notion is that the upbringing of children is still a woman's, and only a woman's, primary responsibility.

Like West Germany, East Germany guaranteed equality of men and women in its constitution and East German politicians invariably pointed to the fact that almost all women in their country worked as evidence of male-female equality. Indeed, if employment is proof of a woman's emancipation, East Germany had a much better record than its neighbor to the west. Women in the German Democratic Republic were not only encouraged to work but they were required to do so because of the severe labor shortage caused by the flight of some 2 to 3 million citizens from their country. To make it possible for women to work full-time, the government had established a tight net of day-care centers. Yet in spite of the fact that so many women were part of the workforce, few rose to the top, fewer than in conservative West Germany. In addition, since men were unwilling to share the household burden, women were often faced with the triple burden of managing the household, working outside the house, and taking care of the children once their offspring had come home from the day-care centers.

Abortion Issue

As in many countries, abortion is a controversial and highly charged political and moral issue. In present-day Germany it is even more complicated because East and West Germany had different laws governing this issue—so far apart indeed that the abortion question was excluded from the unification negotiations in 1990. In East Germany abortion had been legal within the first three months of conception since 1972 and an entire generation of women grew up regarding abortion as their right. In contrast, in West Germany abortion was illegal but could be performed under certain conditions (rape, danger to mother and the unborn child, social hardship). Only in 1992—two years after unification—did the now all-German parliament pass a law permitting termination of the fetus during the first 12 weeks of pregnancy provided the expecting mother had received prior counseling. This law, however, was challenged by a number of conservative politicians, and in 1993, Germany's highest court, the *Bundesverfassungsgericht* (Federal Constitutional Court) invalidated the new law and came out with one of the most curious, logic-defying decisions. It declared that abortion was *illegal* (except when medical or criminal indications existed) but *not punishable* if carried out within 12 weeks of conception, provided a woman seeking an abortion received prior counseling. The aim of that counseling should be to persuade the woman to carry the child to term. After undergoing counseling, a woman would receive a certificate attesting that she had received proper advice from one of the appropriate organizations, including those of the two churches. Under pressure from the pope, and much to the distress of the Catholic laity, the Catholic Church in Germany opted out of this counseling system in 2000, leaving many Catholic women seeking advice somewhere else. In spite of these restrictions, there were 130,890 abortions in 1997; more than 50 percent of the women who had an abortion were married.[10]

MARRIAGE AND FAMILY

The last 30 years have seen profound changes in the way family and marriage are viewed in Germany. There are fewer marriages, fewer children, and more divorces. Alternative lifestyles, such as unmarried couples living together, single mothers and fathers, and same sex partnerships are widely accepted. In talking with young Germans, however, one often gets the impression that marriage is not only on the decline but has disappeared completely. That is not the case. In fact, marriage is still the most preferred form of living together.[11] In the middle of the 1990s, 61 percent of all inhabitants of Germany over the age of 20 were married and for many couples the wedding is still one of the most important events in their lives.[12]

It is surprising that in a country in which the churches have always played a significant role (see chapter 6), only the civil ceremony performed at a *Standesamt* (Registrar's Office) is legally binding. (This law goes back to Otto von Bismarck, the chancellor [1871–1890] during the First German Reich who sought to limit the influence of the churches, especially the Catholic Church.) A church wedding with all the pomp and circumstances might add color and a festive touch—but only that.

Are there typical German customs and rituals associated with a wedding? It is hard to generalize, of course, because customs are shaped by family tradition, exposure to international practices (through travel and friendships), and local and regional differences. Broadly speaking, though, there are some differences between German and American weddings. There is, for instance, no wedding cake to be cut by the newlyweds, no stag party, no wedding (or baby) shower, and no wedding marches by Mendelssohn and Wagner (both German composers after all). Instead of dragging noise-making tin cans behind their car, German newlyweds decorate it with flowers and ribbons. There is, however, still the custom of the *Polterabend* (*poltern* means to make a noise; compare the word *Poltergeist*), especially in rural areas. On the eve of the wedding, friends and acquaintances gather in front of the house of the bride and smash up old pottery, plates, and dinnerware. To ensure a happy marriage, the bride and bridegroom are expected to sweep up the broken pieces together. The custom might go back to the belief that by making a lot of noise, you are driving away any evil spirits lurking in the background; it might also be an evocation of the old German proverb "*Scherben bringen Glück*"—"Broken crockery brings you luck."

The custom of showering the newlyweds with rice—a symbol of fertility—when they emerge from the church or the *Standesamt* seems fairly new. But as one on-line advisor points out,[13] you better make sure that somebody sweeps up the rice afterwards—Germany is an obsessively clean country. Also be prepared to face the ire of your politically correct friends who will point out that with the rice showered on the newlyweds a whole African family could be fed for an entire week. Paper confetti might be a better solution. (There is still the problem of cleaning up.) Finally there are two customs that symbolize the newlyweds' determination to cope jointly with life's difficulties. The first of these customs involves the couple—still dressed in the wedding gown and suit—having to saw through a log of wood. The second custom is more elaborate. Outside the church (or the *Standesamt*) friends armed with objects relating to the couple's hobbies or professions (such as tennis rackets, brooms, and fire hoses, if the bride or bridegroom is working for the fire department) form two rows. The couple has to clear a path through this tunnel. Again, the custom is meant to symbolize the couple's will to overcome all obstacles together, although it could also be regarded as a kind of honor guard.

But, as mentioned before, an increasing number of people feel that they do not need a marriage license to live together. In any case, even if they eventually tie the knot, they will have lived together for a while "to get to know each other." This practice, once frowned upon and condemned as immoral, is widely accepted today. Throughout the Federal Republic, more than 1.9 million couples live without a marriage license, whereby every third of these partnerships also includes a child.[14] Another trend is towards the broad acceptance of unmarried mothers. In contrast to earlier times, there is no stigma attached to this. Still, when the CDU candidate for the German chancellorship, the Catholic Edmund Stoiber, in the 2002 parliamentary election appointed an unmarried woman with a child into his shadow cabinet, a cry of indignation arose from the Catholic bishops. Possibly the clerics would have been less incensed had Mr. Stoiber chosen her for a different cabinet post: she was to head the ministry of family affairs.

One reason for the reluctance of many couples to march off to the *Standesamt* is the high divorce rate. As in all industrialized nations, divorces are on the increase. Every third marriage ends in divorce, a much higher figure than in the 1960s, but considerably lower than in the United States, where every second marriage ends in failure.

In view of all that—the difficulties many women face in reconciling motherhood and career, the growing divorce rate, and the increasing number of people not committing themselves to a marriage—it is perhaps not surprising that Germany, with 1.3 children per family, has one of the lowest birthrates in Europe—only Spaniards and Italians have fewer children. The dropping birthrate has led to worried questions about the future of the German nation. Periodically, illustrated weeklies featuring a cute but lonely baby sporting a black-red-golden hat will anxiously ask, "Will the Germans die out?" The worry seems premature, but of immediate concern is that fewer Germans will pay into the Social Security system, thus endangering the pensions of millions of senior citizens.

The profound changes in societal mores can also be seen in the wide acceptance of homosexuality. Long gone are the days when homosexuality was punishable according to paragraph 175 of the Penal Code; long gone are also the days when the National Socialists placed gays in concentration camps, marking them with a pink triangle. Today, sexual relations between consenting adults of the same sex are not only legal but a non-issue. When in 2001 the mayoral candidate in Berlin, Klaus Wowereit, "outed" himself before the election, saying, "I am gay. And I am proud of it,"[15] the voters agreed and elected him in a landslide. Since 2001, gay partnerships are legal. Homosexuals living in such relationships enjoy almost, but not all, of the rights and duties associated with a heterosexual marriage, such as inheritance and tenants rights, health insurance, and the responsibility for each other.

Other politicians are gay as well but this hardly plays a role in the press. Nor do extramarital affairs or the number of wives politicians have. Willy Brandt, the longtime mayor of Berlin and chancellor of Germany between 1969 and 1974, was a known womanizer. But this did not cost him a vote and the two most popular German politicians in 2002, Gerhard Schröder and Joschka Fischer, had married a total of eight wives, four each—consecutively, of course. Nobody seemed to mind and the Germans followed the

Monica Lewinsky–President Clinton scandal with eagerness but were more fascinated by the reaction of the American press than by the presidential behavior. "What is the big deal?" was a frequently asked question.

Germans in general have fewer hang-ups about sex and nudity than Americans—something you notice as soon as you step off the plane in Frankfurt and walk past a *kiosk*, a newsstand, with its display of hundreds of colorful magazines. Even serious magazines like *Der Spiegel* and *Der Stern* often feature pictures of nude bodies on their covers. During the summer, thousands of sun-worshipers are scattered on the large lawn in the English Garden, Munich's large park, soaking up the sun in the nude. Nobody will get upset seeing naked children on the beaches, in the swimming pools, or in the parks—something which is, in the United States with its Puritan tradition, an impossibility.

EDUCATION

Germans value education. And they are not shy about displaying it. It is not unusual, for instance, to find bookcases in living or dining rooms in German houses. A Ph.D. is not only a qualification for a profession but also a title you proudly wear and enter into your passport. Professors still enjoy a high social prestige in spite of the battering they have endured in the wake of the 1968 student rebellion. Germans also attach great importance to education for another reason. They realize that their export-oriented and resource-poor country can compete in the global market only with a highly trained, well-educated, and skilled workforce. There are aspects of the German educational system that are excellent, such as the "dual system" that combines on-the-job training with schooling in a vocational school. It has rightly received international praise. Other aspects, such as the state-sponsored university system, are in dire need of reform.

The German educational system is complex and highly differentiated. The reason for this complexity is the fact that education is the responsibility of the individual *Länder,* the 16 states that make up the Federal Republic, each with different ideas about what constitutes a good education. Since much of that bewildering variety of school types is of interest only to the educational specialist, what follows is a bare-bones sketch of that system, leaving out many variants.

Surprisingly, there are no state-supported kindergartens in the country that pioneered the concept and gave the word kindergarten to the world. They do exist but correspond more to the American nursery schools . They are private and therefore cost money. German educators therefore do not talk about the K–12 system. Mandatory school attendance begins at age six, when all children begin to attend the *Grundschule* (primary school). The first day of school (*die Einschulung*) is marked by a ceremony attended not only by the parents but also by grandparents and other relatives and friends and is often concluded with an ecumenical service. In the center of the celebration are, of course, the children. To lessen the traumatic experience of entering the "real world" (or possibly to create a common identity) they are given a huge *Zuckertüte* or *Schultüte,* a large cone-shaped bag filled with candy, sweets, chocolate, and, alas, also with some practical items like a pencil sharpener or a key chain. In today's affluent society the young school beginner might even find a wristwatch or a cell phone in that *Schultüte.* Many of the youngsters will also wear bright baseball-style hats, not as a fashion statement or out of group pressure, but for the very sensible reason that these bright hats will make them more visible to drivers. First graders, like older children, generally either walk or take public transportation to school. (School buses are usually only found in rural areas to collect students from widely dispersed villages). Thus, children in Germany are taught from a very early age on to be independent—to an extent that would send most American parents into fits of worry.

After four years children are separated into three distinct tracks, the *Gymnasium,* the *Realschule,* and the *Hauptschule.* The decision about which one of the three school types to attend is an important one since it will determine to a large extent later career opportunities. Because of its importance, a number of factors are taken into consideration such as tests, past academic performance, recommendations of the teachers, and wishes of the parents, and some *Länder* extend the selection process over two years, during the so-called orientation phase (*Orientierungsstufe*). The three school types are usually housed in three different buildings and often in different sections of the city. Attempts by some of the *Länder* to combine the three types on one campus in a so-called *Gesamtschule* (comprehensive school) in order to break down the strict divisions and allow for greater mobility between the tracks have met only with limited success. The well-intentioned school type has never really caught on and today only 15 percent of all students attend a *Gesamtschule.*

The brightest pupils will head for the *Gymnasium,* the university-preparatory academic school from which they will graduate after nine years (grades 5 to 13) with the highly prized *Abiturzeugnis* (certificate of graduation) in their hands, which theoretically grants them admission to the university. Taught by university-trained teachers—some of them with Ph.D.'s—students have to take a broad range of subjects. In the three last years (grades 11 to 13) students can enroll in specialized courses, in addition to a number of mandatory classes, which on the level of difficulty can be compared with college courses in the American system. In recent decades, the number of students attending the gymnasium has constantly risen. Whereas in the 1950s only 5 percent of

Apprentice of a butcher. Photo by Ingo Schneider.

an age group attended the *Gymnasium,* the number has increased to 25 to 30 percent in the late 1990s.

The *Realschulen* (commercial high schools) owe their popularity—almost 40 percent attend a *Realschule*—to the fact that they offer instruction in both academic and business-related courses. *Realschule* students graduate at the end of the 10th grade. The least academically gifted students go to the *Hauptschule,* which has a strong vocational orientation. After finishing the 9th or 10th grade, *Hauptschule* pupils receive a diploma necessary to begin a three-year training or apprenticeship program for technical or clerical professions or go right into the job market.

This vocational training program is a special feature of the German educational system. Praised abroad and largely responsible for Germany's reputation of having well-trained craftsmen and technicians, the dual system, as it is called, combines practical on-the-job training with part-time theoretical instruction in a vocational school. In practice, this means that boys and girls, usually ages 14 or 15, spend three to four days in a factory, an office, or a workshop as apprentices and one or two days a week in school, where they are instructed in general courses but also receive additional training in their specialties. The range of occupations that are officially designated as eligible for vocational training is wide. At present there are around 380 different occupations, ranging from the very popular car repair to baking, from hair dressing to electrical installations, from retail sales to computer repair. The dual system has been recognized as an important factor in Germany's economic success.

The German Universities

German universities were once the envy of the world. Universities like Göttingen, Heidelberg, Leipzig, Munich, and Berlin stood for academic excellence and cutting-edge research, so much so that at the beginning of the twentieth century German had become the language of science. If Nobel Prizes are evidence of a country's eminence in research, Germany did very well indeed. Between 1901 and 1932, a total of 32 German scientists in chemistry, medicine, and physics (twice as many as from France and Great Britain each, the closest contenders for that honor)[16] had been awarded these prestigious prizes. These included such pioneers as Wilhelm Röntgen, the discoverer of X rays; Robert Koch, who established the bacterial causes of many infectious diseases, such as tuberculosis and cholera; the physicist Max Planck, who established the quantum theory; the physicist Werner Heisenberg, who formulated the uncertainty principle; and of course, Albert Einstein, the twentieth century's most famous scientist and "father" of the relativity theory.

Although German universities have existed for at least 600 years—the University of Heidelberg was founded in 1386 and is the oldest German university—the type of university that produced such splendid scientists and scholars in the past was established at the beginning of the nineteenth century by the philologist and educational reformer Wilhelm von Humboldt (1767–1835). According to Humboldt, the university was to be a place where a few privileged students would sit at the feet of great professors and pursue their scholarly work. This Humboldtian model survived all wars, revolutions, and political upheavals, possibly because it was viewed as being successful. All attempts to reform failed, or as one observer says: "Perhaps no institution in Germany has been more resistant to change than the university and, until the 1970s, more successful in preserving its traditional forms of internal governance."[17] In the late 1960s and 1970s, however, two related developments occurred that changed dramatically the nature of the German universities: first, the enormous expansion of the universities, and secondly, the student rebellion of the late 1960s.

The unprecedented growth of the universities was the result of the realization that a highly industrialized nation such a Germany needed more university graduates. Roused out of their complacency by a book by the German educational philosopher Georg Picht, which predicted an "educational catastrophe" (*Bildungskatastrophe*), German politicians quickly expanded the existing universities, founding dozens of new ones in what turned out to be the biggest university construction boom since the Middle Ages. Some of the new universities featured attractive campuses, like Konstanz and Trier, while others consisted of an agglomeration of hideous buildings, such as Bochum or Bielefeld. At the same time, the number of students increased dramatically. Between 1950 and 2000, their numbers rose eightfold, from 200,000 in 1950 to 1.8 million in 1999. The result is that today there exists a number of huge and unwieldy "mass universities." In Berlin alone, 140,000 students study at the three major universities (The Humboldt University, the Free University, and the Technical University). Hamburg University has 62,000 students; Munich, 93,000; Cologne, 31,000; and 52,000 students are enrolled in the relatively small town of Münster.[18] The number of teaching faculty was not expanded correspondingly, with the result that in some popular fields such as German, English, or history, hundreds of students find themselves in seminars and lectures where seats are at a premium. Sometimes, students consider themselves lucky when they see the professor at the end of their studies at the final examination. The large number of students and the lack of individual mentoring also account for the high dropout rate. One in four students leaves the university without a degree.

The second development that changed the character of the German university was the student rebellion in the late 1960s. The revolt of the students was an international phenomenon. But whereas in the United States, students protested against the Vietnam War and participated in the civil rights movement, in Germany their demonstrations were directed on the one hand against their parents' generation, whom they, somewhat smugly, blamed for the Nazi crimes, and on the other hand against the antiquated structures of the universities. Carrying in one famous instance a large banner saying, "*Unter den Talaren der Muff von tausend Jahren*" (under the gowns [of the professors] the mustiness of a thousand years), they demanded a democratization of the rigid hierarchies of the universities and participation in their governance. Though justified in many of their demands, students antagonized large parts of the population not only through their revolutionary rhetoric but also through their radical approach. Demonstrations, sit-ins, and walk-ins occasionally degenerated into violence. Still, reforms were made and today German universities are somewhat more democratic institutions than 50 years ago.

What did not change, however, was the discrepancy between the relatively small number of faculty and the huge number of students. These generally unfavorable student-teacher ratios, however, are somewhat deceiving. Since there is no tuition at German universities, many students just enroll without seriously intending to pursue studies in order to benefit from the numerous perks German students enjoy, such as reduced rates in theaters, cinemas, swimming pools, reduced bus fares, inexpensive health insurance, and so on. There is no shortage of suggestions on how to solve this problem. Attempts by some *Länder* to introduce some modest tuition fees to keep away those students who only enroll for the sake of material advantages have met with loud protests. It is a taboo. The Social Democratic Party (SPD) even wanted to ban by law any attempt to introduce fees, arguing that such fees would discriminate against young people from socially disadvantaged families, forgetting completely that it is the miners in the Ruhr district and the Turkish guest laborers at the assembly line in Stuttgart who through their taxes pay for the studies of a privileged minority. Under the financial strains of recent years, some *Länder* (states) have indeed introduced modest tuition fees.

Unlike the United States, which boasts hundreds of private colleges and universities, among them the splendid Ivy League universities, Germany does not have a tradition of privately financed universities. However, in recent decades, a number of private universities and institutions of higher learning have sprung up to cater to the needs of those students who are dissatisfied with the quality of teaching and lack of counseling at the overcrowded public universities. At present there are about 50 of them, most offering courses in management, business, and law. Although they charge tuition, it is considerably lower than that charged by schools in the United States.[19] The 30, 000 students enrolled represent, of course, only a fraction (less than 2 percent) of the total student population.

Among the 380 institutions of higher learning in Germany, there are many excellent specialized schools that offer students a well-organized education. There are conservatories, art schools, and technical schools with dedicated professors and well-motivated students. The Max Planck institutes and the institutes of the Fraunhofer Society conduct world-class research. In recent years, many universities have initiated reforms, such as evaluation of professors to improve the quality of teaching, once a "sacred cow," or the introduction of Bachelor's and Master's programs to bring German education more closely in line with international standards. And it is surely no accident that more and more international students flock to Germany for study. In 2002, some 140,000 students came from abroad, accounting for more than 11 percent of all students enrolled in German universities and technical schools. Germany is thus the most popular destination after the United States and Great Britain for academic study.[20] Though it is unlikely that Germany will once again become the mecca for students from all over the world, as it was in the nineteenth century, it seems it has reclaimed a place among the top countries for attracting foreign students.

NOTES

1. Christine Guist, *The Family in Germany—Developments in the East and West of the Country* (Bonn: Goethe Institut Inter Nationes e.V., 2002), 3.

2. Ibid.

3. Stern, *Strange German Ways,* 72.

4. Eva Kolinsky, "Non-German Minorities, Women and the Emergence of Civil Society," in *The Cambridge Companion to Modern German Culture,* edited by Eva Kolinsky and Wilfried van der Will (Cambridge: Cambridge University Press, 1998), 122.

5. Benjamin C. Sax and Dieter Kuntz, *Inside Hitler's Germany. A Documentary History of Life in the Third Reich* (Lexington, Mass., and Toronto: D.C. Heath and Co., 1992), 262.

6. Gordon A. Craig, *The Germans* (New York: Putnam Books, 1991), 168.

7. Gros and Glaab, *Faktenlexikon Deutschland,* 81.

8. Stern, *Strange German Ways,* 73.

9. Gros and Glaab, *Faktenlexikon Deutschland,* 83.

10. Gros and Glaab, *Faktenlexikon Deutschland,* 88.

11. Gros and Glaab, *Faktenlexikon Deutschland,* 75. Also Guist, *The Family in Germany,* 3.

12. Ibid.

13. *Voetsch-Webdesign,* http://www.kirchenweb.at

14. Gros and Glaab, *Faktenlexikon Deutschland,* 77.

15. He said: "Ich bin schwul und das ist gut so." (Literally: "I am gay and that is good so.")

16. Heinz, P. Lohfeldt, ed., *Spiegel Almanach 2002. Die Welt in Zahlen, Daten, Analysen* (Hamburg: *SPIEGEL*-Buchverlag, 2002), 528.

17. Craig, *The Germans,* 170.

18. All figures are from Derek Lewis, *Contemporary Germany: A Handbook,* (London: Arnold; New York: Oxford, 2001), 164.

19. Stern, *Strange German Ways,* 149–50.

20. http://www.germany-info.org., (September 2, 2002).

6

Religion

IT WAS A GERMAN philosopher, Friedrich Nietzsche (1844–1900), who at the end of the nineteenth century declared: "God is dead." Although his pronouncement has been echoed by many others after him, rumors of the death of God seem exaggerated, at least in Germany. To be sure, Germany, like most Western countries, has become a largely secular country. But this hardly means that religion has ceased to play an important cultural role. As Gordon Craig, that wise observer of Germany, said: "Considering the number of times that German intellectuals have declared that God is dead, its newspapers devote a surprising amount of space to news about religion."[1] All predictions notwithstanding, the Christian religion has remained a vital force in Germany. Too deeply is it anchored in German culture and history. In addition to Christianity there is a small but once-again growing Jewish community and a large Muslim population in Germany. All three religions and their role in contemporary Germany's culture will be explored in this chapter.

CHRISTIANITY

Although religious freedom in Germany is guaranteed by the constitution and adherents of the major world religions as well as followers of numerous smaller religious groups are free to practice their faiths, religious life in Germany is dominated by the two Christian denominations: Roman Catholicism and the so-called Evangelical Church of Germany (EKD), an association of Lutheran and Reformed Calvinist churches, which we henceforth will refer to as Protestantism. At present there are about 27.4 million Roman Catholics, or 33 percent of the total population, and an equal number (27.6 million) of Protestants.[2] If the members of various other Christian denominations (Greek Orthodox and free churches) are added, the number of Germans who consider themselves Christians is about 70 percent, or, if we look at the two former German states separately, 80 percent of the West Germans and 25 percent of East Germans are church members. The relative strength of the churches in an increasingly secular world might at least be partially explained by the unique status the churches enjoy as public institutions. Although Christianity is not a state religion, as is the Lutheran Church in Sweden, Denmark, Norway, and Finland and the Anglican Church in Great Britain, the two main Christian confessions in Germany, the Protestants and the Roman Catholics, along with the Jewish community (see below) enjoy a privileged position. This status is reflected in the fact that the state collects what is called a church tax (*Kirchensteuer*), even if it applies to non-Christian communities, amounting to eight to nine percent of a person's income tax. After deducting a commission for this administrative service, the state authorities pass on this levy to the churches. The result is that both churches in Germany are enormously wealthy. In 1997, for instance, the EKD received 7.588 billion DM (around $3.7 billion), while the Catholic Church took in 8.1 billion DM (around $4 billion).[3] For that reason, the churches are not dependent on fund-raising or voluntary contributions on Sundays.

The churches, it seems to an outside observer, spend their wealth wisely. They can, for instance, afford to provide generous aid to the developing countries, more so than anybody else. The Protestant Brot für die Welt (Bread for the World) and the Catholic Miserere (Latin, meaning "have mercy") have collected billions of deutsche marks for emergency relief. Their wealth is also reflected in the many churches that have been restored and built since the Second World War. As one observer noted in 1971: "More churches have been built in the postwar Federal Republic—an estimated 10,000 of them— than in the four centuries between the Reformation and World War II."[4] And that was more than 30 years ago. But the main portion of the churches' expenditures goes to providing a host of social services that otherwise the state would be required to perform. Both the Evangelical and the Catholic church run kindergartens, hospitals, nursing homes, counseling and rehabilitation centers, family planning centers, and telephone ministry. With 700,000 employees, the two main charitable organizations, the Catholic Caritas-Verband and the Lutheran Diakonische Hilfswerk, are among the largest employers in Germany.

But "the well-functioning, synergic relationship"[5] between state and churches goes beyond providing an indispensable service to the needy, handicapped, infirm, and old and young. Christianity is deeply embedded in German culture. All but three of the 12 legal holidays (or 15, depending on the

Corpus Christi Procession in Freiburg. Photo by Ingo Schneider.

state) are religious holidays;[6] religion is taught in public schools; Catholic priests and Protestant pastors are trained in publicly financed universities; representatives of the two major Christian denominations and the Jewish community sit on the boards of the two public radio and television corporations; the advice of prominent church leaders and theologians is listened to, if not always followed; and two of the largest political parties, the Christian Democratic Union (CDU) and its Bavarian sister party, the Christian Social Union (CSU), are ostensibly based on Christian principles and have played active roles over the last 50 years in shaping German society.

    That both the Protestant and the Catholic Churches still play such an important role in Germany's cultural and political life is remarkable because the churches have been losing members in significant numbers since the 1980s. With about 180,000 members leaving the church every year, the Protestants are more affected by that trend than the Catholics, who fare slightly better with an average annual dropout rate of about 150,000.[7] Among the reasons given for leaving the churches are disillusionment with an institution that is perceived as having no longer any relevance in today's world. In the case of the Catholic Church, continued discrimination against women is seen in the church's refusal to ordain women, and disagreements with the conservative views on contraception and abortion are frequently cited for leaving the church. For many members of both confessions, the well-known reluctance of people to part with their well-earned money by paying the hefty *Kirchensteuer* is of course also a good reason, if not the most important one, for canceling their church membership. Those who stay in the church seem to be very lax about attending weekly Sunday services. Again, Protestants are more affected by this trend than Catholics. Only 4 percent of Protestants make their way to a church on a regular basis, while 19 percent of Catholics attend Sunday Mass regularly.[8] The only day of the year when both churches can count on a visit of their members is Christmas Eve. On that day churches are packed with believers and non-believers alike. As one observer notes, "Many Germans wear their religious affiliation more like a style of dress, to be put on or taken off mainly for special occasions."[9]

The dismal record of attending Sunday services by a population of which 70 percent still consider themselves Christians points to a paradox, reinforced by a poll. According to this survey, only 44 percent of all Germans consider themselves religious, 47 percent non-religious, and 8 percent atheists,[10] suggesting that almost 30 percent of Germans who are members of a church do not consider themselves religious. In spite of that they stay in their churches. Loyalty and tradition, an appreciation for the essential services the churches provide for the needy, or the thought that one day the church might be needed on particular occasions such as baptism, marriage, and funerals are cited as reasons for remaining in the church. It has been suggested that "individuals, while continuing to see religion as important, have become selective about what features of the established churches and their rituals they are prepared to integrate into their personal life-styles."[11] Though the churches might still have a role to play as cultural and social institutions, their role as providers of spiritual guidance has been greatly diminished. Does this mean that Germany, along with the rest of Western Europe, has become a post-religious society, as an American critic observed?[12] Perhaps. It would be unthinkable in any European country that the prime minister or chancellor starts his cabinet meeting with a prayer, as does U.S. President George W. Bush. Nor is parliament opened with a prayer by an official chaplain. Nor would any politician so frequently insist that God bless his or her country.

The Geographical Distribution

The two major Christian denominations, the Evangelical Church and the Catholic Church, are distributed unevenly over Germany. For historical reasons (to be explained later), Protestants and Catholics lived in fairly distinct geographical areas up until 1945. While Protestants lived in the north, east, and center, Catholics were to be found in the south and west, especially in Bavaria and the Rhineland. These distinctions, while still valid in a general sense, have been considerably broken up by the influx of the 12 million refugees after the Second World War. Settling wherever they could find a job or a new home, Catholics would take up residence in Protestant areas, while Protestants would find new homes in predominantly Catholic areas. This living together of the two denominations, along with the ecumenism embraced after the Second Vatican Council (1962–65) and an awareness that both churches are beleaguered institutions in an age of secularism, has led to a close cooperation of the two Christian faiths on the local, regional, and national levels. They frequently combine their resources in joint welfare activities, occasionally they participate in ecumenical services; mixed marriages, once frowned upon, are on the rise, and for the first time in almost 500 years, Protestants and Catholics celebrated together the Eucharist at the combined Evangelical and Catholic Church Congress in May of 2003.[13] There is, in short, none of the enmity between the two confessions one still finds, for instance, in Northern Ireland. Interconfessional relations in Germany are excellent.

This was not always the case.

A Short History

The historical rivalry between the two major denominations, as well as other peculiarities of state-church relations, calls for a brief look at German history. Why, for instance, are certain regions predominantly Catholic, while others are overwhelmingly Protestant? What is the origin of the close cooperation between state and churches? Why are 80 percent of all West Germans still members of a church, but only 25 percent of East Germans? The answers to these questions are deeply rooted in German history. For some of them we have to go back almost 500 years, for others it is enough to look at divided Germany's more recent history.

When, in 1517, the unknown theology professor Martin Luther (1483–1546) published his 95 theses against the sale of indulgences in the small university town of Wittenberg, neither he nor anybody else was aware that he would precipitate an event of world historical importance whose impact is still felt today. What was initially meant only as a theological debate soon evolved into a widespread protest movement challenging the papal authority and undermining the very foundations of the late medieval church, leading eventually to an unbridgeable rift in the until-then monolithic Catholic Church and the establishment of the Lutheran Church.

Today, Luther is widely revered in Germany as the man who stood up against the authority of the pope. The sites associated with his life have become historical landmarks: the university of Wittenberg where he taught for many decades; the hall in Worms where, in the presence of Emperor

Charles V, he refused to recant his teachings; and Wartburg, where he fled and where he began his magnificent translation of the Bible into German. In his own time, Luther soon realized that he could not implement his reforms within the Catholic Church. He therefore turned to the political authorities, and these were, in the sixteenth century, the territorial princes and the city councils of the free imperial cities. From the very beginning, the success of the Protestant Reformation thus depended on the support of the state. In turn, a key element of Lutheran political theory has always been its unequivocal support of the state. Any resistance against a divinely instituted temporal authority was out of the question. When, for instance, in 1524–25 the German peasants revolted against their oppressors, they were encouraged, as they thought, by Luther's teachings. The reformer, however, denounced the revolutionaries in the strongest possible terms.

By the 1540s the religious conflict had evolved into a military one in which the emperor and his Catholic allies were pitched against the Protestant princes in the so-called Schmalkald War. This military struggle ended only with the Peace of Augsburg in 1555, a treaty that marked one of those important dates in German history that was to have consequences extending to our time. Concluded between the Lutheran and Catholic parties, the Augsburg treaty stipulated that the princes of Germany would be free to choose between Catholicism and Lutheranism in their territories, but also that only a single religion was recognized within the boundaries of these lands.[14] In addition, in many cases the prince was automatically the head of the territorial church. The treaty explains not only that certain regions in Germany are Protestant and others are Catholic but also accounts for the alliance of state and church, or throne and altar, remnants of which still can be seen in contemporary Germany.

Though far from perfect, the Ausgburg treaty assured peace in German lands for the next 60 years. When war broke out in 1618, starting what is called the Thirty Years' War, religious differences certainly played a role, as both confessions tried to extend their territories or roll back the gains made by their opponents since the 1520s. But religious dissensions were only one aspect of this conflict. Rather, dynastic and political considerations played as much a role in that war. When the war ended with the Peace of Westphalia in 1648, after a third of the German population had perished, as some historians claim, the result was twofold: it reconfirmed the principle that the religion of the prince determined the religion of the people, and, secondly, it cemented the confessional divisions along geographical boundaries. This is not the place to trace the development of the churches in the eighteenth and nineteenth centuries and the challenges they faced in times of increasing secularization and industrialization. Suffice it to remember that the Peace of

Augsburg and the Peace of Westphalia left two important legacies for the twentieth century: the clear boundaries between Catholic and Protestant areas and the alliance between state and church.

Especially the latter, the close cooperation between state and church, left the churches poorly prepared for resisting the National Socialists, who after all had come to power legally. In 1933 the newly installed National Socialist regime concluded a concordat with the Vatican. In it, the Catholic Church was granted certain privileges, such as maintaining confessional schools and youth groups in exchange for a promise to abstain from political activity. This recognition by the powerful and widely respected church represented a diplomatic triumph for the Nazi regime. The concordat, however, did not prevent Hitler from violating certain provisions of that treaty and from harassing individual clergy. The Protestants, lacking a central authority, were even more vulnerable to the encroachments by the new state authorities. Brazenly, the Nazis tried to unify the various Lutheran churches in the "German Christian" movement, a staunchly nationalist movement that was purged of its Jewish roots. Rejecting this attempt to bring the Lutheran Church under Nazi control, the Confessing Church (*Bekennende Kirche*) was founded in 1934, and although 18 of its ministers died in concentration camps, its resistance was largely confined to theological and ecclesiastical matters. Yet in both churches there were also numerous individual clergymen who spoke out courageously against the abuses of the regime, men like Martin Niemöller, who spent seven years in a concentration camp, and Dietrich Bonhoeffer, who paid with his life for his resistance, or the Catholic Cardinal Clemens von Galen, who denounced from the pulpit Hitler's euthanasia program, and the Berlin cleric Bernhard Lichtenberg, who was sentenced to imprisonment and died on his way to a concentration camp for praying publicly for the Jews. On the whole, however, the churches, as institutions, offered little resistance to the Third Reich and failed to speak out and denounce the persecution of the Jews.

In spite of the less than heroic role they had played during the Third Reich, the churches assumed an important role in the newly founded West Germany after the Second World War. Compared with almost all other organizations that had been brought under Nazi control, they were seen as institutions that were least tainted by association with that regime. They also could claim that they represented a return to traditional Christian values. By the same token, their very failure to withstand the Nazis prompted them to get involved in the democratic reconstruction of their country. Both churches cooperated in the founding of the CDU, the Christian Democratic Union. This party, along with its Bavarian sister party, the Christian Social Union (CSU), has formed the government for 36 of the more than 54 years of the history of West Germany.

The situation in East Germany, however, was quite different. Here an atheistic Communist regime under Walter Ulbricht made every effort to undermine the churches, especially the Lutheran Church, historically the dominant religious institution in that part of the country, waging a persistent campaign of harassment against those who practiced their religion. Over the years, century-old traditions were abolished: in 1956, for instance, the church tax was repealed, two years later, mandatory religious education in schools was prohibited. Practicing Christians were frequently denied educational and professional opportunities. In some cases, Protestant ministers were jailed; confessional youth groups were outlawed; the Lutheran confirmation was replaced by the *Jugendweihe* (literally, youth dedication), a secular ritual marking the acceptance into the socialist community. Relations between church and state improved, however, when Erich Honecker assumed the leadership of Communist East Germany in 1971, and by the mid-1970s the Protestant Church made an uneasy peace with the regime. In the last decade of the GDR, the churches provided a haven for all sorts of dissenters, ranging from environmentalists to activists of the peace movement, and in the final year of East Germany the Protestant Church played a key role in the peaceful revolution that led to the eventual collapse of the East German regime in 1989. It not only provided venues for prayer meetings and discussions but also made sure that the demonstrations that eventually led to the collapse of the Communist regime remained nonviolent. As the further development of the churches in the former East Germany has shown, it would be wrong to interpret the flocking of dissenters to the Lutheran Church as a revival of Christianity. Forty years of Communist government have been surprisingly successful in almost eradicating the "opiate of the people," as Karl Marx called religion. Church membership has dropped from 14 million after the war to a mere 3.8 million at the end of the millennium;[15] two-thirds of all East Germans are not members of the a church, and 70 percent of them do not believe in God, according to polls."[16]

THE JEWISH COMMUNITY

In contrast to the Catholic and Protestant churches, the Jewish communities in Germany experienced a dramatic increase in the 1990s. As Susan Stern observed, "no other country in the world, including Israel, has experienced such a growth, from 30,000 in 1990 to about 100,000 a decade later."[17] The some 80 Jewish communities are located in all major German cities, but as before the war, it is Berlin where the Jewish presence is most apparent. The German capital is home of the beautifully restored, impressive golden-domed New Synagogue as well as the architecturally striking new Jewish Museum designed by Daniel Libeskind. A Jewish high school has acquired an excellent reputation within a few years and is attracting many non-Jewish students. The revival of Jewish life is also reflected in the fact that Germany has become the third-largest publisher of Jewish books, after the United States and Israel. Many of these books are aimed at a non-Jewish audience to satisfy the growing interest in and fascination with Jewish subjects. Not only do Germans snap up books on Jewish topics but they also stream to lectures on Judaism, learn Hebrew, and travel to Israel.[18]

In spite of the impressive growth, the Jewish community represents a tiny minority compared with the two major Christian confessions and the sizable Muslim population. Yet for historical reasons, it enjoys privileges that other non-Christian religions such as Islam do not have. Susan Stern calls it "a group whose exceptional past has led to an unexpected present."[19] As one of the three privileged religions, Judaism benefits from the church tax and receives state subsidies. Its representatives sit on the broadcasting corporation councils. The head of the Central Council of the Jews in Germany is listened to and his voice is taken seriously.

The dynamic growth of 300 percent of the Jewish community in the last decade in the country that is responsible for the genocide of Europe's Jewry is remarkable and requires an explanation.

Ironically, after the war, Allied-occupied Germany provided a safe refuge for those Jews who had survived the concentration camps and the death machinery of the Nazis or those who had fled from the postwar anti-Semitic purges in Poland. The result was that in the immediate postwar years, 250,000 Jewish displaced persons, or DPs, found themselves in the country that had tried to murder them. Although by 1950, 90 percent of those had emigrated to the United States or to the fledgling state of Israel, 30,000 stayed in Germany, leading a somewhat uneasy existence and sitting on the proverbial packed suitcases, ready to leave in cases of an upsurge of anti-Semitism. By the late 1980s, however, members of this small Jewish community had overcome the so-called packed suitcase syndrome and had decided to stay in Germany and to make the Federal Republic their permanent home. Then an event occurred that marked the most significant development in postwar German-Jewish history. In the wake of Mikhail Gorbachev's perestroika, an agreement was negotiated between the Russian and German governments providing for an open immigration quota for Russian Jews wishing to come to Germany. Since Germany never considered itself an immigration country, this treaty represented an exception and has to be understood as a gesture of atonement to the Jewish people. Neither the German Jews who advocated this arrangement nor the Russians who negotiated it foresaw the consequences. The expected small trickle turned into a broad stream: in the first decade since this policy went into effect, an estimated 160,000 Russians have settled in Germany, of whom, however, only about half are considered Jews by strict laws defining Jewishness. For historical reasons, the German government wisely stays out of the process of deciding a person's Jewishness and errs rather on the side of admitting more than fewer applicants, even if their Jewish ancestry is in doubt. The massive influx of Russian Jews has created considerable problems for the old Jewish community. Having grown up in a very secular society, the Russian Jews are in general more secular, less-versed in Jewish traditions than those already living in Germany. They are also younger and well-educated. Their primary goal in moving to Germany is to integrate themselves quickly into German society and not necessarily into the Jewish community. Although this has inevitably led to resentments and tensions on the part of the older native German Jews, it is also clear that they have revitalized the Jewish community. Ironically, Israel has consistently opposed this immigration to Germany. As Susan Stern put it: "One of the few discords in the German-Israel relationship is caused by the refusal of Germany to turn away Jewish immigrants. Israel wants every Jew for itself."[20]

The Historical Dimension

That Israel resents the immigration to Germany is indicative of this very sensitive, highly complex, and emotionally charged relationship between Jews, Germans, and the state of Israel. Even after 60 years, the Holocaust looms large. However, as one observer noted, "The Holocaust marks a singular historical moment that has everything to do with German-Jewish relations today. But one damages the past by conflating all of German-Jewish experience with the Holocaust, or by reading events of the last centuries as simply a prelude to National Socialist atrocities."[21] A brief look at the history of German-Jewish relations might be helpful in putting the German-Jewish relations in perspective.

Jews have been living in what is now Germany for at least 16 centuries. Emperor Charlemagne (768?–814; emperor 800–814), who in 782 did not hesitate to have thousands of heathen Saxons massacred in an attempt to convert them to Christianity, permitted Jews to own houses and to participate in public life. During the Middle Ages, however, these privileges were rescinded. Fanned by a church-sponsored, religious anti-Judaism, sporadic anti-Jewish outbursts, pogroms, forced conversions, and expulsions were frequent occurrences in Europe. Everything from the black death to bad harvests were blamed on the Jews. Luther, disappointed that the Jews did not accept his version of Christianity, launched vicious verbal attacks on them. The situation changed only during the Enlightenment, the age of reason, when the Jewish philosopher Moses Mendelssohn (1729–86) argued that German Jews should accept German culture as their own while retaining their faith, and free themselves of outworn rituals. At the end of the eighteenth century, literary salons, hosted by Jewish ladies and attended by Jews and Gentiles alike, flourished in Berlin. But it was only in 1872, in Bismarck's Second Empire that Jews were formally granted full and equal rights. Within a few decades, Jews integrated and assimilated to a remarkable degree into German society. Jews fought in the First World War, and 12,000 died. They considered themselves Germans first and Jews second. And they were successful in business, in literature, and in the arts. At the same time, although neither Bismarck nor the Emperor Wilhelm II were anti-Semitic, anti-Semitism was on the rise. In 1880 the respected German historian Heinrich Treitschke published a treatise with the title, "The Jews Are Our Misfortune"; composer Richard Wagner attacked Jews in his essay, "Judaism in Music"; and the influential court preacher Adolf Stoecker launched his anti-Semitic tirades from the pulpit. During the Weimar Republic (1919–1933), whose constitution had been drafted by the Jewish legal scholar Hugo Preuss, Jews contributed immensely to the flourishing culture: there was the architect Erich Mendelssohn (1887–1953); the philosopher Walter Benjamin (1892–1940); the composers Kurt Weill (1900–1950) and Arnold Schönberg (1874–1951); and the writers Alfred Döblin (1878–1957) and Kurt Tucholsky (1890–1935); to name only a few. In spite of latent and sometimes open anti-Semitism, German Jews had become part of German culture and therefore totally unprepared for what became known as the Holocaust, a program that evolved from a state-ordered boycott of Jewish stores on April 1, 1933, to the Nuremberg Laws of 1935 that prohibited marriages between Jews and non-Jews, to the *Kristallnacht,* that nationwide pogrom on November 9, 1938, to the forced deportation and murder in the death camps of the east.

It took Germans a considerable time until they began to deal with that terrible chapter of their history. It was only in the 1960s that German intellectuals and writers such as Günter Grass, Heinrich Böll, and Rolf Hochhuth seriously took up the confrontation with the Nazi past. Triggered by the Adolf Eichmann trial in Jerusalem in 1960 and the Auschwitz trials in Germany itself (1963–1965), intensive discussions about the Nazi atrocities began. But it was the American mini-series "Holocaust," broadcast to 20 million in 1979, a melodramatic and vivid portrayal of the fate of a German-Jewish family during the Third Reich, that brought home the gravity of the crimes committed against their countrymen. Since then the Holocaust has become an obsessive preoccupation. Education about the persecution of the Jews has become mandatory in schools. As Susan Stern observes: "Certainly there was

The restored New Synagogue on Oranienburger Strasse.
Reprinted by permission of Stiftung "Neue Synagoge
Berlin—Centrum Judaicum."

far more knowledge of the Holocaust than anywhere else, and less anti-
Semitism than in many other countries including the United States."[22]

The Federal Republic has also lived up to its historical responsibility in
other respects. Beginning in the 1950s, it has paid enormous sums, a total of
135 billion deutsche marks, to both the state of Israel and to individual Jewish survivors or their relatives in restitutions. Daniel Goldhagen, one of the
harshest critics of Germany's historic anti-Semitism, a scholar who in his
book *Hitler's Willing Executioners,*[23] accused the Germans of having an anti-
Semitic "eliminationist strain," in 1998 wrote about postwar Germans:

"Their [the Germans'] attitudes toward the past will continue to be complex as will be their conduct. Yet compared with how the peoples of other countries including the United States, deal with the dark and inglorious chapters of their pasts, Germans have done better—indeed very well. How many other nations have so publicly and intensely aired the criminal and sordid episodes in their histories?"[24]

ISLAM IN GERMANY

Not Judaism, however, but Islam is the second-largest religion in Germany, if we consider Protestantism and Catholicism as variations of the same Christian religion. As of 2003, approximately 3.2 million Muslims lived in the Federal Republic of Germany.[25] Although they come from 41 different countries and represent the entire spectrum of Islam, the largest group, or around 75 percent, comes from Turkey.[26] Yet in books on modern Germany you are likely to find only a cursory treatment of Islam. If it is mentioned at all, it is in the context of "guest workers" or "multicultural society." Islam, it seems, is not considered a German phenomenon by most observers. The fact that only 450,000 of the 3.2 million Muslims in Germany are German citizens might contribute to this impression as might the fact that the phenomenal growth of the Muslim population in Germany is a recent phenomenon. Up to the mid-1950s, West Germany had virtually no Muslim communities. Then, in the wake of the German "economic miracle," as the country's rapidly growing demand for labor could not be supplied from within, Germany began recruiting workers from other countries, such as from Italy, Spain, Portugal, Yugoslavia, and Turkey. The idea was to bring into the country laborers for only temporary employment, a fact that was reflected in the term *Gastarbeiter* (guest workers). After a few years these guest workers were expected to return to their home countries and be replaced by a new wave of workers. This principle of rotation never worked. German employers were reluctant to let go the people they had spent money on training; and the workers found the freedom and the good pay too attractive to give up after a few years. So most of them stayed and many were joined by their families. By the 1970s, however, West Germany's labor shortage had turned into a labor surplus and unemployment was rising. The German government not only stopped the recruiting of *Gastarbeiter* but offered cash incentives to those who were willing to return to their native countries. Few took up the offer but instead brought their families to Germany. As a result Germany has now a large population of foreigners, about 10 percent, swelled by the hundreds of thousands of so-called asylum seekers who have sought and found political asylum in Germany. Among the *Gastarbeiter* and their descendants, the Turks—overwhelmingly

Muslims—represent by far the largest individual single group, about 1.8 million.

The presence of such a large Muslim population in the midst of a still predominantly Christian country has created problems that have to do as much with cultural as with religious fears on the part of the Germans. A case in point is the appearance of mosques in Germany. As long as the Muslims practiced their religion in so-called backyard mosques, that is, small rooms tucked away in apartments, or old factories, there was no problem. When the Muslims, however, began building larger mosques with their distinctive architectural features of domes and minarets in cities, objections were raised: the Arab architecture was seen as too alien to fit into the traditional German cityscape, the minarets too tall, the muezzin's calls to prayer too loud, and the traffic jams created by the worshipers flocking to the mosque too chaotic. In spite of these objections numerous mosques have been built in recent years in most German cities and acceptance of them by the German population has been growing. According to estimates there are currently 2,200 simple prayer rooms and 77 mosques in Germany; another 123 are under construction.[27] Hamburg has more mosques than any other city in Europe.

Muslims, like all religious groups, enjoy complete freedom of religion according to the Basic Law, Germany's constitution. But although Islam is, as noted previously, the third-largest religion in Germany, after Protestantism and Catholicism, or the second largest if you count the two Christian denominations as one, it is not recognized as a legal public body, as these two Christian religions and Judaism are. The explanation is that there is no single official organization that represents the interests of all Muslims. In spite of that lack of recognition, Islam is flourishing and is generally well-accepted. The undeniable problems that exist have relatively little to do with religion itself but with the realization that Germany is being transformed from a fairly homogeneous into a multicultural society. While some Germans welcome that change, others oppose it, fearing that it will change the very identity of their country. The problem with the large Islamic Turkish population is compounded by the fact that many of the Turkish Muslim immigrants have come from a pre-modern, patriarchal society in rural Anatolia with different cultural assumptions and value systems than those prevalent in liberal and largely secular West Germany. Especially the diametrically opposed treatment of women in these two societies has often led to cultural clashes. Integrating these immigrants into German society has therefore proven a major challenge.

The events of September 11, 2001, have had relatively little effect on the situation of the Muslims in Germany. The leaders of the largest Islamic organizations in Germany were quick to denounce the terrorist attacks in New

York and Washington, while German politicians of all parties admonished their countrymen not to equate the tiny minority of Islamic extremists responsible for the attacks with the large minority of peace-loving Muslims living in their country. Ironically, "9/11" seems to have had the positive effect of increasing the interest in Islam as a religion and deepening the dialogue between Christians and Muslims. Germany has become a multicultural society, whether the Germans like that or not. People of different faiths and cultural backgrounds will have to learn to live together. This is the challenge for the twenty-first century.

NOTES

1. Craig, *The Germans*, 83.
2. According to http://www.germany-info.org (February 18, 2003). Other sources provide slightly lower figures: 26.6 million Catholics and 26.6 million Protestants (Religionswissenschaftlicher Medien-und Informationsdienst e.V, http://www.remid.de/remid_info_zahlen.htm).
3. Gros and Glaab, *Faktenlexikon Deutschland*, 133.
4. Craig, *The Germans*, 380.
5. Stern, *Strange German Ways*, 86.
6. The three secular holidays are New Year's Day, May 1 (Labor Day) and October 3 (Day of German Unity).
7. Harenberg, *Aktuell 2002*, 326–27.
8. According to Federal Republic of Germany, *Questions and Answers*, 109.
9. Lord, *Culture Shock*, 70.
10. Gros and Glaab, *Faktenlexikon Deutschland*, 135.
11. Lewis, *Contemporary Germany*, 212.
12. Michael Elliott, *Newsweek*, Special Edition, December 2000/February 2001, 18.
13. *Der Spiegel* 7 (2003): 18.
14. Thus, it did not grant religious freedom on an individual basis; only the prince or the authorities had this right. Individuals who embraced a different religion could either emigrate to another territory or had to practice their faith in secret.
15. *Der Spiegel* 2 (2003): 65.
16. Solsten, *Germany. A Country Guide*, 175.
17. Susan Stern, *Jews in Germany, 2001* (Bonn: Inter Nationes, 2001), 1.
18. Cf. Andrew Nagorski, "A Strange Affair. Germans Are Fascinated with All Things Jewish. Is It Contrition?" *Newsweek*, 15 June 1998, 36–38.
19. Stern, *Strange German Ways*, 82.
20. Stern, *Jews in Germany*, 1.
21. Andrei Markovits, Beth Simone Noveck, and Carolyn Höfig, "Jews in German Society," in *The Cambridge Companion to Modern German Culture*, edited by Eva Kolinsky and Wilfried van der Will (Cambridge: Cambridge University Press, 1998), 86.
22. Stern, *Jews in Germany*, 11.

23. Daniel Goldhagen, *Hitler's Willing Executioners. Ordinary Germans and the Holocaust* (New York: Alfred Knopf, 1996).

24. Nagorski, "A Strange Affair," 38.

25. The figures vary according to the sources: Gros and Glaab, *Faktenlexikon Deutschland*, 137, gives the number as 1.8 million; Stern, *Strange German Ways*, 85, says 2.6 million; Harenberg, *Aktuell*, says 3 million. The 3.2 million comes from REMId (see above).

26. Andreas Goldberg, "Islam in Germany," in *Islam, Europe's Second Religion*, edited by Shireen Hunter (Westport, Conn., and London: Praeger, 2002), 29.

27. According to Steffen Rink, "Under the Banner of Dialogue and Transparency. Mosques in Germany." In <http://www.goethe.de/kug/ges/pur/thm/en30158.htm>.

7

Literature

ALMOST 200 YEARS AGO, the French woman of letters Madame de Staël (1766–1817), an exile from Napoleon's France and a keen observer of other nations, called Germany the country of "poets and thinkers."[1] Ever since then the Germans have eagerly embraced that label, pointing to the impressive number of philosophers, such as Immanuel Kant, Georg Wilhelm Friedrich Hegel, Friedrich Nietzsche, Arthur Schopenhauer, and Martin Heidegger, as well as writers, such as Johann Wolfgang von Goethe, Friedrich Schiller, Franz Kafka, Thomas Mann, and Hermann Hesse, to name only a few. Asked whom they are proud of, educated Germans are unlikely to name a historical figure as Americans would, but rather Goethe, Schiller, or Thomas Mann. Even today, in an increasingly materialistic world dominated by television's light entertainment, literature plays an important role in public life in Germany. New literary works are reviewed and heatedly debated in the pages of the "Feuilleton," that section in any German newspaper devoted to culture. For years, a monthly television program called "Literarisches Quartett" (Literary Quartet), consisting of four literary critics, attracted millions of viewers. Some contemporary authors like Günter Grass, Hans Magnus Enzenberger, or Christa Wolf are public figures in the sense that their pronouncements and advice on current affairs are listened to and debated, if not always followed.

The following survey will concentrate on the literature written in twentieth-century Germany, with special emphasis on those works written in both Germanys between the end of the Second World War in 1945 and the present. However, to completely ignore the literature of the past would be to disregard an important part of the German literary heritage. The chronicle of postwar German literature will therefore be preceded by a quick sketch of some important literary works from the past.

THE PAST

Every European country had its golden age in literature. For Spain it was the seventeenth century when writers like Cervantes, Calderón, and Lope de Vega created their works; for Italy it was the Renaissance with Dante, Boccaccio, and Machiavelli. For Germany the great age of literature was the late eighteenth and early nineteenth century, the era associated with the two giants of German literature, Johann Wolfgang von Goethe (1749–1832) and Friedrich Schiller (1759–1805). Between 1794 and 1832 (Goethe's death), the tiny town of Weimar in central Germany became a leading cultural center.

This does not mean that no important literary works were produced earlier. In fact, the beginnings of German literature go back to the ninth century; it reached a first climax in the Middle Ages with such magnificent works as Gottfried von Straßburg's *Tristan und Isolde,* Wolfram von Eschenbach's *Parzifal,* and Walther von der Vogelweide's poems and songs. During the following centuries, during the Renaissance and the Baroque, important works appeared. But it was Goethe and Schiller who, at the end of the eighteenth and beginning of the nineteenth centuries, inaugurated an unprecedented flowering of German literature, the age of *German Classicism.* Today every schoolchild in Germany knows their names and has read at least some of their works. As *the* German national poet Goethe has given his name, for instance, to the hundreds of culture and language institutes, the Goethe-Institutes, whose mandate it is to acquaint other countries with German culture.

Goethe was a man of prodigious talents: a sensitive and innovative poet, a dramatist, novelist, essayist, and scientist, a genius in many fields of human endeavor. His complete works collected in the Weimar edition comprise 143 volumes. Of all his works, none is more famous than his poetic drama *Faust,* one of the immortal works of world literature. In Goethe's drama, the scholar Faust concludes a pact with Mephistopheles, the sharp-tongued and witty devil. As long as Faust continues to strive for happiness and knowledge, the devil shall serve him. If, however, Faust believes he has reached that state of happiness and satisfaction, the devil can have his soul. Goethe's major innovation is that Faust, at age 100, is indeed happy for a brief moment and should therefore, by the terms of the pact, surrender his soul to Mephisto. Yet in a last final mystical scene he is saved by God. *Faust* is such a complex drama that it was performed in its entirety only in 1875 for the first time, more than 40 years after the poet's death.

Along with Goethe, Friedrich Schiller is considered the second master of German literary classicism. Today he is primarily remembered for his brilliant historical dramas, such as his trilogy on the imperial general in the Thirty Years' War, Wallenstein; his drama on Joan d'Arc (1801; *Johanna von Orleans*); the Swiss national hero *Wilhelm Tell* (1804); the son of the Spanish king Philip II, *Don Carlos;* and his most popular play, *Maria Stuart* (1800; *Mary Stuart*). A lifelong champion of freedom from repression, Schiller also contributed a treasure trove of quotable lines to the German language. In addition to his plays, Schiller also wrote a number of ballads and poems, including "Ode to Joy," which Beethoven used in the last movement of his Ninth Symphony. With its noble sentiments of universal brotherhood, the piece has become the official hymn of the European Union.

German Romanticism of the early nineteenth century, which followed the classicism, is probably the most fascinating of all literary periods. It was the time when the Brothers Grimm wrote down their fairy tales, when authors like Ludwig Tieck (1773–1853) and Joseph von Eichendorff (1788–1857) published their charming novellas, when E.T.A. Hoffmann (1776–1822) wrote his bizarre tales of madness, horror, and the supernatural; it was also the time when Adelbert von Chamisso (1781–1838) produced with his novella *Schlemiehl,* about a man who sold his shadow, one of the great works of literature; it was finally the time when the young poet Novalis (1772–1801) created the symbol of Romantic yearning, the blue flower. In their works, these writers tried to bring together the world of reason and emotion and the world of the subconscious and the conscious.

Twentieth-Century German Literature

The twentieth century in Germany was a period of ruptures and continuities. Imperial Germany ended in 1918 with the defeat of the German army; following a revolution, the democratic Weimar Republic was established. But this republic was destroyed in 1933 when Hitler came to power and established a dictatorship. The Second World War, unleashed by Hitler in 1939, ended with the total collapse of the Third Reich. In the following years, Germany was divided into two states and only reunited in 1990.

The literature written during that time reflected these ruptures. Following the First World War, Expressionists sketched utopian visions of the "new man," while the Dadaists, the most radical of the avant-garde artists, denied any meaning of art. Although their works are largely forgotten, their legacy to modern literature is ubiquitous. Experimentation with texts, concrete poetry, collage techniques—all derive from this unconventional anti-art. Germany also saw the emergence of important playwrights, such as Bertolt Brecht,

Frank Wedekind, and Peter Weiss, who had a profound influence on the development of the international stage (see chapter 9). Poets such as Gottfried Benn and Rainer Maria Rilke had considerable impact on European poetry. But even more than these playwrights and poets, three German novelists left their mark on world literature in the first half of the twentieth century: the two Nobel Prize winners in literature, Thomas Mann and Hermann Hesse, and Prague-born Franz Kafka.

Thomas Mann (1875–1955)

His place of honor in German literature is undisputed. With his reputation approaching that of Goethe, he was the most famous German novelist of the twentieth century. His books are sold all over the world and there has always been a keen interest in him and his family. A mini-series on his family broadcast in 2001 in Germany drew millions of viewers to the television screen.

With his first novel, *Die Buddenbrooks* (1901; *The Buddenbrooks*), Mann won instant acclaim as a major writer. With irony and humor he describes the decline of a family of Lübeck corn merchants over four generations, roughly between 1835 and 1877. As the representatives of each successive generation decline biologically, they gain in artistic sensibility. The novel, which by 2000 had sold over 10 million copies worldwide, won Mann the Nobel Prize in Literature in 1929. Of his numerous masterly shorter narratives, the novella *Der Tod in Venedig* (1912; *Death in Venice*) is perhaps the best known in this country. On a visit to Venice, the aging Gustav von Aschenbach, a German writer of iron discipline, falls in love with the 15-year-old Polish boy named Tadzio. In spite of the outbreak of cholera, he stays in Venice and dies of that disease and of love on the very day when the Polish family departs from the stricken city. *Death in Venice* has been turned into a visually stunning film by the Italian director Luchino Visconti (1971) and an opera by Benjamin Britten (1973).

Der Zauberberg (1924; *The Magic Mountain*) is set in the exclusive atmosphere of a Swiss sanatorium in Davos, where the young Hamburg engineer Hans Castorp visits his sick cousin. When a small spot on his lung is discovered, he stays for years and is exposed to the major European philosophical approaches in the figures of two men, the Italian Settembrini and the Jesuit Naphta. With unfailing irony, Mann has created not only a *Bildungsroman* of an individual but also a critique of European civilization and its underlying intellectual foundations. In 1933, the year when Hitler came to power, Mann immigrated to America. With his *Doktor Faustus* (1947), written in American exile, Thomas Mann probes the German national character by creating the

fictitious composer Adrian Leverkühn as the modern Faust who sells his soul
to the devil.

Hermann Hesse (1864–1947)

In the 1960s and 1970s, Hermann Hesse became a cult figure for a whole
generation of readers. His novels *Siddhartha* (1922) and *Steppenwolf* (1927),
written decades earlier, suddenly became bestsellers in America. Hesse himself
was seen as a guru for all those who were on a pilgrimage of self-discovery. A
famous bar in Berkeley, California, and a rock band bear the name "Steppenwolf." What appealed to these readers were Hesse's rejection of bourgeois
society, his admiration of Eastern mysticism and philosophy. All his heroes
are outsiders. Already his first novel, *Demian* (1919), published after the end
of the First World War, had, in the words of Thomas Mann, "an electrifying
influence on a whole generation... With uncanny accuracy this poetic work
struck the nerve of the times and called forth grateful rapture from a whole
generation who believed that an interpreter of their innermost life had risen
from their midst."[2] *Steppenwolf* is also a very modern novel that struck a
chord with modern readers. Apparently millions could identify with Harry
Haller, the Steppenwolf, the outsider who cannot come to terms with the
world around him.

Chronologically between *Demian* and *Steppenwolf* falls the novel *Siddhartha,* a work that was inspired by Hesse's study of Indian philosophy and
religion. What made *Siddhartha* so attractive at the time of its publication, and
in subsequent decades, was the central character's search for self-fulfillment. In
an increasingly secular world in which universal values have all but disappeared, each reader is encouraged to create his own meaning. Like Hesse's
other works, *Siddhartha* has been translated into many languages, including
nine Indian languages and dialects.

Some critics consider *Das Glasperlenspiel* (1943; *The Glassbead Game,* also
known in English as *Magister Ludi,* 1949) his best novel. Set in the distant
future in the twenty-third century, but in a landscape that is more reminiscent of the nineteenth century, the novel recounts the life of Joseph Knecht,
who from humble beginnings rises to the top of the semi-monastic order that
has devoted itself to the cultivation of the arts.

In spite of the skepticism by some academics who are distrustful of Hesse's
irrationalism and romanticism, the Hesse boom shows no sign of abating.
Over 100 million copies of his works have been sold worldwide.[3] In 2002,
many towns associated with the author's life celebrated his 125th birthday.
His Swabian hometown of Calw, for instance, staged no fewer than 200

events, including a concert by the legendary American rock band Steppen-wolf.

Franz Kafka (1883–1924)

No rock bands are named after Kafka's novels, as far as we know. Yet no other writer in the twentieth century has articulated the anxieties of our age with more precision and clarity than the German-Jewish writer Franz Kafka. The word *kafkaesque* has become a household word. The English poet W. H. Auden said: "Had one to name the artist who comes nearest to bearing the same kind of relations to our age that Dante, Shakespeare, and Goethe bore to theirs, Kafka is the first one would think of... Kafka is important to us because his predicament is the predicament of modern man."[4] During his lifetime only a few short stories were published and known only to a relatively small circles of admirers. In the meantime such stories as *Das Urteil* (1913; *The Judgment,* tr. 1945), *Die Verwandlung* (1915; *The Metamorphosis,* tr. 1937), and *In der Strafkolonie* (1920; *In the Penal Colony,* tr. 1941) have become modern classics. His three novels were published after his death: *Der Prozeß* (written in 1914–15, published in 1925; *The Trial), Das Schloß* (1926; *The Castle*) and *Amerika* (1927; *America*). Common to *The Trial* and *The Castle* is that the central characters try to get in touch with some unseen, unidentifiable power—and fail. That failure gives these narratives their nightmarish qualities. Their plight is made even more poignant in that they both suffer from an inborn feeling of guilt, a guilt that they also accept. In *The Trial,* for instance, Joseph K. is arrested for reasons he never learns. At the end, he is killed. Similarly in *The Castle,* K., a land surveyor in a mountain village dominated by a huge castle, is unable to get in contact with the inhabitants of the castle. He never obtains entry.

The literature during the first 30 years of the twentieth century was not limited to these literary giants, although, in retrospect, they tend to overshadow the numerous other novelists, poets, essayists, and playwrights who contributed to a flowering of literature. There were many others. For instance, with his novel *Berlin Alexanderplatz* (1929), Alfred Döblin portrayed the German capital in all its contemporary complexity and vibrancy. Focusing on one lower-class individual, Franz Biberkopf, "a criminal unable to escape from criminality,"[5] Döblin used a variety of narrative techniques, such as interior monologues, montage, reportage, and fragments from newspapers to evoke the Berlin of the late twenties. Towards the end of the Weimar Republic, Erich Maria Remarque created a sensation with his antiwar novel *Im Westen nichts Neues* (1929; *All Quiet on the Western Front*), in which he portrayed the suffering of the front soldier in the First World War. Translated into many languages it became a worldwide best-seller and was made into a movie in 1930.

Literature during the Third Reich

When the National Socialists came to power in 1933, the conditions under which literature was produced changed radically. In their attempt to control all aspects of cultural life, including literature, the new rulers created the Reich Chamber of Literature, an organization in which membership was obligatory for those who wanted to get published. Political opponents and Jewish writers were excluded. Book burnings of works by "un-German" and Jewish authors on May 10, 1933, took place in Berlin and other cities. Hundreds of writers emigrated, including Thomas Mann, his brother Heinrich, an accomplished writer himself, the playwrights Bertolt Brecht and Ernst Toller, and the novelists Alfred Döblin, Erich Maria Remarque, and Anna Seghers, to name only a few. Those writers who stayed in Germany and who were opposed to National Socialism went into what later was called "inner emigration," that is, although they remained physically in Germany, they either remained silent during the 12 years of the Nazi terror or wrote nonpolitical books such as children's books and historical novels. Others produced works that subtly criticized the regime, but in such a way that they eluded the literary censors. There were finally those writers who, even before 1933, had written books that were welcomed by the new rulers. Frequently these books extolled the virtues of hard-toiling peasants and battle-scarred soldiers.

POSTWAR GERMAN LITERATURE

The impact of the Second World War on German life and letters was severe. When the war ended with Hitler Germany's unconditional surrender on May 8, 1945, Germany lay in ruins. Within a few years, the Cold War had created two blocs with totally different ideological foundations and leading to the establishment of two German states in 1949. From that year on, it is impossible to speak of *one* German literature. East and West German literature therefore have to be treated separately.

West German Literature

The year 1945 is often called "*die Stunde Null*" (the Zero Hour) in West Germany. The term refers not only to the total destruction of German cities but also to the low point German history had reached in the wake of the Nazi regime. Among young intellectuals there was a feeling that a new beginning was necessary, that a clean sweep of the inhuman Nazi ideology had to be made. In an attempt to purge the German language of what they considered the abuse by the Nazis, young writers sought to write in a simple and straightforward way. Another term often used to describe the works written in the immediate postwar period is "literature of the ruins" (*Trümmerliteratur*), a term coined by Heinrich Böll, referring to the subject matter of the short stories written by these writers.

The best known exponent of the *Trümmerliteratur* is Wolfgang Borchert (1921–1947). Drafted at the age of 20 into the German army, he was a reluctant soldier who was sentenced to jail a number of times for his sarcastic remarks against the leaders of the Third Reich, but pardoned only to be shipped off again to the Russian front. He returned from the war a sick man and died of a liver ailment at age 27 in 1947. Between 1945 and 1947 he created a small but important oeuvre consisting of poems, short stories, and one drama, *Draußen vor der Tür* (1947; *The Man Outside*), premiered in Hamburg one day after Borchert's death. It captured the deep disillusionment of an entire generation. After years in Russian captivity, the soldier Beckmann returns to bombed-out Hamburg only to find out that his wife had married somebody else, that his parents have committed suicide, and that the colonel who had ordered him to command a reconnaissance troop during which 11 of his comrades were killed refuses to "take back the responsibility." Everywhere Beckman finds himself as "the man outside."

The same year in which Borchert's drama was premiered saw the founding of a group that was to dominate West Germany's literary life for the next 20 years, the Gruppe 47 (Group 47). Founded in 1947 (hence the name) as an informal discussion group by Hans Werner Richter (1908–1993), it met every year, and by the mid-1950s the modest gatherings had developed into media events, attended by publishers in search for new talents, and by radio, and later television, crews. By the early 1960s the annual meetings, always held at a different place, had "turned into a kind of Cannes for the literary stars and starlets."[6] In 1967, however, in a climate of increasing political radicalization, the group dissolved.

The Gruppe 47 was an informal gathering. There were no membership dues or statutes. Members were invited by postcard by Hans Werner Richter. Still, in spite of the lack of formal by-laws, certain rituals had evolved: after Richter had called the meeting to order with a bell, the invited author would sit in what became to be known as the "the electric chair" and would read from his or her manuscript. The readings would be followed by instant criticism by members of the audience, to which the author was not allowed to respond. The audience could also end any author's reading by the old imperial gesture of thumbs-down.

The impact of the group on literary life in West Germany, Austria, and Switzerland was immeasurable. The two outstanding exponents of postwar German literature, Heinrich Böll and Günter Grass, both winners of the prestigious Nobel Prize in Literature, received their first public exposure at meetings of the Gruppe 47.

Heinrich Böll (1917–1985)

"Christian moralist," "conservative anarchist," "Adenauer's gadfly," these are some of the labels that point to the core of Heinrich Böll's morals stance. In his short stories and novels, he chronicled with a critical eye the first 40 years of the Federal Republic. Shaped by his Catholic upbringing and his experiences during the Nazi period—he had to serve in the German army for six years—he had little patience with hierarchies and authority, but always compassion for the poor, wounded, defenseless, and disadvantaged.

His early stories and novels, among them *Wo warst Du, Adam* (1951; *Where were Thou, Adam,* tr. 1955) and *Der Zug war pünktlich* (1949; *The Train was on Time,* tr. 1956), belong to the literature of the ruins dealing with the suffering of soldiers and civilians, during and after the war. During the 1950s, the period of the remarkable reconstruction of Konrad Adenauer's Germany, Böll attacked the complacent materialism and the rat-race work ethos of his countrymen while he described with sympathy those who have been excluded from the "economic miracle." His criticism and satire are always tempered by humor and irony, such as in his story "Dr. Murkes gesammeltes Schweigen" ("Dr. Murke's Collected Silences," 1958) , a spoof on West Germany's busy *Kulturbetrieb* (culture business).The culmination of his early work is the novel *Billiard um halb zehn* (1959; *Billiards at Half-Past Nine,* tr. 1961). From a technical narrative point of view, this work is the most ambitious because it compresses, by means of a series of flashbacks and interior monologues, into one day the story of three generations of a prominent Cologne family of architects. As in earlier works, his moral universe is one of black and white. Those who are weak and disadvantaged are the "lambs," while those who are powerful, successful, and influential are said to have partaken of the "host of the beast." While *Billiards* deals with a panoramic view of German society over several generations, *Ansichten eines Clown* (1963; *The Clown,* tr. 1965) concentrates on one individual, Hans Schnier, the son of a prominent family of Rhenish industrialists, who has defied tradition by becoming a clown, an outsider, in a society that has become increasingly successful and affluent.

The 1960s and early 1970s were a time of increasing politicization in Germany. There were student protests, terrorist attacks, and the backlash of a nervous government and a militant right-wing press. In this climate of hysteria against the real and suspected terrorists, Böll wrote an article in the news magazine *Der Spiegel* warning against a witch hunt against the alleged terrorists and demanding that they should be entitled to the same due process as other citizens. In response to his measured article, Böll was suspected of harboring sympathies and became himself the victim of a witch hunt. His houses were searched and he himself was denounced by the conservative newspaper *Bild-Zeitung*. Böll turned his experiences into a novel, *Die verlorene Ehre der Katharina Blum* (1974: *The Lost Honor of Katharina Blum,* tr. 1975), which was later made into a successful movie by Volker Schlöndorff. At a carnival party, Katharina Blum meets a young man, falls head over heels in love with him, and spends the night with him in her apartment. As it turns out, he is wanted as a terrorist. Since he escaped, the police concentrate on her as the alleged "sympathizer." In particular, a reporter of the tabloid *Die Zeitung,* a thinly veiled allusion to the *Bild-Zeitung,* hounds her, her mother, and her friends mercilessly. With her reputation destroyed, the desperate Katharina shoots the unscrupulous journalist when he visits her for an interview.

While *The Lost Honor of Katharina Blum* offers a snapshot of German society at a particular critical junction, *Gruppenbild mit Dame* (1971; *Group Portrait with Lady,* tr. 1973), probably his most accomplished and ambitious work, presents a comprehensive and panoramic picture of German history between the 1920s to the early 1970s. The cast of some hundred people, including a Russian prisoner of war, a Turkish guest laborer, and some "good" Nazis are all connected to the central figure of Leni Gruyten, a "saintly slob," as one critic called her.[7] *Gruppenbild mit Dame* is a departure for Böll on two counts: it has a remarkable narrative structure (the author tries to reconstruct the life of the central figure with the help of conversations with those who knew her); and it is also less dogmatic in the sense that Böll gives up his tendency of schematically dividing his cast of characters into lambs and beasts, as in *Billiards at Half-Past Nine.* Böll has become more tolerant for the gray, for those who are less than perfect.

Günter Grass (born 1927)

It is not often that a writer is featured on the cover of *Time;* it is even rarer that a *German* author is depicted on that magazine's cover page. But this is exactly what happened in April 1970 when *Time* devoted a lengthy story to Günter Grass. The occasion was the publication in English of his fourth novel, *Örtlich betäubt* (1969; *Local Anesthetic,* tr. 1970). *Time* wrote: "At 42, Grass certainly does not look like the world's, or Germany's, greatest living novelist, though he may be both."[8] Whether Grass is the world's greatest nov-

Grass (left) in 1960. Courtesy of Deutsches Literaturarchiv in Marbach.

elist is debatable—there are so many talents from all over the world, although his international stature was recognized when he was awarded the Nobel Prize in Literature in 1999—but there is no doubt that he is contemporary Germany's greatest novelist. For more than 45 years, since he first burst on the literary scene with his novel *Die Blechtrommel* (1959; *The Tin Drum,* tr. 1962), Grass has dominated Germany's literary scene.

Born in 1927 in the free city of Danzig (now Gdansk in Poland), Grass was drafted into the German army at age 17, was taken prisoner by the Americans in 1945, and worked as a field worker, miner, jazz musician, and stonecutter before he began writing. In 1958 he was invited to read at the annual meeting of the Gruppe 47 from his work-in-progress *Die Blechtrommel,* receiving the coveted prize of that group. The publication of that novel in the following year was an immediate success. Translated into many languages and having sold more than 4 million copies by 1999, it also brought back German literature to the level of world literature.

Grass and his artwork in 1997. Courtesy of Deutsches Literaturarchiv in Marbach.

The Tin Drum is a complex work, brimming with satire, grotesque distortions, and exuberant bawdiness that has prompted some public libraries in the United States to ban it from its bookshelves, even today. The story is told from the perspective of the narrator-protagonist Oskar Matzerath, a person who at age three decides to arrest his growth through an intentional fall down the basement stairs. Meant as a kind of resistance against the adult world, Oskar has the mind of an adult but the physical appearance of a three-year-old. Equipped only with a children's tin drum and a glass-shattering voice, Oskar recounts his life in Danzig, the rise of the Nazis, the Second World War and his adventures in postwar Germany. In 1979 *The Tin Drum* was made into a successful film by Volker Schlöndorff, winning an Oscar for the best foreign movie in 1980 (see chapter 8).

The Tin Drum was followed in 1961 by the novella *Katz und Maus (Cat and Mouse,* tr. 1963) and in 1963 by *Hundejahre (Dog Years,* tr. 1965). All three works comprise the so-called Danzig trilogy. But while *Cat and Mouse* is a tightly constructed novella focusing on a single German teenager, Joachim Mahlke, growing up during the Third Reich, *Dog Years,* like *The Tin Drum,* and written with the same kind of verbal virtuosity, offers a rich panorama of colorful characters.

From the very beginning of his career to this day, Grass has never been shy about speaking out on political issues. In the 1960s he went one step further than that. He actively campaigned twice, in 1965 and 1969, on behalf of the Social Democratic Party's chancellor candidate, Willy Brandt. Crisscrossing Germany in a VW van, he delivered over 100 campaign speeches. His experiences during these long campaigns are recounted by Grass in his work *Aus dem Tagebuch einer Schnecke* (1972; *From the Diary of a Snail*, tr. 1973). In it Grass rejects all ideologies and magic cures but embraces a patient, slow, "snail-like," evolutionary approach to solve Germany's problems. That Grass is very skeptical of revolutions, such as demanded by the students in the late 1960s, becomes clear from his novel *Örtlich betäubt* (1969; *Local Anesthetic*, tr. 1970). It is a work about the generational conflict between a high school teacher and one of his students. In protest against the use of napalm in Vietnam by the United States, this student wants to burn his dachshund in one of the busiest streets in West Berlin, on the assumption that a dog-burning would arouse more anger than a human immolation in dog-crazy Berlin.

With *Der Butt* (1977; *The Flounder*, tr. 1978), Grass proved that he had not lost his linguistic inventiveness, his Rabelaisian humor, his ability to spin a good yarn and evoke distant periods. With over 550 pages, *Der Butt* is a massive work with two major themes: the eternal power struggle between men and women and the history of cooking and food. The author follows these themes by evoking nine different characters from nine different periods, from the three-breasted Awa from the Stone Age to a fiancee of a Danzig dock worker in the 1970s.

With his novel *Die Rättin* (1985; *The She-Rat*, 1987), Grass articulated the anxieties of many Germans in the 1980s when the two superpowers contemplated stationing medium range missiles armed with nuclear warheads on German territory. In the event of a war Germany would have been transformed into a lunar landscape. But that is exactly the scenario Grass develops in the novel, in which the narrator orbits in a small space capsule around our planet devastated by a nuclear holocaust that has extinguished all life on earth except those of rats. His latest work, *Crabwalk*, will be discussed subsequently.

East German Literature

In 1945 the beginnings of East German literature looked promising. Intent on establishing an "anti-fascist democratic order" in their zone of occupation, the Soviets invited many emigrant writers, both Communist and non-Communist, to return to the country. However, this period of relative freedom was short-lived. In the 1950s the Communist government under the leadership of Walter Ulbricht advocated and imposed on writers the dogma of Socialist Realism, a set of guidelines that had been formulated in Stalin's Soviet Union in the 1930s. According to this doctrine a work of literature had to show unequivocal commitment to the Communist party, had to present typical characters, and had to be easily understood. Formalism, that is, the emphasis on modern, experimental narrative techniques, was condemned. Writers who did not conform were excluded from the Communist Writers' Union.

In order to encourage workers to write, Ulbricht, in a speech in the industrial town of Bitterfeld in 1959, encouraged workers to write about their experiences, hoping that workers, untainted by the knowledge of such formalists as Alfred Döblin or James Joyce, would write the kind of Socialist Realist literature desired by the Communists. "Pick up the pen, buddy" (*Greif zur Feder, Kumpel*) was the motto. Conversely, established writers were encouraged to go into the factories, mines, and fields to acquaint themselves with the world of the workers. The "Bitterfeld Way," as it became known, was a failure on both counts. Intimate knowledge of a workplace does not automatically translate into good literature; and very few authors actually dirtied their hands in the factories and fields.

Like the rulers of any totalitarian state, East Germany's Communists kept a close eye on literary production. Without going into details of the relationship between writers and state authorities, it can be said that the literary history of East Germany is one of alternate tightening and loosening of the leashes on which writers were kept. Using a different metaphor, East German literature experienced thaws followed by freezes, followed again by thaws. In 1971, for instance, the new head of East Germany's Communist government, Erich Honecker, declared that there should be "no taboos in the spheres of art and literature, if artists were proceeding from a firm position of socialism." Indeed for about five years, relative freedom prevailed. But when the East German singer and poet Wolf Biermann criticized the East German government in a concert in West Germany in 1976, he was immediately stripped of his East German citizenship, an action which prompted numerous East German writers and artists to sign a letter of support for their beleaguered colleague. This in turn resulted in a new wave of persecutions. Between 1976 and 1981, over 300 writers and intellectuals left East Germany.[9] Some were expelled, and others left the country on their own.

Although the dogmatic rigidity of Socialist Realism was later relaxed, the East German authorities, up to the very end of their state in 1989, kept a tight control over writers. In general, then, writers who did not conform were silenced, prohibited from publishing, harassed, imprisoned, or expelled from East Germany.

It is a tribute to the human spirit that, in spite of these adverse conditions, important works were produced in the German Democratic Republic. East Germany's most prominent writer was Christa Wolf (born 1929). A Socialist and member of the Communist party, she began writing short stories in the Socialist Realist style, even worked in a railway wagon factory following Ulbricht's admonishments in Bitterfeld. But in her first major novel *Der geteilte Himmel* (1963; *Divided Heaven: A Novel of Germany Today,* tr. 1965) she broke with part of that doctrine. Although not exactly an avant-garde novel, it uses flashbacks and other narrative techniques that in the 1950s would have been denounced as formalistic. *Divided Heaven* is the story of the love of a young East German woman, Rita, for a young East German man, Manfred, who uses a conference in West Berlin to defect. Shortly before the Wall goes up in Berlin, she visits him in West Berlin but decides to return to the GDR, her true home, while her friend easily finds a well-paying job as a chemical engineer in the West. Although the ending is in line with Communist political correctness, the novel is much more sophisticated than to be dismissed as a Communist propaganda piece. For one thing, Wolf shies away from a black-and-white portrayal of the two characters, but rather describes Manfred as a skeptic disappointed with the system. With this semi-positive portrayal of a *Republikflüchtling* (refugee from the republic)—the official term for those who turned their back to the GDR—and the acknowledgment of the devastating effect of the Berlin Wall on personal relationships, Wolf broke with two East German taboos. *Divided Heaven* was very successful, both in East and West Germany, and was translated into 15 languages and made into a successful film in the GDR.

By the time Christa Wolf published *Nachdenken über Christa T.* (1968; *The Quest for Christa T.,* tr. 1970) and *Kindheitsmuster* (1976; *A Model Childhood,* tr. 1980), she had largely freed herself from the constraints of Socialist Realism. Both these novels, in very different ways, explore individual lives, and they do this with sophisticated narrative techniques. In *The Quest for Christa T.,* the narrator tries to reconstruct through letters, diaries, and memories how a friend, Christa T., who had died of leukemia, lived, dreamed, and worked. In her largely autobiographical novel, *A Model Childhood,* Christa Wolf explores her childhood and youth in Nazi Germany, asking herself why she, her friends, and her family fell under the spell of Hitler. Criticism of her own country, however, remained a taboo.

The publication of Ulrich Plenzdorf's (born 1934) *Die neuen Leiden des jungen W.* (1973; *The New Sufferings of Young W.,* tr. 1979) catapulted this young writer to the top of the GDR literary scene. Although only five years younger than Wolf, Plenzdorf seemed to belong to a new generation. There is none of the self-reflection, of the tormented search for the true self in him, and none of the guilt feelings because of the Nazi past. In this novel, Plenzdorf describes a Berlin teenager, Edgar Wibeau, who is fed up with being viewed as the model GDR boy and frustrated by the conformity of his life in school. He drops out of school and escapes to a garden shed outside Berlin, where he meets and falls in love with a young kindergarten teacher, works briefly in a brigade that renovates houses, and accidentally kills himself while building a spraying machine. Skeptical of the omniscient narrator, Plenzdorf presents the story from a number of perspectives. As the father who had never much contact with him tries to reconstruct the last weeks of his son's life in a number of interviews, the son, "from beyond the Jordan," as he says, corrects the interviewees, offering, in the hip slang of a Berlin adolescent, his version of the events.

Edgar is a dropout, to be sure. But he is not an anti-Communist, and he never questions the foundations of Socialism. What he rebels against is the conformity, the petty regulations, and the narrow-mindedness of individual representatives of that system. But even this kind of criticism was a breath of fresh air in the stuffy atmosphere of East German provincialism.

RECENT GERMAN LITERATURE

In 1968, amidst the student rebellion, noisy protests against America's war in Vietnam, and the West German government's clampdown on terrorists, the German poet and essayist Hans Magnus Enzensberger proclaimed "the death of literature," arguing that fiction contributed little to solving society's social and political ills. His call for an end of literature proved premature. To be sure, the 1970s saw a surge of politically committed "documentary literature," produced in the belief that such works were more authentic than pure fiction. But this fad was short-lived. In a deliberate reaction to this kind of "objective" writing, German-speaking authors of the 1980s deliberately turned to recording their innermost feelings often at the expense of good storytelling. The last two decades, however, have seen a resurgence of precisely that storytelling. Today German literature offers a colorful kaleidoscope of different themes and voices. There are of course the established authors, such as Christa Wolf, Patrick Süskind (born 1949) who created an international sensation with his novel *Das Parfüm* (1985, *The Perfume*) and Hans Magnus Enzensberger (who obviously did not follow his own advice), and, above all, Günter Grass. But there is also an entire generation of younger authors, the grandsons and granddaughters of Grass, so to speak, who have discovered the simple art of telling a good story. In addition, German literature has been enriched by a number of authors whose parents came to Germany as guest laborers. These so-called multicultural authors, such as Gino Chiellino (born in 1946 in Italy), Rafik Schami (born in 1946 in Syria), Franco Biondo (born in 1947 in Italy), and Emine Sergi Özdamar (born in 1946 in Turkey), have articulated the precarious situation of growing up between two different cultures. German-Jewish authors like Edgar Hilsenrath (born 1926), Jurek Becker (1937–1997), Barbara Honigmann (born 1949), and Rafael Seligmann (born 1947) have begun to make themselves heard. Women's literature, which in the 1970s emerged as a major development in German literature with such novels as Ingeborg Bachmann's *Malina* (1971) and Verena Stefan's *Häutungen* (1975; *Shedding*, tr. 1978), continues to flourish. With her novel *Kassandra* (1983; *Cassandra,* tr. 1984), Christa Wolf has written one of the most significant feminist novels of the 1980s. In order to illuminate the perennial problem of the relationship of men and women and how this relationship is shaped and determined by political power relationships, Christa Wolf turned to the ancient past. The setting is ancient Troy after it has been conquered by the Greeks; the protagonist is the Trojan seeress Cassandra, whose fate it was that nobody believed her. As she awaits her death at the hands of the Greeks, she reminisces, in a series of flashbacks and interior monologues, about the war, which she views as a consequence of patriarchy.

Although there are as many themes as there are authors, two typical German themes can, in addition, be isolated: the unification of the two Germanys in 1990 and the preoccupation with the German past.

The fall of the Berlin Wall and the subsequent German unification spawned a number of novels, works in which the days of the revolution are reconstructed, the life in East Germany is depicted or the involvement of the Stasi—East Germany's secret police—are recounted. Some of these works are serious, others satirical. While Ingo Schulze (born 1962) describes the hopes and helplessness, the expectations and disappointments of ordinary East Germans in his unsentimental novel *Simple Storys* (1998), Thomas Brussig (born 1962) creates with his provocative and hilarious novel *Helden wie wir* (1996; *Heroes Like Us,* tr. 1997) "the juiciest story of Germany in our time."[10] Günter Grass, who never disguised his skepticism toward the hasty German unification, contributed a massive novel, *Ein weites Feld* (1995; *Too Far Afield*) to the debate. It is a multilayered work that includes a subtle homage to the nineteenth-century German novelist Theodor Fontane and a sharp criticism of West Germany's alleged "takeover" of East Germany.

The second German theme that preoccupies some authors is the legacy left by the Nazis. After almost 60 years since the end of the Third Reich, Hitler still casts a long shadow. The painful process of *Vergangenheitsbewältigung,* the coming to terms with the past, is never finished, as Bernhard Schlink's short novel *Der Vorleser* (1995; *The Reader*) seems to suggest. Translated into 27 languages, selected by Oprah Winfrey as a "book of the month," and for months at the top of the *New York Times* bestseller list, the novel had sold 2 million copies by 1999 and is scheduled to be made into a Hollywood movie. The work relates the sexual relationship between a 15-year-old boy, Michael Berg, and a 36-year-old woman, Hanna Schmitz, in the late 1950s. Seven years later, the boy, now a law student, discovers that his former lover had been a concentration camp guard. His attempt to comprehend what happened in the war and his continuing preoccupation with his ex-lover constitute a powerful symbol for the never-healing wounds left by Hitler on the German psyche. The second generation represented by Michael Berg becomes involved in the crimes of the Third Reich through its association with the generation of the perpetrators, Schlink seems to say. In contrast to Schlink, W.G. Sebald (1944–2001) took a different approach to the problem of *Vergangenheitsbewältigung* (coming to terms with the past): In his melancholy novel *Die Ausgewanderten* (1993; *The Emigrants*, tr. 1996), he tries to retrace and thus recover the lives of four exiles who have left their home country. Most recently, Günter Grass has given the "coming to terms with the past" effort a new twist. In 2002 he published a novella called *Im Krebsgang* (2002; *Crabwalk;* tr. 2003). It revolves around the sinking of the gigantic ocean liner *Wilhelm Gustloff* in January 1945 by a Soviet submarine in the Baltic Sea. It was one of the greatest maritime catastrophes in which, according to estimates, more than 9,300 persons, six times as many as in the Titanic disaster in 1912, mostly women and children fleeing from the Red Army, drowned. With this description of German suffering, Grass broke one of the taboos of postwar German literature. For decades, any attempt to mention the ordeals the German civilians endured at the hands of the Allies (500,000 killed in Allied air raids; 1 to 2 million died while fleeing from the Red Army) was viewed as an attempt to relativize the Nazi crimes and to lighten the burden of the German guilt. It took Günter Grass, a liberal who had always described unflinchingly the Nazi past in his books, to disregard this unspoken prohibition. Just at the time when the *Wilhelm Gustloff* was sinking into the icy waters of the Baltic Sea—so Grass's story goes—Tulla Pokriefke, a character from the Danzig trilogy, gives birth to a son. It is this son who is the fictional narrator of the story. With this masterfully crafted novella, Grass once again has demonstrated that at age 70 he is still at the top of his art.

When Madame de Staël, almost 200 years ago, called Germany the country of "poets and thinkers," she added that in its literature there was a "mild and peaceful anarchy." In a way, this characterization is still valid today. The literature written today in many places in the German-speaking world is colorful, vibrant, varied, and has many different voices.

NOTES

1. In Madame de Staël's book *De l'Allemagne* (On Germany) (1813). Also see Madame de Staël, *On Politics, Literature and National Character,* translated and edited by Morroe Berger (Garden City and New York: Doubleday, 1965), 254.

2. Thomas Mann, introduction to *Demian. The Story of Emil Sinclair's Youth,* by Herman Hesse (New York: Bantam Books, 1985), ix.

3. *Tagesthema,* DW-tv, 8 October 2002.

4. Quoted on rear cover of Franz Kafka, *The Penal Colony. Stories and Short Pieces* (New York: Schocken, 1978).

5. H. B. Garland, *A Concise Survey of German Literature* (Coral Gables, Florida: University of Miami Press, 1971), 111.

6. Peter Demetz, *After the Fires. Recent Writings in the Germanies, Austria, and Switzerland* (New York: Harcourt Brace Jovanovich, 1986), 3.

7. Demetz, *After the Fires,* 100.

8. "The Dentist's Chair as an Allegory of Life," *Time,* 13 April 1970, 68.

9. Demetz, *After the Fires,* 142.

10. Uwe Greiwe in *Abendzeitug München.* Quoted on rear cover of American edition.

8

The Media and Cinema

GERMANY IS BY FAR the largest media market in Europe. Since the media (newspapers, magazines, books, television, and radio) both reflect and shape the mentality of a people, a discussion of them is essential for understanding a foreign culture. This will be done in the first part of this chapter. The second and longer part of this survey will deal with the contributions German cinema has made to world cinema from the beginning of that art form to the present. It will chronicle the evolution of the film industry during the Weimar Republic, the Third Reich, and in the two Germanys, and conclude with observations about some recent developments in united Germany.

THE PRESS

With their penchant for concrete language, Germans often refer to the rich and colorful kaleidoscope of newspapers, magazines, and periodicals as the German *Blätterwald,* meaning literally "forest of leaves or papers" (*Blätter* denoting both these things). A forest indeed it is: colorful, dense, and huge, as even a cursory look at any well-stocked newsstand in Germany will tell you. You will find plenty of daily newspapers, a number of excellent weeklies, and hundreds of illustrated magazines and periodicals tailored to specialized interests.

In spite of the competition of radio and television Germans are still avid newspaper readers. Every day, 25 million newspapers are sold,[1] and since a paper is usually read by several persons, the total readership is estimated at around 50 million. That means that 8 out of 10 Germans over the age of 14 read a paper daily.[2] After Japan, Great Britain, and Switzerland, Germany has the largest density of newspaper readers in the world. And since freedom of the press is anchored in the German constitution, Germans have a wealth of different sources of information. The success of the Federal Republic as a democratic state would not have been possible without a watchful free press that represents such a wide variety of opinions in Germany.

By far the largest number of these newspapers are local or regional papers. In 2000, there were 337 such papers.[3] The number, however, is somewhat misleading and gives a distorted picture of the diversity, since many of the local papers share the same political, travel, and cultural sections and are distinguished only by their local sections. The reason, as so often is the case in the newspaper business, is economic. Local papers cannot afford large editorial staffs for national and international news.

Germany has no single national newspaper such as *The Times* of London and *Le Monde* of Paris. This lack of a single national newspaper has to do with a deeply rooted sense of federalism. Instead there are a number of excellent regional newspapers with a national distribution. They have a total circulation of about 1.6 million. With *Die Süddeutsche Zeitung, Die Frankfurter Allgemeine Zeitung,* and *Die Welt,* Germany boasts some of the best and most respected daily papers in the world. Although all of them are politically independent, their editorial stances differ considerably. Common to all is superb international coverage provided by a host of correspondents abroad, a thorough business section, and extensive discussions of cultural issues in the so-called *Feuilleton.* What you will not find in these papers, however, are comics.

The largest of these daily newspapers with a nationwide circulation is *Die Süddeutsche Zeitung,* published in Munich with a circulation of 434,000.[4] Established in 1945, the *Süddeutsche,* as it is commonly referred to, is considered a liberal paper. It is much praised for its journalistic brilliance in its glosses and reports and its intolerance toward all those who try to subvert the free democratic order of Germany. The *Frankfurter Allgemeine Zeitung* (FAZ), is probably Germany's best-known paper, though its circulation is somewhat smaller (408,000). Its strength is its worldwide net of correspondents, which provide superb international coverage independent of news agencies and services. Read by leaders in business, politics, and culture, it tends to be more conservative. Since April 2000 an eight-page English summary of the paper appears as a supplement to the *International Herald Tribune.*

Die Welt (circulation 250,000), the journalistic flagship of the powerful Axel Springer Publishing House, Germany's largest newspaper publisher, is conservative in its outlook and was fiercely anti-Communist during the Cold War.

In addition to the local, regional, and national papers that are mostly sold by subscription, there are a number of papers that are exclusively sold at the newsstands. By far the best known of these tabloids is the *Bild-Zeitung*, another product of the Axel Springer house. With its attention-grabbing layout, sensational headlines, numerous pictures (*Bild* actually means picture), often including topless models, and its titillating stories of the small and big scandals of the rich and famous, it has become Germany's largest newspaper with a daily circulation of 4.2 million (approximately 11 million readers) and the sixth-largest newspaper in the entire world. What explains its success? Its language is simple and easily understood; the articles are short, quickly scanned while you are sitting in your commuter train, its coverage of sports is extensive—and sports is a passion in Germany just as it is in America.

Another source of information for many Germans are a number of well-established weekly newspapers and magazines. In contrast to the daily press, these papers offer less up-to-date news but rather more extensive analyses and commentaries in an attempt to place political events in a larger context. Because of the high level of discourse and their national distribution, these weeklies contribute substantially to the national debate on important cultural and political issues.

Best known is the weekly news magazine *Der Spiegel* (circulation 1.1 million). Founded in 1946, it has become Europe's largest and probably one of its most influential magazines. *Der Spiegel* takes the press's watchdog function very seriously. Famed for their excellent investigative reporting and backed up by the legendary *Spiegel* archive in Hamburg, which is said to be bigger than that of Germany's security service and, as the London *Economist* said, "a darn sight more reliable,"[5] *Spiegel* journalists have uncovered numerous political scandals. Every Monday when *Der Spiegel* hits the newsstands, politicians are said to anxiously open up that magazine to find out whether they are the object of a report. Though originally modeled on *Time* magazine, *Der Spiegel* is as thick as *Time, Newsweek,* and *U.S. News & World Report* put together. With its ability to transform news items into suspenseful stories, with its clever language, superb sources, and in-depth reporting on other parts of the world, *Der Spiegel* remains indispensable weekly reading for millions of Germans.

Der Spiegel lost its monopoly position when the weekly news magazine *Focus* was founded in 1993. With shorter articles, more graphics, and a generally less-critical tone, it appeals to a different sector of society and has, in a relatively short time, reached a circulation of 800,000. It seems, though, that it has not reduced *Der Spiegel*'s readership but has attracted new readers to the news magazine market.

The third widely read weekly is *Die Zeit* (circulation 450,000). Different from both *Der Spiegel* and *Focus* in that it is printed in the classical newspaper format, *Die Zeit* is a demanding newspaper that debates political and cultural topics at excruciating length. Its political stance is hard to pin down. Theo Sommer, one of the editors, conceded that the paper is actually three different newspapers rolled into one and held together by a common typography: in its politics *Die Zeit* is centrist, in its cultural section leftist, and in its business section it tends to be conservative.

In addition to these weeklies, German readers can turn to a astonishing variety of magazines, journals, periodicals, illustrated weeklies, scholarly journals, and specialized magazines. It is estimated that approximately 20,000 magazines are published in Germany with a total circulation of 200 million. Of these, the magazines that are targeted at a broad audience comprise 750 titles, including the illustrated weeklies, women's magazines, and trashy pulp magazines. The most serious is *Der Stern* (circulation 1.1 million). Other magazines, like *Die Neue Revue* (circulation 320,000), concentrate on erotic topics, health advice, and celebrities, while *Die Bunte* (725,000) reports on Europe's old aristocracy and the stars and starlets of film and television. A number of magazines, like *Brigitte* and *Für Sie* cater especially to women, featuring articles on fashion, cosmetics, beauty aids, hospitality, and health. Their wide circulation suggests that these topics are not sufficiently covered in the dailies and weeklies. *Emma,* a magazine exclusively written by and for women, was founded by Alice Schwarzer, the icon of the German feminist movement.

There is no dearth in pulp magazines, called in German *die Regenbogenpresse* (rainbow press), with titles such as *Bild der Frau, Neue Post, Neues Blatt*—all with circulations of over 1 million each. They fill their pages with stories of the trials and tribulations of today's celebrities from TV and film and the European aristocracy, a phenomenon, as the cult around Princess Diana has shown, not confined to Germany.

The economic boom of the 1990s has led to an upsurge in business magazines. Old established magazines like *Capital* and *Wirtschaftswoche* were joined by an impressive number of new publications with titles like *Telebörse, Focus Money,* and *Financial Times Deutschland.* Entrepreneurs have obviously discovered a new market.

Finally, there are a number of magazines catering to the specialized interest groups. Home builders, surfers, sailors, and computer freaks have their own magazines just as much as cigar aficionados, antique furniture collectors, and model railroaders.

BOOKS

Perhaps it is not surprising that in the country in which Johann Gutenberg invented printing with movable types more than 550 years ago, books still flourish. After the United Kingdom and China, with their infinitely larger markets, Germany ranks third in the world in terms of book production. In 1998, for instance, almost 80,000 first and new editions were published in Germany.[6] There are about 3,000 publishing houses, some small and concentrating on specialized market niches, others large and internationally known, as the Bertelsmann Group, Europe's biggest publishing house. The annual Frankfurt Book Fair that takes place every year in October is by far the largest book fair in the world. It is an event of superlatives. In 2002, for instance, a total of 6,000 exhibitors from 110 countries exhibited over 300,000 titles. This keen interest in books is evidence that Germans, in spite of the competition of other media such as television and radio, still do read a lot. According to statistics, every fourth German uses a book, either fiction or nonfiction, as a source of information. Especially if they want to deepen their knowledge of history, the social sciences, other countries, and philosophy, Germans often resort to the printed page. And they can buy books in any of the 5,000 bookstores or borrow them in one of the 13,500 public libraries.[7] Surprising also is the intense interest in foreign cultures and literatures. Books by non-German authors frequently rank at the top of the best-seller lists.

RADIO AND TELEVISION

Any visitor to Germany is struck by the variety of channels on German television. Whether you are interested in news, sports, talk shows, financial matters, feature films, entertainment, or the arts, you will find what you want on one of the 40 channels. This bewildering variety has not always been the case. In fact, up to 1984, Germany had basically only two major television networks, the ARD and the ZDF. When the airwaves were opened up, a number of private channels sprung up, which since then have proliferated due to the introduction of cable and satellite television.

Germany, then, has a dual system of public and private radio and television.

In contrast to the United States, where public radio and television is financed by private sponsors, voluntary donations from "viewers like you" and by the alms handed out by a reluctant Congress, with the result that it leads a marginal, albeit important Cinderella existence, German public radio and television are lavishly funded and have virtually no commercials (commercials on television are restricted to 20 minutes per day, between 5 and 8 P.M. and are banned on Sundays and holidays). So who pays for them? Every owner of a radio and TV set in Germany is required to pay a monthly fee (around 16 euros a month), which is distributed according to a key to the various public TV and radio stations. Consequently the two main public radio and TV corporations, ARD and ZDF, have at their disposal billions of euros. With 3,600 employees, including correspondents in 18 different countries, ZDF, for instance, is one of Europe's biggest networks with a budget, in 2001, of 1.6 billion euros,[8] a huge sum that allows them to offer high-quality, commercial-free programs. It needs to be stressed that both ARD and ZDF are run not by the government but by supervisory boards consisting of representatives from all segments of society, such as political parties, churches, and labor unions, thus guaranteeing a balanced view.

Journalists from other countries are often impressed by the overall caliber of German television. In-depth documentaries are surely among the best in the world. But in addition, both channels offer a mix of shows, films, miniseries, entertainment, and mysteries. While in the eighties, *Dallas* and the *Denver Clan* were the most successful series, more recently products "made in Germany," such as the soap operas *Lindenstrasse* and *Gute Zeiten, schlechte Zeiten* (*Good Times, Bad Times*) or detective shows (*Derrick, Der Alte, Tatort*), have become more popular. And being relatively independent of the ratings, the two networks also offer, more often than American channels, programs of artistic and literary merit. The strength of both ARD and ZDF, however, are the news departments with their own worldwide net of correspondents. For millions of Germans watching either the ARD's *Die Tagesschau* at 8 P.M. or ZDF's *Heute Journal* an hour earlier has become a family ritual. Millions trust the impartial and reliable news, even at a time when other commercial stations present their news with much more hype and fanfare.

In contrast to the public stations, the private channels finance themselves exclusively through commercials. The largest ones, SAT, RTL, and Pro 7, have certainly evolved into real competition to the established and well-heeled public ones. With an attractive mixture of sports, talk shows, boulevard magazines, homegrown TV series, feature films, and, more recently, reality TV, they have managed to lure viewers, in increasing numbers, from the established channels, so that in 2000 the public ARD and the private RTL were in a head-to-head race for the largest market share of the viewers.[9]

The *Deutsche Welle* occupies a special position in the German media landscape. Financed by the federal government, and with a staff of 1,600 employees, including 400 editors from 70 different countries, its radio programs are broadcast in 29 languages, including Hindi and Swahili, via short wave and satellite, its signal rivaling that of the BBC and the Voice of America in power and constancy. Since 1992 *Deutsche Welle* also broadcasts, worldwide and 24 hours a day, a television program in German, English, and Spanish. Programs are often rebroadcast by local and regional stations. Because of its impartiality and objective reporting, *Deutsche Welle* is often listened to in countries where the press and other media are censored or banned. Since April 2002, viewers in North America can enjoy the best of German television in their own living rooms on *Germantv,* a program featuring highlights from the two public television channels as well as from *Deutsche Welle.*

INTERNET

Of all the media, however, the Internet has experienced the most dramatic growth in Germany in recent years. Germans, it seems, have taken to the Internet like fish to water. In 2000, for instance, there were 25 million Germans, or every third German, using the World Wide Web. These figures are probably out of date as soon as they are published, as every day more people make use of that revolutionary medium. An indication of the popularity of the Internet is also that the domain name ".de" (for Deutschland) ranks second in use after ".com."

CINEMA

Weimar Republic

Politically and economically, the period of the Weimar Republic, the time between the end of World War I and the appointment of Adolf Hitler as chancellor in January 1933, was a time of unrest, humiliation, and misery for millions of Germans. Culturally, however, the Weimar years saw an unprecedented flowering in the fine arts, in architecture, music, and cinema. Indeed, the German cinema achieved a "golden age" not only in the quality but also in the quantity of the films put out, making it "perhaps the world leader during the great years of the silent films in the 1920s".[10] In Europe, Germany produced by far the largest numbers of films. In 1925, for instance, 228 feature films were released in Germany compared to 74 in France and 44 in Great Britain.[11] Only the United States rivaled Germany in the number of films produced per year.

But what makes Weimar Cinema so remarkable is not only the quantity but also the quality of the films made during that period by celebrated directors such as Robert Wiene, Fritz Lang, F. W. Murnau, and Ernst Lubitsch. Especially, the relatively small body of the so-called Expressionist films has exercised a lasting influence on the development of subsequent filmmaking, extending from Orson Welles to the film noir of the 1940s, such as *The Maltese Falcon (*1941), Hitchcock's *Psycho* (1960), and Charles Laughton's *The Night of the Hunter* (1962).

The era of Expressionist films began with *Das Cabinet des Dr. Caligari* (*The Cabinet of Dr. Caligari,* 1919; director, Robert Wiene), a film that already displays all the features of its genre: its fantastic sets with its distortions, wedge-shaped doors, oblique windows, angular houses; its exaggerated acting, and the stark contrasts between light and shadow. The haunting atmosphere is intended to evoke states of anxiety.

The plot is complicated. In a small town in northern Germany, a number of murders is committed by a somnambulist, Cesare, whose actions are controlled by Dr. Caligari, a crazy old mountebank and fortune-teller who murders all those whose deaths his hypnotized victim predicts. When a certain Alan is murdered, his friend Francis is determined to find his friend's murderer. After many adventures he finally suspects Cesare and with him Caligari. Francis pursues him and discovers that Caligari is the director of a mental institution, who has become interested in the story of the ancient Caligari and has been conducting the same sort of experiments as the historic Caligari.

In spite of its complicated, intricate, and possibly confusing plot, which is made even more difficult by a frame story in which Francis is revealed to be the inmate of a mental institution, *Caligari* remains one of the masterworks of the Expressionist film, spawning a particular style of filmmaking, Caligarism (from the French *caligarisme*).

Expressionist in style are also the early films by F. W. Murnau, who has been called the greatest film director the Germans have ever known.[12] His *Nosferatu. Eine Symphonie des Grauens* (*Nosferatu, A Symphony of Horror*, 1922) was the first of a whole series of vampire films. Based loosely on Bram Stoker's famous story of Dracula (1897), the film tells the story of the vampire who lies by day in his coffin in his castle and at night goes out and preys on the civilized world, bringing the plague wherever he appears. Challenged by the positive forces of good embodied by a girl who refuses to be scared by him, Nosferatu is finally destroyed.

By the mid-twenties, Expressionism had run its course and a "new sobriety" (*Die Neue Sachlichkeit*) dominated not only literature and the arts but also filmmaking. Fritz Lang, one of the representatives of that new trend, a director who had established his reputation with films like *Marbuse, der Spieler* (*Marbuse, The Player*, 1922) and *Die Nibelungen* (1924), masterfully handled huge crowds of people, as in probably his most famous film, *Metropolis* (1927). It was the most expensive film made during the Weimar period. Its shooting took almost a year; in addition to the main characters, the film employed 750 secondary roles and 35,000 extras.[13] *Metropolis* depicts an imaginary city of the future, divided in an underground world where thousands of tired workers slave away at machines, while above ground a leisure class enjoys itself in elaborate pleasure gardens and stadiums. The gap between the two worlds is bridged when Freder, the son of the Master of

Metropolis, falls in love with Maria, representative of the workers. The message is simple if not naive: only love can heal the wounds of social injustice, symbolizing the union of the brain and the hands. Like *Caligari, Metropolis* had a significant impact on subsequent filmmaking, as one critic observes: "The cityscape of the modern cult movie *Bladerunner* (1982), which, in turn, left clear marks on movies like *Batman* (1989), would have been impossible without the influence of the seminal silent movie *Metropolis.*"[14]

When sound films were introduced in the late twenties, the German film industry embraced this new technology quickly and by 1930, 84 percent of all the films made were already sound films. One of the first and most famous sound films was *Der Blaue Engel* (*The Blue Angel,* 1930), directed by Josef von Sternberg. Based on a novel by Heinrich Mann, *Professor Unrat* (1905), the film tells the story of the self-destructive passion of an elderly schoolmaster for a cabaret singer, played by Marlene Dietrich. It was this film that launched the young actress on an international career that included numerous films made in Hollywood.

Thus by the end of the Weimar Republic, the German film industry had established a reputation for producing artistically and technically sophisticated films that represented a real challenge to Hollywood.

Film in the Third Reich

When the National Socialists came to power in 1933, they quickly brought under their control all cultural activities. Everybody involved in culture had to be a member of the Reich Chamber of Culture, an organization that covered all areas of cultural activities including the cinema. Excluded from membership were Jews and political opponents of the new regime, leading to the emigration of a number of famous directors and actors. Dr. Joseph Goebbels, the newly appointed minister of propaganda and enlightenment, made himself head of the Chamber of Culture. Like Hitler, Goebbels was fascinated by film and often was involved personally in the planning and production of films. The cinema became thus part of the all-encompassing ideological control the Nazis exercised over Germany.

Given the high priority accorded to cinema by the Nazis, one would expect that a large number of the films made between 1933 and 1945 were propaganda films. In fact, only a small fraction of the more than 1,110 films produced under Goebbels's aegis can be termed "Nazi propaganda." The large majority of feature films released during the 12 years of Hitler's regime were apolitical and included a large number of melodramas, detective films, comedies, musicals, and spectacular historical epics. They were well-made, since, in spite of the terrible drain of talent in 1933, a majority of the artists and technicians who had brought German cinema to such high standards during the Weimar Republic were not affected by the expulsions in the wake of the Nazi assumption of power. The same is true of the actors. Fewer than a third of the popular film stars before 1933 emigrated between 1933 and 1939, a year when emigration became virtually impossible.[15] In other words, great talent remained in Germany.

Understandably, the relatively few propaganda films have attracted considerable attention since they give us insights into the aims and mentality of the National Socialists. The most famous propaganda film is Leni Riefenstahl's *Triumph des Willens* (*Triumph of the Will,* 1935), a "documentary" of the 1934 National Socialist party congress. The film, the result of six months of intensive editing of the 62 hours of filmed material, transformed the prosaic events of the party congress into a spellbinding self-portrait of the National Socialists. The initial scene depicting Hitler's arrival by plane in Nuremberg sets the tone. The viewer first sees clouds; only after a while the "Führer's" small plane emerges from the clouds, casting a crosslike shadow on the columns of Hitler's faithful followers marching toward the city. The plane lands, and Hitler steps out into the cheering crowds. Hitler's open car moves briskly toward the hotel where another throng of admiring fans awaits him. With one brilliant stroke, Leni Riefenstahl has established one of the principal themes of the party congress and the film: Hitler as Germany's savior who descends from the sky/heaven (in German the same word: *Himmel*), but who at the same time mixes with the people and is therefore one of them. In subsequent scenes this theme is repeated and Hitler remains the main focus of the entire film (as of the party congress), while the more than half a million visitors are reduced to cheering crowds or, as in the memorable scene of the commemoration of the war dead, to ornamental patterns and gigantic blocks.

At the time of the release, *Triumph des Willens* brought fame and numerous prizes to the film director. In 1936 she was commissioned by the International Olympic Committee to produce the official film of the 1936 Berlin Olympic Games. After the defeat of the Third Reich in 1945, however, Leni Riefenstahl was ostracized, her archives were temporarily confiscated, and she had to defend herself in a number of trials. In the intervening more than 50 years she remained, until her death in 2003 at age 101, the Third Reich's most controversial filmmaker. Her numerous admirers, mostly in the United States, including George Lucas, Steven Spielberg, Kevin Costner, and Jodie Foster, who wants to make a feature film about her (there exists already a two-hour documentary), brushed off her former Nazi sympathies and admired her cinematic genius. In 1999 *Time* magazine elected her as the only woman of the 100 most important artists of the twentieth century. Her detractors, on the other hand, mostly found in Germany, accused her of having aided the

Third Reich by her glorification of the Nazi dictator. Public screening of *Triumph des Willen* is still forbidden in Germany.

Cinema in East Germany

Postwar Germany's division into two states had a profound impact on the cultural developments of the two dissimilar states. Since the large studios of the former Nazi-controlled UFA in Potsdam-Babelsberg happened to be in the Soviet zone, the Soviets, together with the German Communists, established as early as 1946 the first German postwar film company, the DEFA. From then on, film production was controlled financially, politically, and artistically first by the Soviets and then by the Communist party. DEFA was to remain the only film company in the GDR.

With the major production facilities located in the East, it is not surprising that the very first German postwar film in the East or West, was made by DEFA. It was Wolfgang Staudte's *Die Mörder sind unter uns* (*The Murderers Are Among Us,* 1946), an early attempt to come to terms with the Nazi past. Set in bombed-out Berlin, the film tells the story of Dr. Mertens, who returns from the war. He meets his former commander, now a manufacturer, who had ordered the execution of hostages in occupied Poland and who now has switched from producing steel helmets to pots and pans. Outraged by this opportunist who is unwilling to accept any responsibility or guilt for his crimes, Mertens wants to take justice in his own hands and kill him. He is, however, dissuaded from doing so by a woman he has met among the ruins. This former concentration camp inmate pleads, "We are not allowed to condemn to death." Whereupon he retorts, "But we are allowed to accuse."

Since antifascism was one of the pillars of East Germany's self-understanding, antifascist films were to become staples of the East German cinema. Frank Beyer's *Jakob der Lügner* (*Jacob the Liar,* 1974), is one of the finest in this genre and the only GDR film ever nominated for an Oscar. Locked up in an East European ghetto, Jakob pretends to own a radio on which he hears news about the approaching Red Army. It is this hope for liberation by the Soviet army that keeps his fellow sufferers alive, although in the end, the hope turns out to be an illusion.

GDR filmmakers were less successful in depicting their depressing reality. That had nothing to do with their ability or willingness to do so but rather with the restrictive cultural policies of the Communist authorities, who by the early fifties had fully embraced the precepts of Socialist Realism, "the doctrine that demanded uplifting filmic portrayals of positive working class heroes." Critical films such as *Berlin-Schönhauser Ecke* (Berlin-Schönhauser Corner, 1957), depicting the problems a group of adolescent, unintegrated "rowdies" faced in conformist East Germany, were criticized, others banned. Only after the building of the Berlin Wall in 1961, which closed the last escape route to the West, did East German cultural functionaries feel secure enough to relax the leash somewhat, as in Konrad Wolf's *Der geteilte Himmel* (*Divided Heaven,* 1964), based on Christa Wolf's novel with the same title. In the following decades, the pendulum repeatedly swung back and forth between repression—in 1965 half a year's film production was shelved after the intervention of the party[16]—and liberalization, between hope and paralysis. Films like Frank Beyer's *Spur der Steine* (*Trail of Stones,* 1968), a film that could hardly be considered a threat to socialism but a plea for a more open, humane, albeit socialist society, were banned, while others such as Heiner Carow's *Die Legende von Paul und Paula* (*The Legend of Paul and Paula,* 1973) were released. With 1.8 million visits in one year,[17] this erotic melodrama advocating the right to private happiness and self-realization became one of DEFA's great successes.

The eighties, however, were again a time of repression. Gorbachev's glasnost and perestroika were not welcomed by the East German Communists. Reforms were blocked and the realistic portrayals of the increasingly difficult situation in East Germany were discouraged. At that time one of the young frustrated directors summed up the dilemma facing filmmakers: "We are facing our reality as if we were standing before a house on fire—and we aren't even allowed to take pictures of it."[18]

In 1989 the Berlin Wall came down. A year later, West Germany absorbed East Germany. The GDR ceased to exist and with it, East German Cinema.

Cinema in West Germany

Germans emerging from the rubble of their bombed-out cities wanted to be entertained and not to be reminded of the nightmare that lay behind them. Hollywood's dream factories quickly seized the opportunity and flooded the West German market with movies that had been banned during the Third Reich in Germany in the previous 12 years. The Germans themselves produced mainly entertainment films, or as the critics would have it, "escapist fare." Sentimental *Heimatfilme* (home-sweet-home films) set in rural idyllic landscapes such as *Grün ist die Heide* (Green Is the Heath, 1950), romantic adventure comedies, detective films, westerns based on the novels of the immensely popular Karl May, and, in the wake of the sexual revolution of the sixties, innumerable sex comedies—this was the common fare for the cinemagoer. Not surprisingly, these films were popular. The fifties, when few families had TV sets, especially became the boom years at the box office. In 1955, for instance, 128 films were released, and in 1956 there were a record 817 million cinema visits.[19] Though popular with the audiences, the films were regularly panned by the critics for their triviality and remoteness from political reality. To be sure, there were notable exceptions to this trend: films like Bernhard Wicki's powerful antiwar film *Die Brücke* (*The Bridge*, 1959), showing the senseless fight of a group of young high school students drafted into the army in the last weeks of the war, or Helmut Käutner's *Des Teufels General* (*The Devil's General*, 1954), the story of a Luftwaffe General's resistance to Hitler, or Kurt Hoffmann's *Wir Wunderkinder* (The Prodigies, 1958), the biting satire on an ex-Nazi who had become a wealthy industrialist.

The New German Cinema

In 1962 a group of young filmmakers signed a manifesto at the Oberhausen film festival, brashly declaring the death of "*Opa's Kino*" (Grandpa's cinema) and calling for a new cinema. It should take almost a decade before a number of young directors emerged who actually produced films that soon would be hailed by critics at home and abroad as the "New German Cinema." In 1978 *Time* magazine declared, "The Germans are now producing the most original films outside America."[20] Another critic echoed these sentiments: "The New German Cinema of West Germany has probably been the most important movement in international cinema during the 1970s."[21]

Within a few years, the names of Werner Herzog, Rainer Werner Fassbinder, Wim Wenders, Volker Schlöndorff, and a host of less renowned colleagues attracted the attention of cinephiles from New York to Paris, from San Francisco to Berlin. The directors grouped under that name formed no school and had no common program. What they had in common was a break with "*Opa's Kino*," a joy in artistic experimentation and a willingness to deal with topical social and political problems facing the West German affluent society in which they had grown up.

Celebrated by *Newsweek* as "by far the most remarkable of the young German directors," the eccentric and brilliant Werner Herzog (born 1942) was fascinated by the bizarre and abnormal, by outsiders, social outcasts, and obsessive visionaries, whether it is in his early nightmarish film *Auch Zwerge haben klein angefangen* (Even Dwarfs Started Small, 1969/1970), the story of the collapsed uprising of dwarfs, or the failed dream of the three ill-assorted Germans who go to America in *Stroszek* (1977), or the mad delusions of the protagonists in the two films that established his reputation in the United States, *Aguirre, der Zorn Gottes* (*Aguirre, the Wrath of God*, 1972) and *Fitzcarraldo* (1980/81). Aguirre leads a band of conquistadors across the Andean into the Amazon jungle in search of El Dorado. After two months of hunger, exposure, and attacks from native Indians, he is the only survivor. From the very first scene, as the sixteenth-century Spanish expedition descends on a narrow, precipitous path from the Andes to the steamy landscape of the Amazon jungle to the ending when the mad Aguirre slowly drifts down the Amazon on a raft dreaming of founding the purest dynasty there ever was to rule the whole of New Spain, *Aguirre* abounds in breathtaking images and stunning photography.

With *Fitzcarraldo* (1982), Herzog returned to the same exotic setting as in *Aguirre*. The film again features a man with obsessive dreams that include building an icemaking factory and an opera house in the Amazon jungle. His latest dream involves buying a rubber-tapping license in a remote part of Peru that is inaccessible by boat due to rapids and hostile Indians. To reach the area and avoid the rapids, Fitzcarraldo has the ingenious idea of steaming up a river parallel to the one made inaccessible by the rapids and having a steamship dragged across a mountain, past the rapids, thus opening up the area. Once this feat is accomplished, drunk Indians cast off the lines and the steamer and its crew tumble down the rapids.

Of all the filmmakers who made up the heterogeneous group of the New German Cinema, Rainer Werner Fassbinder (1946–1982) has attracted the most attention. A man of prodigious productivity—during his short career he directed about 50 films including the 15-hour film for television called *Berlin-Alexanderplatz*—Fassbinder was a workaholic who concealed his discipline behind a scruffy exterior of dirty jeans, a leather jacket, and a mean "Hell's Angels" look. Unlike Werner Herzog, who tends to choose exotic places for his films. Fassbinder always dealt with contemporary German issues: "I am a German, making German films for a German audience."[22] His themes are bigotry and racism, xenophobia, the isolation of the elderly, and exploitation, sexual and otherwise. Fassbinder began directing films in the mid-sixties and by 1973 he had already made an amazing 18 films, some of which were made for television. His breakthrough with the wider public, however, came with his film *Angst essen Seele* (*Fear Eats Soul,* 1973), the love story of an older woman and a young Moroccan *Gastabeiter* (guest worker). Five years later, in a trilogy consisting of *Die Ehe der Maria Braun* (*The Marriage of Maria Braun,* 1978), *Lilli Marleen* (1979), and *Lola* (1981), Fassbinder dealt with recent German history. The first, *Maria Braun,* became one of his most successful films, winning him critical acclaim abroad and in West Germany. Set for the most part in the first decade following World War II, the film chronicles the rise and fall of a successful business career of an attractive, strong-willed and opportunistic West German woman, Maria Braun. But the film is more than the melodramatic story of an individual. *Maria Braun* can also be interpreted as a parable for postwar Germany. This is sug-

Schlöndorff's *The Tin Drum,* which won an Oscar as best foreign film in 1980. Reprinted by permission of *Der Spiegel.*

gested not only by the portraits of Hitler and the West German chancellors flashed on the screen but also by the soundtrack featuring the sound of exploding bombs, the reading on the radio of endless lists of missing persons, excerpts from Chancellor Adenauer's speeches, and, at the end, the breathless voice of the radio reporter describing Germany's victory in the world championship soccer match in 1954.

Whereas Fassbinder's characters are unmistakably German, Wim Wenders, the third of the best known filmmakers, strives for internationality in his films. *Der amerikanische Freund* (*The American Friend,* 1976–77), for instance, takes place in Hamburg, Paris, and New York and features American, Swiss, German, and French actors, whereas *Paris, Texas* (1983–84) tells the story of a man who had vanished for years and who is involved, like most of Wenders' characters, in a search, in this case a search for his language, his son, and his wife. In the modern fairy tale *Himmel über Berlin* (*Wings of Desire,* 1986–87), two extraterrestials look down on Berlin. One of the them falls in love with a trapeze artist, renounces his heavenly existence and becomes an earthling.

While Fassbinder and Herzog often wrote their own screenplays, Volker Schlöndorff (born 1939) likes to transform literary texts to the screen. After filming *Der junge Törless* (*Young Törless,* 1966) after a novel by the Austrian writer Robert Musil, Schlöndorff made the successful *Die verlorene Ehre der Katharina Blum* (*The Lost Honor of Katharina Blum,* 1975) based on a novel by Nobel prizewinner Heinrich Böll. Even more successful was Schlöndorff's film *Die Blechtrommel* (*The Tin Drum,* 1979), again a film adaptation of a novel, this time of Günter Grass's monumental novel of the same name, which had appeared in 1959. Both at home and abroad the film was widely acclaimed, winning *La Palme d'Or* (the golden palm) in Cannes in 1979 and an Oscar for the best foreign film in 1980, the first German film to receive such an award (see chapter 7). In the same year, Helma Sanders-Brahms's *Deutschland, bleiche Mutter* (*Germany, Pale Mother,* 1979) appeared. Unabashedly autobiographical, the film narrates "a conventional love story, except that it happened in that time and that place," as the voice-over of the female narrator tells the viewer. "That time" is the Third Reich and the Second World War and the postwar period. While the father is away in the war, the mother and her small daughter develop a tight bond strengthened by their shared horrible experiences. With the return of the father and the reassertion of his authority, the mother's newly discovered role as provider is no longer needed, her freedom gone. This loss of her independence results in a psychosomatic affliction expressing itself in a facial paralysis and in a suicide attempt.

The 1990s: A New German Film Miracle?

By the mid-eighties, a new generation of directors emerged who managed to make films that were suspenseful, entertaining, well-crafted, and sophisticated at the same time. *Time* magazine's verdict of 1982, "The Germans are coming! The Germans are coming!", referring to the appearance of a few successful German films on the American market, might be dismissed as hype. It is true, however, that the 1980s and 1990s saw the release of a number of films that were very successful in Germany and were even able attract respectable audiences in the United States, a notoriously hard market to crack for foreign films. Among the films produced in the 1990s, comedies were particularly successful at the box office and also gained a measure of respect abroad. Sönke Wortmann's *Der bewegte Mann* (*The Most Desirable Man*, 1994), Doris Dörrie's *Keiner liebt mich* (*Nobody Loves Me*, 1996), and *Männer* (*Men, 1985)* played to full houses in Germany. In the course of the 1990s, Helmut Dietl produced three films dealing with the mass media. *Schtonk* (1992), nominated for an Oscar, is a satire on the fiasco surrounding the publication of the forged Hitler diaries, while *The Late Show* (1998–99) is a spoof on the emptiness of the talk shows popularized by the emergence of private television. The latest entry into this genre, *Der Schuh des Manitu* (*Manitou's Shoe*, 2001) brought an unprecedented 11 million visitors into German cinemas, "raising the country's market share to 18.4 per cent and making it the most successful German film of all time."[23]

Films about the Third Reich continue to fascinate viewers at home and abroad. Wolfgang Peterson's two-and-a-half-hour epic *Das Boot* (*The Boat*, 1985), depicting the claustrophobic world of a German World War II submarine, attracted large audiences. Joseph Vilsmaier's *Stalingrad* (1992) shows one of World War II's fiercest battles from the simple soldier's point of view; Agnieszka Holland's *Hitlerjunge Salomon* (*Europa, Europa*, 1991) tells the bizarre and wrenching story of a Jewish boy who survived World War II and the Holocaust by joining the Hitler Youth. Vilsmaier's *The Comedian Harmonists* (*The Harmonists*, 1997) chronicles the bittersweet story of the brilliant vocal sextet that charmed German audiences between 1927 and 1935, the year they were banned by the Nazis because two of the singers were Jewish; Michael Verhoeven's *Das schreckliche Mädchen* (*Nasty Girl*, 1990) pits a high school girl determined to find out about the Nazi past of her town against her elders equally bent on hiding that past; Max Fäberböck's *Aimée and Jaguar* (1998) recounts the lesbian love affair between a Jewish woman, living under a false identity in wartime Berlin, and a German mother of four married to a Nazi soldier. All these films are based on true stories. The Holocaust is also the emotional backdrop for Caroline Link's film *Nirgendwo in Afrika* (*Nowhere in Africa*, 2002), which won the Oscar for the best foreign film in 2003. The film, which follows Stefanie Zweig's autobiography of the same title, chronicles the life of a German-Jewish lawyer and his family, who flee Nazi Germany in 1938 and settle in Kenya as tenant farmers. The most recent entry into this genre, Margarethe von Trotta's *Rosenstrasse* (2003), deals with the successful resistance of a group of German women against the deportation of their Jewish husbands.

The end of the 40 years of Communist dictatorship in East Germany in 1989 has also spawned a number of films. Some of these are comedies, such as Peter Timm's *Go Trabi Go* (1991) and Sebastian Peterson's *Helden wie wir* (Heroes Like Us, 1999), others deal on a more serious level with the legacy of the German partition. Such a film is, for instance, Margarethe von Trotta's

Das Versprechen (The Promise, 1994), a story of two lovers trapped on oppo-
site sides of the Berlin Wall. Frank Beyer's *Nikolaikirche* (St. Nicholas
Church, 1995), on the other hand, examines the 1980s resistance movement
centered around this church in Leipzig. The film focuses on "one family and
its variant members functioning as a microcosm of the wider socialist state."[24]

Finally, with about 10 percent of Germany's population being foreigners,
Germany has become a multicultural society. This trend is reflected in an
increasing number of films by young directors of Turkish descent who very
often depict the classic dilemma of immigrants being caught between the
desire to maintain their cultural identity and the need to assimilate into the
new culture. Among these Turkish directors, the best known is Fatih Akin.
His film *Kurz and schmerzlos* (Short and Painless, 1997), set in the tough
underworld of a large German city, has been called a *Multikulti Gangsterbal-
lade* (a multicultural gangster ballad),[25] while his film *Im Juli* (In July, 2001),
featuring a German-Turkish cast, narrates the love story of a frustrated German apprentice teacher and a beautiful Turkish woman whom he pursues in
a hilarious odyssey through southeastern Europe all the way to Istanbul.

In 2001, films made in Germany had captured a market share of 18 percent of the Hollywood-dominated German market. This was seen as a triumph and the word of a new German "film miracle" was heard occasionally.
This is certainly premature. But it shows that the German cinema is alive and
well. Though some of these films were moderately successful in the United
States, such as the hip-hop fantasy *Lola rennt* (*Run, Lola, Run,* 1998) by Tom
Tykwer starring one of the German cinema's rising actresses, Franka Polente,
and Sandra Nettelbeck's *Bella Martha* (*Mostly Martha,* 2001), there is no danger that the American market will ever be flooded by European, let alone German films. The number of films from non-English-speaking countries shown
in the United States has steadily decreased in recent decades and represents
less than one percent of the market share in this country. The last thing, it
seems, American viewers want to do when they go to the movies is to read.
And subtitles are an unavoidable feature of any foreign-language film.

NOTES

1. Hermann Meyn, *Massenmedien in Deutschland* (Konstanz: UVK Medien,
2001), 85.

2. Gros and Glaab, *Faktenlexikon Deutschland,* 171.

3. Meyn, *Massenmedien in Deutschland,* 85.

4. Meyn, *Massenmedien in Deutschland,* 105.

5. *The Economist,* 16 November 2002, 46.

6. The Federal Government, *Facts About Germany,* 460.

7. All figures from The Federal Government, *Facts About Germany,* 462.

8. *Der Spiegel* 45 (2001): 121.

9. Harenberg, *Aktuell 2002,* 279.

10. Warren French quoted in Robert Amour, *Fritz Lang* (Boston: Twayne Publishers, 1977), 8.

11. Roger Manvell and Heinrich Fraenkel, *The German Cinema* (New York and Washington: Praeger, 1971), 12.

12. Lotte Eisner, *The Haunted Screen: Expressionism in the German Cinema and the Influence of Max Reinhardt* (Berkeley and Los Angeles: University of California Press, 1973), 97.

13. Manvell and Fraenkel, *The German Cinema,* 25.

14. Ingo R. Stoehr, *German Literature of the Twentieth Century. From Aestheticism to Postmodernism,* vol. 10, *Camden House History of German Literature* (Rochester and New York: Camden House, 2001), 82.

15. After David Welch, *The Third Reich: Politics and Propaganda* (London: Routledge, 1993), 63.

16. Martin Brady and Helen Hughes, "German Cinema," in *The Cambridge Companion to Modern German Culture,* edited by Eva Kolinsky and Wilfried van der Will (Cambridge: Cambridge University Press, 1998), 311.

17. Wolfgang Gersch, "Film in der DDR," in *Geschichte des deutschen Films,* edited by Wolfgang Jacobsen, Anton Kaes, and Hans Helmut Prinzler (Stuttgart: Metzler, 1993), 347.

18. Quoted in Gersch, "Film in der DDR."

19. Brady and Hughes, "German Cinema," 314.

20. *Time,* 20 March 1978, 51.

21. Warren French, foreword to *New German Cinema: From Oberhausen to Hamburg,* by James Franklin (Boston: Twayne Publishers, 1983), 11.

22. Quoted in Franklin, *New German Cinema,* 140.

23. Jan-Christopher Horak, "German Film Comedy," in *The German Cinema Book,* edited by Tim Bergfelder, Erica Carter, and Deniz Göktürk (London: bfi Publishing, 2002), 36.

24. Dickon Copsey, "Scene Change: Pluralized Identities in Contemporary German Cinema," in *Contemporary German Cultural Studies,* edited by Alison Phipps (London: Arnold, 2002), 252.

25. Copsey, "Scene Change," 256.

9

Performing Arts: Theater, Music, Opera, Dance, and Cabaret

IN GERMANY, the performing arts, that is the spoken theater, the opera, operetta, classical music, and dance theater, enjoy financial public support unparalleled in the world. There are approximately 180 state-supported theaters, a total of 141 professional orchestras, and over 80 opera houses. The funds Germany spends on the performing arts are staggering. As two English critics point out, "State and municipal subsidies to German theaters now [1988] stand at about seven times the amount of public funding the United States provides for all the arts, and the Berlin Opera House alone receives almost as much as the British Arts Council has at its disposal for all the theaters it supports."[1] Germany's theaters alone employ approximately 45,000 people and so represent an important economic factor. It is also estimated that, for instance in 1991, Germany spent a total of 7.7 billion DM (around $3.5 billion) on music, an amount that corresponds to the total investment in hospitals and road construction.[2] Because of the generous subsidy system, the German theater, opera, and music scene is not only of high quality but also affordable: a German theatergoer normally pays only a third or less of the actual cost of a ticket.

The exceptionally lavish public patronage of the arts is the result of two factors: first, Germany's political fragmentation prior to unification in 1871. Up to that time each kingdom, dukedom, earldom, and free city had its own opera, ballet, and theater and was ready to compete with similar institutions in other territories. After Germany's unification in 1871, the system of subsidizing the arts was taken over by the newly created states and not the central government, surviving revolutions and political upheavals, two world wars, and fascist and communist systems. For that reason, even today, it is not the federal government but the individual states (*Länder*) and municipalities that are responsible for the arts. The second explanation for the governmental generosity towards the arts has to do with the pivotal role music, the opera, and the theater play for the German national identity. Germans always regarded themselves as members of a "*Kulturnation.*" This high regard is reflected in the very buildings that house the performing arts. Theaters and opera houses are often magnificent, stately edifices. While in the eighteenth and nineteenth centuries they often resembled classical temples with rows of Greek columns adorning the main entrance, today they often are architecturally stunning structures with imposing entrances and beautiful lobbies where during intermission visitors leisurely promenade, a glass of champagne in hand, under the brightly lit chandeliers.

In many cases, a theater, an opera house, and a ballet company are housed under the same roof and are under the same direction. In fact, Germany has 76 such multipurpose or three-part (theater, opera, ballet) houses, offering a broad range of plays, dance, and music theater (opera, operetta, musical). In any given season, the permanent ensemble of such a institution will perform a repertoire of 20 to 30 different works.

THEATER

Germany is a paradise for theater lovers. Nowhere in the world are there so many theaters relative to the size of the population. The approximately 180 publicly supported theaters are complemented by roughly 190 private theaters and more than 30 festival theaters.[3] The rich theatrical scene is not concentrated in one city as it is in Great Britain and France but, as noted above, highly decentralized. To be sure, after the recent unification of the two Germanys in 1990, Berlin has probably again the highest number of theaters, but there are world-class theaters in Hamburg, Bochum, Frankfurt, Stuttgart, and Munich, and even medium-sized cities often have excellent three-part houses.

The wealth and diversity of theaters reflect the place theater has occupied in German cultural life since the middle of the eighteenth century, when for the first time a serious literary theater emerged in German lands. In a seminal essay, Friedrich Schiller (1759–1805), one of Germany's most brilliant playwrights, defined the theater as a "moral institution" (*moralische Anstalt*). Ever since then, theater in Germany has been viewed more than mere entertainment, as it is primarily in the English-speaking world; it has also been regarded as a forum for serious political, philosophical, and moral discussions. It is not surprising that there is no German equivalent to the English term "show business."

Since theaters also view themselves as guardians of the canon of the Western dramatic literature, they stage plays from the classical Western tradition much more often than the commercial theaters in the Anglo-Saxon world, including classic plays by the Greek writers Euripides, Sophocles, and Aeschylus, modern classics by Molière, Ibsen, Chekhov, Shaw, Shakespeare, Strindberg and, of course, the German classics by Lessing, Goethe, Schiller, and Kleist. Producing these well-known classics and making them relevant to today's audience present a perennial challenge to directors. This has led to what in German is called *Regietheater,* or director's theater, meaning that the emphasis has shifted from the playwright and play to the director. In an effort to shed new light on old plays, directors often employ shock tactics, such when Othello "appears in tails with black paint running down his face, hanging the dead Desdemona nude over a clothes line,"[4] or when in a performance of Friedrich Schiller's *Maria Stuart,* the two queens Mary Stuart and Elizabeth anachronistically scoot on roller skates on the stage.

The Development of German Theater

Unlike England, Spain, and France, Germany was late in developing a serious theater tradition. Here, drama of high literary standards emerged only in the second half of the eighteenth century. Credit for this development must go to three men: Gotthold Ephraim Lessing (1729–81), Friedrich Schiller (1759–1805), and Johann Wolfgang von Goethe (1749–1832).

Lessing rightly has been called "the father of serious German theater." His importance is twofold: first, he was the first German literary critic to direct the Germans' attention to Shakespeare, away from the slavish imitation of French classical theater, thus initiating an enthusiasm for the English playwright that has lasted to this day. Secondly, he created a number of "bourgeois tragedies" (*Miss Sara Sampson,* 1755, and *Emilia Galotti,* 1772), that is, plays in which bourgeois or middle-class persons (and not members of the aristocracy and important historical personalities) are the protagonists. Most of his plays have become staples in the classical repertoire and one, *Nathan der Weise* (*Nathan the Wise,* 1779), that enlightened plea for religious tolerance, is even occasionally performed abroad, as it was in 2002 in New York.

But it was Friedrich Schiller, who through his theoretical writings and above all through his own plays, became the master of the German classical theater. His plays, revolutionary at the time, have retained their freshness, and it is hard to find any theater in the German-speaking world that does not feature at least one Schiller play per season. His plays include: *Die Räuber* (*The Robbers,* 1782), *Kabale und Liebe* (*Intrigue and Love,* 1784), *Don Carlos* (1787), the *Wallenstein* trilogy (1778–99), *Maria Stuart* (*Mary Stuart,* 1800),

Die Jungfrau von Orleans (*The Maid of Orléans,* 1801), and *Wilhelm Tell* (*William Tell,* 1804). Goethe, Germany's undisputed literary giant, a man of monumental accomplishments in many different fields, was also for 26 years the director of the court theater in the small duchy of Saxe-Weimar, and as such became acquainted with the practical problems of the theater. His dramas include *Götz von Berlichingen* (1773), the psychological drama *Torquato Tasso* (1789), the historical play *Egmont* (1788), and above all his *Faust* (part 1, 1808; part 2, 1832), one of the great poetic and philosophical works of world literature. Because of its length and difficulty, directors rarely mount productions of the entire two-part play, although the first part, the so-called Gretchen tragedy, is often staged.

If Lessing, Schiller, and Goethe gave the German theater the high status it enjoys up to this day, it was Georg Büchner (1813–1837) who deserves to be called "the father of *modern* theater." His plays—*Dantons Tod* (*Danton's Death,* 1837) and *Woyzeck* (1837)—were so modern that they were not performed until decades after his death, and anybody reading them today or seeing them performed will be surprised that Büchner died only five years after Goethe. He seems to belong not only to a different generation but to a different century. His impact on twentieth-century naturalist, expressionist, and political theater was enormous. Woyzeck, for instance, is a soldier and a barber, a simple man. By portraying him as an oppressed human being, dependent on milieu and origin, Büchner anticipated Gerhart Hauptmann (1862–1946), Germany's main exponent of Naturalism. Best known is Hauptmann's *Die Weber* (*The Weavers,* 1892). Written 50 years after Büchner, it deals with the uprising of the Silesian weavers in the middle of the nineteenth century. That play exhibits all the characteristics of a naturalistic drama: a close reproduction of the spoken word including dialect, a seemingly accidental plot, the mass of the weavers as the collective hero, a focus on social problems, and sympathy with the oppressed.

The Twentieth Century

"If God ever came to Berlin, he would make sure he got tickets to see a Reinhardt play,"[5] said the Austrian Arthur Schnitzler. However, Max Reinhardt (1873–1943), "the innovator of a poetic realism on the stage...and master of gigantic productions and a genius of the mob scene,"[6] was only one of the brilliant directors and playwrights who had come to Berlin in the 1920s, making the German capital, with its 33 theaters, the liveliest and most innovative theater city in the world. There would have been many more reasons for God to secure tickets for theatrical productions. As a matter of fact, Reinhardt, immensely popular as he was, was looked down upon by the two avant-garde directors, Leopold Jessner (1878–1945) and Erwin Piscator (1883–1966). Jessner was influenced by the prevailing style of Expressionism (see the chapters on art and literature), with its focus on the typical and "essential." For his stage productions he favored stylized, abstract sets, even for those plays that were not Expressionist, such as Friedrich Schiller's *Wilhelm Tell*. For that production, for instance, Jessner created a stage consisting of abstract ramps, stairs, and bridges, instead of the traditional bucolic Alpine landscape.

But perhaps the boldest of Berlin's great directors was Erwin Piscator. Unabashedly placing his considerable theatrical talents in the service of leftist political and social reform, he employed in his productions the newest technology of the age, including film and slide projections, conveyor belts, and revolving sets, making his plays into spectacular multimedia shows with a strong political message. At the same time, by creating essentially an anti-illusionist theater, he appealed to the intellect rather than to the emotions. These two aspects of Piscator's work, the political message and the break with the illusionist theater, intrigued the young Bertolt Brecht (1898–1956), who was to emerge as the most influential theatrical figure of the first half of the twentieth century. Throughout his career, which spanned the Weimar Republic, the Third Reich (which he spent in exile), and Communist East Germany, Brecht was a playwright, theorist, and theater practitioner. He not only wrote a number of plays that have become classics, such as *Die Dreigroschenoper* (*The Threepenny Opera,* 1928), *Mutter Courage und ihre Kinder* (*Mother Courage and Her Children,* premiered 1941), *Das Leben des Galileo* (*Galileo,* premiered 1943), *Der gute Mensch von Sezuan* (*The Good Woman of Setzuan,* premiered 1943) and *Der kaukasische Kreidekreis* (*The Caucasian Chalk Circle,* premiered 1954), but also profoundly changed our understanding of drama. Rejecting the traditional, Brecht developed what he called "the epic theater," a term he had borrowed from Piscator. For the Marxist Brecht, theater had the function of changing social conditions, of becoming "a tool of social engineering, a laboratory for social change."[7] Believing that this could be best accomplished by encouraging the audience to keep its distance and look critically at the stage action, Brecht discouraged the audience to get emotionally involved. To this end Brecht developed a number of techniques, causing the *Verfremdungseffekt,* usually translated as the "alienation or distancing effect," through which the stage action was meant to be seen by the audience in a new, unfamiliar way. Through the inclusion of songs, a narrator, posters announcing the action of the next scene, and other techniques, he constantly interrupted the theatrical illusion. The focus was no longer on what happened but why it happened. Though Brecht's politics were often viewed with considerable skepticism, his influence on German and international theater was profound.

Weimar's flourishing theater came to a halt with the assumption of power by the National Socialists in 1933. Many of the playwrights and directors who for a short time had made Germany the center for cutting-edge theatrical experimentation went into exile. The theaters of the Third Reich reverted to the safe classics and introduced a few new playwrights who wrote plays about Nazi heroes and German historical figures.

Postwar German Theater

In 1945 German cities lay in ruins. But amidst the hopelessness and desolation of the ruined cities, a theater life sprang up with surprising speed. It is a sign of the importance Germans attach to the theater that some of the first buildings being rebuilt were theaters. If no theaters were available, plays were performed in schools, churches, cellars, in anything that had survived the war. Initially, there was a tremendous hunger for those foreign playwrights who had been banned during the Nazi dictatorship, such as Jean-Paul Sartre, Albert Camus, Jean Anouilh, Thornton Wilder, G. B. Shaw and T. S. Eliot, and later in the 1950s, the playwrights of the theater of the absurd, Eugene Ionesco and Samuel Beckett. Among the few contemporary German plays that could match the success of the foreign dramatists, two stand out: Wolfgang Borchert's *Draußen vor der Tür* (*The Man Outside*, 1947), a play about a disillusioned soldier who returns from Russian captivity to his destroyed hometown of Hamburg (see chapter 7), and Carl Zuckmayer's *Des Teufels General* (*The Devil's General*, 1946), the story of resistance by an air force general who, though a Nazi opponent, is such a passionate flyer that he joins the newly created Luftwaffe and becomes an important general and thus an unwilling accomplice of Hitler. In the end he falls victim to this pact with the "devil" and out of desperation kills himself. The 1950s were also dominated by two successful German-speaking Swiss playwrights, Max Frisch (*Biedermann und die Brandstifter, The Firebugs*, 1958, and *Andorra*, 1961) and Friedrich Dürrenmatt (*Der Besuch der alten Dame, The Visit*, 1956, and *Die Physiker, The Physicists*, 1962).

The 1960s

The 1960s brought the breakthrough for German playwrights. Within a few years a number of dramatists emerged who changed the German theatrical landscape, prompting W. G. Sebald, a German writer and literary critic living in England, looking back in 1988, to declare: "There can be no doubt that the dozen or so years from 1968 to the early 1980s were among the most inspiring in the history of twentieth-century German theatre."[8] The breakthrough can be dated to the premiere of Rolf Hochhuth's play *Der Stellvertreter* (*The Deputy*) in 1963. Directed by Erwin Piscator, who had returned from exile, the play caused a sensation not so much through its form—Hochhuth employed the traditional five-act structure—but through its theme: the playwright accused Pope Pius XII of having failed to condemn the Nazi atrocities against the Jews. What was new, however, in Hochhuth's play was not only the attack on one of the most revered figures of the Catholic Church but also that the play claimed to be based on a careful study of historical documents intended to support its main thesis. With this play Hochhuth initiated a whole new trend, the "documentary theater." Heiner Kipphardt's *In der Sache J.Robert Oppenheimer* (*In the Matter of J.Robert Oppenheimer,* 1964) and Peter Weiss's *Die Ermittlung* (*The Investigation,* 1965) were the best-known plays of that genre.

Transcending the documentary theater, however, though including elements of it, was Peter Weiss's *Die Verfolgung und Ermordung Jean Paul Marats dargestellt durch die Schauspielgruppe des Hospizes zu Charenton unter der Anleitung des Herrn de Sade* (*The Persecution and Assassination of Jean-Paul Marat as Performed by the Inmates of the Asylum of Charenton under the Direction of the Marquis de Sade,* 1964). A phenomenal success in Europe and the United States, it was called by the usually restrained *London Times* "a dramatic milestone of the first order." It is total theater; seeing it an unforgettable experience, or as Peter Brooks, who staged the play in London and directed the 1967 film version, observed: "Starting with its title, everything about the play is designed to crack the spectator on the jaw, then douse him with ice-cold water, then force him to assess intelligently what has happened to him, then give him a kick in the balls, then bring him back to his senses again."[9]

East German Theater

During the 40 years of its existence East Germany boasted as healthy a state-supported theater system as West Germany. If anything, with 68 theaters and 200 venues, this small state, the size of Ohio and with a population of a mere 16 million, had an even more developed theater landscape than the Federal Republic. To be sure, there was censorship and the occasional interference by the state, but the technical and artistic standards were high. Brecht's Berliner Ensemble attracted visitors from all over the world, as did East Berlin's Komische Oper (Comic Opera) under the direction of Walter Felsenstein. Moreover, many a provincial theater further removed from the watchful eyes of the cultural functionaries in East Berlin, staged surprisingly daring productions. In addition, in view of the lack of critical newspapers and other news media able to criticize openly the government, the theaters

Production of *Germania Tod [Death] in Berlin,* 1978. Courtesy of
Deutsches Theatermuseum, Hildegard Steinmetz Archive.

became "a major medium of communication."[10] Using veiled language,
directors would often challenge the political system of the GDR. This became
especially important in the last years of East Germany, when the old Communist guard under Erich Honecker refused to follow Mikhail Gorbachev's
reform course. A line from a classical drama, such as from Schiller's *Wilhelm
Tell,* "Das Alte fällt, es ändern sich die Zeiten" (The old collapses, times are
changing), could prompt a round of knowing and sympathetic applause. Nor
had the audience any difficulty in identifying the old tired knights at King
Arthur's round table who had failed to find the holy grail (in Christoph
Hein's play *Die Ritter der Tafelrunde* [The Knights of the Round Table,
1989]) with their current senile Communist leaders.

East Germany also produced a number of highly gifted playwrights such as
Peter Hacks, Volker Braun, Ulrich Plenzdorf, and Heiner Müller. Müller
(1929–1995) emerged in the mid-1970s as the most important dramatist,
receiving international acclaim in Europe and America. If for Weiss (in his
Marat/Sade) the world was a madhouse, for Müller, in his *Germania Tod in
Berlin* (*Germania Death in Berlin,* 1978), the world had become a slaughter-
house. The play presents a grotesque and blood-soaked panorama of German
history replete with bizarre appearances of Hitler and Goebbels, dismem-
bered German soldiers, whores, and Communists. Müller's *Hamletmaschine*
(1979) was meant as "a sweeping critique and rejection of the entire male-

dominated civilization, of capitalism and communism alike."[11] Müller's theater is total theater depending on nonverbal action and powerful images. The text itself in the *Hamletmaschine* has become secondary and amounts to a mere nine pages in the printed edition.

The heavy burdens associated with German unification, combined with a worldwide recession beginning in 2001, have had a profound effect on the theaters in Germany, dependent as they are on public funding. Many theaters in former East Germany had to close, while the West German theaters had to tighten their belts. Dismayed by these cuts, directors conjured up the end of the German theater as it has existed. This is certainly premature. An outsider might be in a better position to judge the present situation. In the mid-1990s, an English critic gave the following flattering appraisal of the contemporary German theater: "Today Germany with directors like Peter Stein, Peter Zadek and Claus Peymann, continues to boast not only the best funded theaters of the world but also the most innovative."[12]

MUSIC

Germany is a land of music. Visitors to Germany invariably are impressed by the richness and variety of its musical life. The country of Bach and Beethoven, Brahms and Wagner, Schumann and Stockhausen, (and Schubert and Mozart, if we add composers from Austria, which of course was part of the German empire at that time) has a total of 141 professional orchestras,[13] some of which look back at long and distinguished traditions. The flagship of the German symphony orchestras is the Berlin Philharmonic, led currently by the Englishman Sir Simon Rattle. But other ensembles, such as the Munich Philharmonic, the Bamberg Symphony Orchestra, the Gewandhaus Orchestra in Leipzig, and the Dresden Staatskapelle have won world renown, and so have individual artists like the violinist Anne-Sophie Mutter, the viola player Tabea Zimmermann, the trumpet player Ludwig Güttler, and the singers Hildegard Behrens, Waltraud Meier, Gabriele Schnaut, Kurt Moll, Peter Hoffmann, René Kollo, Dietrich Fischer-Dieskau, and others.

The important role music plays in German life becomes even clearer when we look at some statistics: around 8 million Germans, that is every tenth person, is actively engaged in music in one form or the other.[14] There are 21,000 choirs, thousands of amateur orchestras, ensembles, and groups making music on every level. The number of rock, pop, and jazz bands is too large to count. In addition, there are about 30 music festivals in Germany, of which the Bayreuth Wagner festival, the Schleswig-Holstein Music Festival, and the Munich Opera Festival are the most famous. Germany also still boasts of 10 radio orchestras—in the United States long a thing of the past—some of them with international reputations.

German Composers

Composers from the German-speaking countries have enormously enriched the world's musical heritage. Indeed, it would be difficult to find any program of classical music anywhere in the world that does not include at least one work by a German composer. Johann Sebastian Bach (1685–1750), the "superstar of the Baroque,"[15] gave the world such magnificent classics as the Brandenburg concertos, the B Minor Mass, hundreds of cantatas, the *St. Matthew Passion*, and the sublime *Christmas Oratorio*, which belongs to a German Christmas as much as a candlelit Christmas tree. But it was the classical era, that short period comprising the second half of the eighteenth and the first quarter of the nineteenth century, which brought forth two masters: Wolfgang Amadeus Mozart (1756–1809) and Ludwig van Beethoven (1770–1827). Mozart was a musical wunderkind, a child prodigy. At the age of 3 he played the piano and violin, at the age of 5 he began to compose, at 9 he wrote his first symphony, and at 13 he became concertmaster in his native Salzburg. His works, written in almost every conceivable genre including trios, quartets, sonatas, symphonies, concertos, and operas (see below), blend gracious beauty with classical serenity. It is perhaps not surprising that this "darling of the gods" has become the subject of many legends. The (false) rumor, for instance, that he was poisoned by his rival Salieri was made into the central theme of Peter Shaffer's play *Amadeus* (1979), a play that was turned into an Oscar-winning movie (1984) by Milos Forman. The classical period culminated in the music of Ludwig van Beethoven, acknowledged as one of the greatest composers who ever lived. He was primarily a composer of instrumental music, including piano and violin concertos, sonatas, songs, string quartets, and, above all, his nine symphonies, works in which he broke all formal conventions. Beethoven's impact on succeeding generations of composers was tremendous. However, he is not only universally admired for his monumental musical accomplishments, but also for his struggle against one of the worst afflictions that can befall a musician, his deafness. It began when he was in his late twenties and became progressively worse until he was totally deaf. Yet it was at that time that he wrote some of his greatest works, including the Ninth Symphony with its choral finale based on Schiller's poem "Ode an die Freude" ("Ode to Joy"). It is a work that seems to encapsulate the triumph of the human spirit over adversity, whether this is a terrible condition like deafness or political repression. How fitting it was, then, that Leonard Bernstein conducted that work in Berlin to celebrate the fall of the

Beethoven Monument in Bonn. Photo by Eckhard Bernstein.

Berlin Wall at the end of 1989, replacing the word "Freude" (joy) with "Freiheit" (freedom). It is equally appropriate that the "Ode to Joy" has become the official "national" anthem of the European Union.

Beethoven's late works have been called Romantic, but the term Romanticism is so fluid that it covers virtually all works from the entire nineteenth century ranging from Franz Schubert's (1797–1828) intimate lieder (songs) to Gustav Mahler's (1860–1911) mammoth symphonies involving hundreds of musicians. The outstanding representatives of the Romantic music were Felix Mendelssohn-Bartholdy (1809–47) and Robert Schumann (1810–56). Today, Mendelssohn might be primarily remembered as the composer of the "Wedding March," a work that accompanies wedding celebrations around the globe. But in addition to this march he also composed five symphonies, piano and chamber music, oratorios, and the frequently performed Violin Concerto in E minor. Robert Schumann, a brilliant piano virtuoso, composer of piano and orchestral works, also wrote 250 lieder. His wife Clara Schumann (1819–96) was not only one of the outstanding pianists of her time but also a composer of numerous piano pieces and songs. The towering figure of German Romantic music, however, was Richard Wagner (1813–83), who revolutionized German opera (see below). Johannes Brahms (1833–97), more or less a contemporary of Wagner, rejected Wagner's progressive ideas and composed more in the traditional style, while the late Romantic composer Richard Strauss (1864–1949) was strongly influenced by Wagner's music.

In the twentieth century, German composers continued to make important contributions to the musical repertoire. Especially the Weimar Republic, that is Germany between the end of the First World War and the assumption of power by the National Socialists, demonstrated in music an openness for fresh ideas, making it "one of the richest periods in German musical history."[16] It was, as the satirist Kurt Tucholsky wryly remarked, as if the revolution "that had been canceled because of bad weather was taking place in music."[17] At that time Austrian-born Arnold Schönberg (1874–1951, since 1941 Schoenberg) abandoned tonality and developed his revolutionary 12-tone music. It was also the time when the annual Festival for Modern Music in Donaueschingen was established in 1921 to provide a forum for avant-garde composers. It is hard to generalize about the music composed during that time. Indeed, what makes this period so fascinating was "the bewildering variety of musical styles."[18] Next to the music written in the neo-Romantic style there were the dissonant compositions of the avant-garde.

With the beginning of the Third Reich, many composers of Jewish descent emigrated. Hindemith's music fell out of favor with the new regime. The avant-garde dispersed. But music is not so easily tainted by ideology as literature and the visual arts. And so it continued to flourish in Hitler's Germany. The classical repertoire was cultivated and under Wilhelm Furtwängler the Berlin Philharmonic Orchestra was able to retain its high standards. Richard Strauss became the head of the Reich Chamber of Music and Wagner the favorite composer of the Nazis. In 1937 Carl Orff composed his immensely popular *Carmina Burana*.

It is perhaps not surprising that the 12-tone music and other forms of experimental and avant-garde music, which had been suppressed during the Third Reich, would experience a strong revival after the war. The first decades of the postwar period were dominated by three composers who would attract international attention: Karl Heinz Stockhausen (born 1928), Hans Werner Henze (born 1926), and Bernd Alois Zimmermann (1918–1970). Of these, Stockhausen was the most radical. Considered one of the most inventive of the avant-garde composers and a pioneer in electronic music, he established his own electronic studio in Cologne where he composed a number of outstanding works for the medium. Although his music makes demands on performers and listeners, he became a cult figure in the 1960s and 1970s, drawing admiration not only from avant-garde musicians, but also from rock performers such as Frank Zappa and the German band Kraftwerk.[19]

In the 1970s, however, a certain disillusionment with the avant-garde music set in; parallel to the emergence of the New Savages (*Die Neuen Wilden*) in the visual arts (see chapter on arts), who had returned to figurative painting, a new traditionalism in music was favored. The models became the great composers between Beethoven and Mahler and the young German composers returned to classical genres, like symphonies and string quartets. The most prominent representatives are Wolfgang Rihm (born 1952), Manfred Trojahn (born 1949), Hans Jürgen von Bose (born 1953), and Detlev Müller-Siemens (born 1957).

OPERA

Germany—the land of the opera? That is certainly not one of the images foreigners associate with the country in the center of Europe. Does not this title traditionally go to Italy, the home of Verdi, Puccini, and Rossini? Yet with 80 opera houses dispersed all over the country, from Aachen to Zwickau, Germany takes a lead in comparison with other countries. There are opera houses in the large metropolitan cities but also in smaller cities like Freiburg, Trier, and Hildesheim. The densely populated Ruhr-district in Western Germany has no fewer than nine opera houses, so that an opera buff could go to a different opera each night of the week. In the 2000/2001 season, no fewer than 8,000 opera performances took place in the Federal Republic.[20] Some of the German opera houses are world renowned, such as those in Hamburg, Berlin, Frankfurt am Main, and Stuttgart.

Common to all German opera houses is that they are financed by public funds. These subsidies amount to about 80 to 85 percent of the budget, while ticket sales cover only the remaining 15 to 20 percent. To give an example of the extraordinary public support German opera houses enjoy: the three taxpayer-financed Berlin opera houses, the Deutsche Oper, the Staatsoper, and the Komische Oper, in 2001 had a combined budget of 147 million euros (about $147 million); of these, 115 million euros (78 percent) were subsidies. Because of the large number of singers and instrumentalists needed to staff the some 80 opera houses, Germany employs a large number of foreigners. Of the 25 to 40 percent foreigners on staff, half of them come from the United States. America, it seems, trains its musicians well but because of the paucity of opera houses cannot provide jobs for them.

Because of the relative independence from ticket sales, German opera house directors can occasionally dare to stage a new opera or commission a new opera. The result is that the program of the average opera house in Germany is slightly more varied and modern than the American one. But it also has to be conceded that few of these new works make it into the regular repertoire. Most disappear after one or two seasons to be replaced by traditional works. German opera directors are as reluctant to play to half-empty houses as their American colleagues, with the result that they revert to the stock of the 30 or so classics by Mozart, Bizet, Verdi, Richard Strauss, Puccini, Rossini, Lortzing, and Wagner, the towering figure of the German opera.

German opera of course did not begin with Richard Wagner. In the eighteenth century Christoph Willibald Gluck (1714–87), and of course Mozart, delighted their audiences with operas, and Mozart's *Zauberflöte* (*Magic Flute,*

1791) remains one of the most popular operas in Germany to this day. Perennial favorites with German audiences are also the Romantic operas *Der Freischütz* (The Hunter, 1820) by Carl Maria von Weber (1786–1826) and *Zar und Zimmermann* (Csar and Carpenter, 1837) by Albert Lortzing. But it was Richard Wagner who represented a new stage in the development of opera, revolutionizing the genre in several ways. While the traditional opera consisted of individual numbers, such as arias, duets, and choruses, connected by the spoken word and the recitative, Wagner introduced the "continuous melody." To structure the music, the composer introduced the leitmotif, a short musical passage associated with a specific character, object, situation, or emotion. Wagner's most remarkable innovation centers around his effort to fuse all the arts making up an opera into a unified work of art, a *Gesamtkunstwerk*. Thus the music, the lyrics, the staging, the stage design, and the choreography are blended to form this new "music drama," a term he preferred for his own works. For his subjects Wagner turned to the Nordic sagas and the German medieval past. Of all his operas, the four-part *Ring* cycle consisting of *Das Rheingold, Die Walküre, Siegfried,* and *Die Götterdämmerung* (*Twilight of the Gods*), first performed in Wagner's own festival house in Bayreuth in 1876, is his most monumental achievement, while his *Die Meistersinger von Nürnberg* (1868) remains his most popular opera.

As in other artistic areas, the Weimar Republic proved to be a time of experimentation. The new republic's openness to new ideas is also reflected in the extraordinary variety of operas composed at that time. In the 1927–28 season alone, 60 new operas were premiered[21] in the some 100 opera houses in Germany. On the one hand Richard Strauss continued to compose operas in the neo-Romantic style, such as *Frau ohne Schatten* (A Woman Without a Shadow, 1919) and *Arabella* (1933); on the other hand Arnold Schönberg and Alban Berg pushed the frontiers of music further with their compositions and operas, as Schönberg did with *Moses und Aron* (composed 1930–32; premiered 1957) and Berg with his *Wozzeck* (1925). But their music was appreciated only by a small elite; for the uninitiated it remained largely inaccessible. It was partly against this kind of elitist music that Ernst Krenek, Kurt Weill, and Paul Hindemith composed their *Zeitopern* (topical operas), works in which they broadened the definition of opera by incorporating musical styles previously considered inappropriate for serious opera, such as jazz, as well as by placing their works in modern office buildings, elevators, trains, and train stations. In Hindemith's opera *Neues vom Tage* (*News of the Day,* 1929), for instance, there is a chorus of secretaries who happily (and rhythmically) pound their typewriters while singing. The best known of these *Zeitopern* is *Ernst Krenek Jonny spielt auf* (*Jonny Strikes up the Band,* 1927). It is the story of a black jazz violinist whose free-living style and carefree attitude is contrasted with the cerebral attitude of Max, a white Central European. *Jonny spielt auf* was taken up by more than 50 opera houses in Europe and America and was so popular that even a cigarette was named "Jonny." However, of all the operas composed during the Weimar Republic, the *Dreigroschenoper* (*The Threepenny Opera*, 1928), with the text by Brecht and the music by Kurt Weill, has remained the most popular one. Many people might not even remember that the very hummable "Mack the Knife" song comes from that opera. Loosely based on John Gay's eighteenth century *Beggar's Opera*, the *Dreigroschenoper* is a bitter satire on the bourgeois society of the Weimar Republic.

Among postwar Germany's opera composers, Bernd Alois Zimmermann (1918–70) made musical history with his *Soldaten* (Soldiers, 1965). Combining influences of Schönberg and jazz, he created a work that has been called "the most significant German opera since Berg's Lulu."[22] The prolific Hans Werner Henze won praise for his *Elegie für junge Liebende* (Elegy for Young Lovers, 1961), the *Bassarids* (1966) and *Die englische Katze* (The English Cat, 1983). Udo Zimmermann's (born 1943) *Weisse Rose* (White Rose, premiered 1986) has been received by audiences like few other musical works of the twentieth century. The opera depicts the final hours in prison before their execution of two young German resistance fighters against Hitler, Hans and Sophie Scholl. Among the young composers, Wolfgang Rihm (born 1953) has emerged as an important voice with his *Jacob Lenz* (1979) and *Die Eroberung von Mexico* (The Conquest of Mexico, 1992), as did Siegfried Matthus (born 1934) with his opera *Die Weise von Liebe und Tod des Cornets Christoph Rilke* (The Lay of Love and Death of Cornet Christopher Rilke, 1985) and *Graf Mirabeau* (Count Mirabeau, 1989). They are accessible but at the same time musically complex and challenging. In evaluating these talents, Erik Levi came to the conclusion: "In charting the turbulent history of German music over the past hundred years, the presence of such considerable musical talent in a united Germany augurs well for the future."[23]

DANCE THEATER

Unlike France and Russia, Germany does not have a strong ballet tradition, and the ballet companies that put Germany on the international map have been directed by foreigners: John Cranko (born in South Africa) who directed the Stuttgart Ballet Company from 1960 to his death in 1973 and won international recognition for that company, and the American John Neumeier who has made the Hamburg ballet into one of Europe's leading companies.

But it was in the area of modern dance that German dancers and choreographers made, and are still making, significant contributions. Modern dance, like modern art, was developed at the beginning of the twentieth century. It was a revolt against the classic, formalized, and highly controlled ballet. Called *Ausdruckstanz* (expressive dance) in German, it is much more spontaneous than the classical ballet or, as Pina Bausch, one of the contemporary representatives of that art form, said: "I am not interested in how people move but in what moves them."[24] It is of course no accident that this experimental and novel genre flourished in the Weimar Republic known for its joy in experimentation. The most outstanding German representatives of the *Ausdruckstanz* in the first half of the century were Mary Wigmann (1886–1973), a pioneer and extremely influential teacher, and Kurt Jooss (1901–1979). Jooss's, to take but one example, *Der Grüne Tisch* (*The Green Table*), has become a classic. The title of the piece refers to the table around which aging politicians argue until war breaks out with all its known horrors. Premiered in 1932, it has been called "the first major dance sequence of the tragedy of war" and "has been performed throughout the world and has been staged by more dance companies than any other work in the modern repertory."[25]

Today dance theaters in Germany are flourishing under many creative and talented directors. But without a doubt the best-known figure in contemporary German dance theater is Pina Bausch. Typical of Germany with its decentralized cultural scene, her dance company is located not in Berlin or Munich but in the industrial city of Wuppertal at the edge of the Ruhrdistrict, a city perhaps better known for its unique suspension railway than for its culture. Her works, among them *Frühlingsopfer* (Rite of Spring, 1975), *Blaubart* (Bluebird, 1977), and *Nelken* (Carnations, 1982), for which she covered the entire stage with white and pink carnations, are "a highly emotional mix of mime and dance, theatre and circus, acrobatics and incantation."[26] Bausch's multicultural ensemble frequently goes on tour to other countries. The language of music and the body is understood everywhere.

CABARET

It seems a large step from publicly financed, magnificent opera houses, concert halls, and dance stages with their lavish productions to the small, intimate, and privately-run cabarets. But the German cabaret (*Kabarett*) is just as much part of German performing arts culture as the opera, the theater, and classical music.

The basic ingredients of a German *Kabarett* are a cramped stage, an intimate setting and a small troupe of performers led by a conferencier who is engaged in a witty, satirical discussion of current events. In their skits and songs, actors lampoon political events and figures with wit, irony, and satire. Indeed, the very names of some of the famous cabarets of the last hundred years point to their satirical character: one of the best-known cabarets of imperial Germany, for instance, was called "Die elf Scharfrichter " (The Eleven Executioners); two of East Germany's foremost cabarets were "Die Distel" (The Thistle) and "Die Pfeffermühle" (The Pepper Mill) and one of West Germany's preeminent establishments named itself "Die Stachelschweine" (The Porcupines).

The *Kabarett* in Germany is basically a twentieth-century phenomenon. It first thrived in Wilhelminian Germany when it satirized the prevailing rigid sexual morality, its pervasive militarism, and Germany's imperialistic ambitions. But the heyday of the political cabaret was the tumultuous years of the Weimar Republic, when Berlin became the European capital of popular entertainment. Targets were Germany's continuing militarism, capitalism, the judiciary, generals, and individual politicians. Towards the end of the republic, in the early thirties, the rising Nazis increasingly became the butt of cabaret performers. Not surprisingly, when the National Socialists came to power in 1933, many of the cabarets with their Jewish producers, performers, and composers were closed down. Other cabaretists, however, continued to poke fun at the Nazis, men like Werner Finck, one of the bravest of the cabaret performers. For years he battled the Nazis in his small *Kabarett* "Die Katakombe" (The Catacomb). Finck's specialty was the political double-entendre. One day he came on stage clutching in his hands a framed picture of Adolf Hitler (whose portrait every German family was expected to have in its living room). In his typical, somewhat awkward way, he wandered around the stage, asking himself loudly: "Where should I hang him? Here or there? Or should I put him against the wall?" Finck's "Katakombe" was shut down in 1935, although other cabarets continued to perform under the watchful eye of Dr. Goebbels, the minister responsible for culture, until all were closed down in 1941.

After the end of the Nazi dictatorship, political cabaret experienced a comeback in West Germany in the 1950s and 1960s, when Konrad Adenauer's conservative politics became the prime targets of the cabaret's satirical barbs. In spite of its tight clamp on all cultural activities, Communist East Germany also accepted the cabaret as a vent for the numerous frustrations encountered in their daily life by its citizens.

Today, however, in united Germany when a Social Democratic/Green coalition is governing and Germany has become a very open society, the classical *Kabarett* has lost much of its punch. In addition, satirical programs on national television with an infinitely larger audience, have assumed much of the function of letting off steam previously held by the *Kabarett*. Still, cabarets do exist. Even in a free society like contemporary Germany there is still a lot to grumble about.

POP, ROCK, ET CETERA

In the fields of jazz, rock, and pop music, German groups are internationally less known. Anglo-American rock and pop groups dominate this market. In spite of the overpowering influence of the English-speaking rock scene, a few artists from the German-speaking countries have managed to attract, at certain times, international attraction in the last decades. Hit songs, such as Nena's "99 Luftballons" (99 air balloons), or "Rock Me Amadeus" by the late Austrian Falco made it to the charts in the United States and in Great Britain. In the 1970s the bands Einstürzende Neubauten and Kraftwerk, one of the first bands to use the potential of computer-assisted music, attracted international attention. The rock band BAP was one of the first Western bands to tour China. These and other groups were known under the somewhat disparaging name "German Kraut Rock." Internationally recognized also are the Scorpions, a band that sings in English. Since the 1990s, German techno music has been recognized internationally and each year in July techno fans from all over Europe gather in Berlin to celebrate the "Love Parade" in what is called the biggest party of the world.

In spite of the predominance of music sung in English, there are quite a number of artists who have not "sold out" by abandoning their native tongue. That they are quite successful should not surprise us. With over 100 million people speaking German in Central Europe (Germany, Austria, and German-speaking Switzerland), this area is the third-largest music market in the world, after the United States and Japan. German artists, then, do very well performing in their own language.

Such an artist who sings mainly in German is Udo Lindenberg, well-known for his social-critical songs, though considered slightly passé by the younger generation. He received notoriety when in the 1980s he provoked the East German leader Erich Honecker with the song "Sonderzug nach Pankow" (Special Train to Pankow [Honecker's residence]) sung to Glenn Miller's "Chattanooga Choo Choo Train" and a video showing Honecker jumping over the Berlin Wall. Die Fantastischen Vier are Germany's best-known rap group. Rock aficionados also go wild about the provocative and loud heavy metal band Rammstein and fans in other countries don't seem to mind that they sing in German. Compared with the earsplitting music of the rock bands, the music of the so-called Liedermacher (literally, songmakers) is definitely more subdued. Accompanied only by a guitar, these Liedermacher sing of love, relationships, and politics. For decades the poetic and sophisticated Reinhard Mey has attracted a loyal following. During the existence of East Germany, three East German Liedermacher, Wolf Biermann, Bettina Wegener, and Stephan Krawczyk, played an important role. Their albums, banned in the East, were secretly recorded in the East, smuggled out into the West, where they were produced, and then smuggled back into the GDR, giving hope and encouragement to dissidents.

Virtually unknown outside the German speaking world, but immensely popular inside Germany, are the two superstars of the rock scene, Marius Müller-Westernhagen and Herbert Grönemeyer. Throughout the 1990s, Müller-Westernhagen was Germany's pop best-seller[27] and for over 20 years Herbert Grönemeyer, dubbed the German Springsteen, has given sold-out concerts to his German fans. His 1984 album *Bochum* stayed on the charts for 79 weeks and his single "Männer" (Men) was another big hit. After a hiatus of several years following the tragic death of his wife, he was able to stage a triumphant comeback in 2002 with his album *Mensch,* the title song of which became an instant success.

NOTES

1. Michael Patterson and Michael Huxley, "German Drama, Theatre and Dance," in *The Cambridge Companion to Modern German Culture,* edited by Eva Kolinsky and Wilfried van der Will (Cambridge: Cambridge University Press, 1998), 228. "All in all, German theaters and orchestras receive public funds totaling DM 4.5 billion [circa $2.2 billion] a year." Also: The Federal Government, *Facts About Germany,* 487.

2. Richard Jacoby, *Musical Life in Germany* (Bonn: Inter Nationes, 1997), 39.

3. The Federal Government, *Facts about Germany,* 481.

4. Ardagh, *Germany and the Germans,* 227.

5. Quoted in Michael Patterson, *The Revolution in German Theatre, 1900–1933* (Boston, London, and Henley: Routledge and Kegan Paul, 1981), 14.

6. Wolf von Eckardt and Sander L. Gilman, *Bertolt Brecht's Berlin. A Scrapbook of the Twenties* (Garden City: Anchor Press; New York: Doubleday, 1974) 77.

7. Martin Esslin, *Brecht. The Man and His Work* (Garden City and New York: Doubleday, 1961), 123.

8. W. G. Sebald, ed., *A Radical Stage: Theatre in Germany in the 1970s and 1980s* (Oxford: Berg, 1988), 3.

9. Peter Brook in his introduction to the English translation (New York: Atheneum, 1969), vi.

10. Sebald, *The Radical Stage,* 110.

11. Stoehr, *German Literature,* 385.

12. Michael Patterson, "The German Theatre," in *The New Germany. Social, Political and Cultural Challenges of Unification,* edited by Derek Lewis and John R. P. McKenzie (Exeter: Exeter University Press, 1995), 160.

13. The Federal Government, *Facts about Germany,* 486.

14. Jacoby, *Musical Life in Germany,* 43.

15. Dietrich Schwanitz, *Bildung. Alles, was man wissen muß* (Munich: Goldmann, 2002), 402.

16. Erik Levi, "Music," in *The Cambridge Companion to Modern German Culture,* edited by Eva Kolinsky and Wilfried van der Will (Cambridge: Cambridge University Press, 1998), 240.

17. Quoted in Lisa Appignanesi, *Cabaret: The First Hundred Years* (London: Methuen, 1984), 97.

18. Levi, "Music," 240.

19. Levi, "Music," 253.

20. *Der Spiegel* 49 (2002): 182.

21. Susan C. Cook, *Opera for a New Republic. The Zeitopern of Krenek, Weill, and Hindemith* (Ann Arbor, Mich., and London: UMI Research Press, 1988), 3.

22. Levi, "Music," 252.

23. Levi, "Music," 254.

24. Quoted in Ardagh, *Germany and the Germans,* 284.

25. Patterson and Huxley, "German Drama, Theatre and Dance," 223.

26. Ardagh, *Germany and the Germans,* 284.

27. *Der Spiegel* 44 (2002): 213.

10

Painting

GERMANY HAS RICH and ancient traditions in the visual arts, ranging from frescoes painted more than a thousand years ago on church walls to internationally recognized works of art by Joseph Beuys and Anselm Kiefer in the present. Like in previous chapters, the emphasis will be on the present. However, ignoring the great masters of the past would create a wrong picture of Germany, for these masters have become part of the identities of at least the educated Germans—and so have the numerous museums in Germany. As one cultural critic pointed out, museums "help to make identities—our sense of who we are—tangible: they help to *materialize* identities."[1] For that reason, a sketch of the German museum landscape and some highlights from the glorious past of German art will precede this account of twentieth-century German art.

MUSEUMS

Germany is a paradise for museum lovers. In fact, it would take a visitor more than 14 years to visit all of the 5,219 museums in the Federal Republic, providing that he or she would take in only one museum per day and does not rest for weekends or vacations.[2] The sheer number of museums is not only impressive but also the variety. There is, it seems, a museum for every taste and interest. There is a museum devoted to printing (the Gutenberg Museum in Mainz); there is a newspaper museum (in Aachen); a musical instruments museum (in Leipzig); an architecture museum (in Frankfurt); and a mining museum (in Bochum). The major German car companies, BMW, Volkswagen (VW), Mercedes, and Porsche have their own museums

The Vitra Design Museum in Weil am Rhein, designed by Frank O. Gehry. Photo by Eckhard Bernstein.

(in Munich, Wolfsburg, and Stuttgart). If you are interested in clocks, head for the clock museum in Furtwangen; if the story of Zeppelin fascinates you, visit Friedrichshafen on Lake Constance; and if you have a weakness for chocolate, put Cologne on your itinerary and pay a visit to the Deutsches Schokoladen-Museum (delicious samples provided); technology freaks should visit Munich's Deutsches Museum, Europe's largest technology museum. In addition, every German composer, poet, and philosopher seems to be honored with a museum.

There are hundreds of art museums; 555 to be exact, according to official statistics. Among them are some of world renown: Hamburg's Kunsthalle, the Alte und Neue Pinakothek in Munich, Dresden's Neue Meister Galerie, Berlin's Neue Gemäldegalerie, the Städel Art Institute in Frankfurt am Main, Stuttgart's new Staatsgalerie, and Cologne's Wallraf-Richartz and Ludwig Museum. Many of them are old and well-established, others were built more recently. In the 1980s a veritable museum construction boom began (see chapter on architecture), with the result that since the beginning of the 1960s the number of museums has doubled. With the growth of musems, the number of visitors has also increased dramatically. While in 1975 the German museums registered 22 million visitors, in the 1990s the number of visitors has risen to 100 million per year.[3] The emergence of a leisure society, a general democratization of culture, and more attractive "packaging" of exhibits might be some of the reasons for the increase in museum attendance.

German museums hold art treasures from all over the world. Understandably, their strength most often lies in the collections of German art. The following sketch of the development of German art can hardly do justice to the wealth of works produced in the last 1,000 years on German soil. It is merely meant as a first orientation.

THE PAST

The earliest art works created in Germany that have survived go back more than a thousand years and are wall paintings or frescoes in churches. Like almost all art of this period, they were created by monks, for monasteries were the cultural strongholds of the time and Christian teachings almost exclusively provided the inspiration for artistic work. The best preserved murals are those in the church of St. Maximin in Trier and those in the church of St. George in Oberzell on Reichenau, an island (now connected by a causeway with the mainland) in Lake Constance in southwestern Germany. Created around 1000, they depict abbots of the monastery Reichenau, as well as six apostles and the miracles performed by Christ.

However, the main source of our knowledge of art of that time, or what is called the Romanesque period (950–1150), are not the frescoes, most of which have perished, or oil painting, which was only discovered at the beginning of the fifteenth century, but book illustrations. Before the invention of printing by Johann Gutenberg around 1450, all books had to be copied by hand and they were illustrated or illuminated, the technical term, with miniature paintings. Again, this was done by monks and the books they illustrated were religious books, such as gospel books, prayer books, psalters, and legends of saints.

Gothic Art

During the Gothic period (c. 1150–1500), new building techniques made the construction of taller churches with larger windows possible. The magnificent cathedrals in France (Chartres, Paris, Rouen, Reims, and Amiens) and in Germany (Cologne, Freiburg, Straßburg, Ulm, and Regensburg) are the most glorious expression of the new Gothic architecture. For art this meant that on the one hand large wall spaces for frescoes had disappeared; on the other, large windows needed to be filled with stained glass, essentially a Gothic invention. Especially impressive are the large rose windows in the west facade of the cathedrals.

The art of manuscript illumination continued to flourish, but in addition to religious motifs, secular themes, such as scenes from tournaments, festivals, and hunting, were depicted. The most outstanding German monument of manuscript illumination is the Codex Manesse (Manesse Handschrift) now preserved at the University Library of Heidelberg, created around 1330. With its 852 pages and 137 colorful portraits of German "Minnesänger," it is not only a compendium of one and a half centuries of German lyric poetry but also one of the most beautiful and valuable manuscripts of the European Middle Ages. With their portrayal of armored knights, the joys of hunting, and courtly festivals and games, the portraits offer a vivid picture of the aristocratic courtly life at that time.

The late medieval period also saw the emergence of oil paintings on panels that sought to represent figures and objects more or less realistically. As with most other art produced during that period, this kind of painting revolved around religious themes, and altarpieces were the primary focus of artistic efforts. Frequently depicted scenes were scenes of Christ's passion, especially the crucifixion; scenes from the life of the virgin, such as the annunciation and the nativity; and episodes from the lives of saints. Since initially painters remained anonymous, art historians refer to them either by the places they worked (the Alsatian master) or by the work they created (the master of the XYZ altar.) Only in the fifteenth century were individual painters identified by their names, such as Conrad Witz (c. 1400–1446), who has been called "the most powerful creative spirit in German painting before Dürer."[4] The vast majority of his 20 surviving panels are remnants of altarpieces. Witz was an artistic innovator. For unlike his predecessors, who usually painted the background in gold or were satisfied with hints of a landscape, Witz, in his "Miraculous Draught of Fishes" (1444; Geneva, Musée d'Art et l'Histoire), part of the Geneva altarpiece, depicts a real landscape, namely that of Lake Geneva and the shoreline near the city. This much-discussed painting is usually considered the first landscape painting in German art.

Renaissance Art

In Germany, Renaissance art is synonymous with one artist, Albrecht Dürer (1471–1528), the greatest artist Northern Europe produced during that time. He was a master draftsman, a printmaker, and a painter, a humanist, a teacher, and a theoretician. Born in the ancient city of Nuremberg, he was first apprenticed by his father as a goldsmith, later trained as a painter by Michael Wolgemut; he traveled widely, first in Germany, later twice to Italy, and once to the Low Countries. At home in all the artistic media of the time (woodcuts, engraving, watercolor, drawing, and painting), he created an impressive work of 70 paintings, 350 woodcuts, and 900 drawings. Among his engravings, three master engravings stand out, "St. Jerome in his Study"

(1514), "Melancolia" (1514), and "Knight, Death and the Devil" (1512), not only because of their technical brilliance but also because of their symbolical meaning. In the latter, a knight in full armor, filling out almost the entire picture, proceeds undaunted by the devil and by death on his way.

Dürer also excelled in another genre, in portrait painting. In that respect, he might be regarded a typical Renaissance man, because that period is often thought of as the age in which the individual was "discovered." A yearning for immortality through a portrait was one of the characteristic features of that time. Wealthy patrons had their portraits painted to insure their fame beyond the grave. And there was no one at the time more skillful in capturing the unique individuality of a person than Albrecht Dürer. His oil paintings of the wealthy Augsburg merchant Jakob Fugger (1518, Munich, Alte Pinakothek), Emperor Maxilimian I (1519, Vienna, Kunsthistorisches Museum), or the Christ-like self portrait (1500, Munich, Alte Pinakothek) are among his best-known portraits.

Like most of the artists at the time, Dürer was a deeply religious man and many of his commissioned paintings were altarpieces. Among his religious paintings, though not an altarpiece, his two-paneled depiction of the four apostles, St. John, St. Peter, St. Paul, and St. Mark in Munich's Alte Pinakothek is world famous.

Though Dürer is clearly the dominant Renaissance artist in Germany, there were others who contributed substantially to the extraordinary flowering of art in Germany during that period. Next to Dürer there were Matthias Grünewald, Hans Holbein, and Lucas Cranach. Cranach (1472–1553) was an artist of prodigious productivity—he left over 400 paintings in addition to a large body of woodcuts, engravings, and drawing. For nearly four decades he was the court painter of the princes of Saxony and was intimately associated with Martin Luther and the Protestant Reformation, whose main representatives he repeatedly painted.

If Cranach immortalized the leaders of the Reformation, Hans Holbein (1497–1543), who was born in Augsburg but spent a large part of his life in Switzerland and England, became a celebrated and sought-after portraitist at the English court of Henry VIII. Trusting the artist's skill, the king, notorious for his six wives, also sent Holbein abroad to portray potential brides. Today, Holbein is considered one of the outstanding portraitists in Western art.

Compared to Dürer, Cranach, and Holbein, Matthias Grünewald (1475/80–1528) left a relatively small body of work to posterity (22 paintings, 37 drawings). Little is known about him, yet his name is forever linked to one unequaled masterpiece, the Isenheimer Altarpiece (Colmar in French Alsace, Museum Unterlinden). Consisting of two hinged sets of wings with a total of nine panels that can be viewed in three different configurations, the altarpiece is impressive not only by its sheer size (24 feet high, 15 feet high) but also by its style. Whereas Dürer favored classical proportions, beauty, and symmetry in his paintings, Grünewald was fascinated by the demonic, the passionate, and the grotesque to dramatize the main theme of the altarpiece, the Christian concept of salvation. The artist's consummate handling of color, the complex iconography (which has kept art historians busy for centuries), the expressive realism depicting the suffering of Christ, and St. Anthony, the patron saint of the monks who commissioned the altar, make this extraordinary work a forerunner of German Expressionism (see below).

Baroque and Rococo Art

The period between the Renaissance and the beginning of the Enlightenment is usually referred to as the Baroque followed by the even more ornate and playful Rococo. While in other European countries great artists emerged (in Italy, Caravaggio and Tintoretto; in Spain, El Greco and Velasquez; in Flanders, Rubens; and in Holland, Rembrandt), Germany cannot boast of any artist of comparable stature, although it produced remarkable artists in other areas such as music (Johann Sebastian Bach, Georg Philipp Telemann) or architecture (Balthasar Neumann).

Romantic Art

Whereas neoclassicism, a widely popular style in Europe and the United States during the last decades of the eighteenth and the first half of the nineteenth century, emphasized clarity, harmony, and rationality, Romanticism, a literary and artistic movement at the end of the eighteenth and beginning of the nineteenth century, stressed the emotional, the subconscious, and the spiritual. In addition, German Romantics often expressed a longing for the German Middle Ages.

The greatest representative of Romantic painting in Germany was Caspar David Friedrich (1774–1840). A superb landscape painter, he always imbued his landscapes with allegorical-symbolic meaning. His "Cross in the Mountains" (1808, Dresden, Gemäldegalerie, Neue Meister), for instance depicts a cross with the crucified Jesus standing on a large rock, surrounded by fir trees and illuminated by the setting sun. The rock symbolizes faith, the fir trees stand for eternal hope, and the sun symbolizes the divine light. Often solitary figures, such as the "Traveler above the Sea of Clouds" (1818) or "Two Men Contemplating the Moon" (1819, Dresden, Gemäldegalerie, Neue Meister), are placed in landscapes, with their back turned to the viewer and contemplating nature, thus inviting the viewer to participate in the reflection of nature as it was created by God. Friedrich's "Sea of Ice" (1823–24, Hamburg, Kunsthalle), depicting the remnants of a crushed ship amidst blocks of ice turned upward, can be interpreted as a symbol of nature's destructive force and man's vulnerability.

Biedermeier Art

Originally designating a type of furniture, the term *Biedermeier,* named after a character in a popular magazine, is often used for the period between Napoleon's defeat in 1815 and the revolution of 1848. It was a time when the old conservative powers reasserted themselves by political repression and censorship, with the result that the average German, apolitical to begin with, retreated even further into his private sphere. It is this world that Carl Spitzweg (1808–1885), one of the most popular and accessible painters of the nineteenth century in Germany, captured in his small paintings. Spitzweg depicted old-fashioned and slightly eccentric figures against the background of typical old German towns with their narrow streets, timber-framed houses, and charming provinciality. The shortsighted bookworm standing on a ladder in his library; the slightly pompous professor in his garden absorbed in the reading of a manuscript; the man carefully cultivating a cactus; and probably, the most famous one, "The Poor Poet" (1839, Berlin Nationalgalerie), are some of his characters. The latter painting shows the poet in his sparsely furnished attic lying in bed, apparently to keep warm. An umbrella is unfolded over his bed to protect him from a leak in the roof.

Realism and Naturalism

The realists rejected the religious symbolism of the Romantics and the escapist genre painting of Spitzweg. Instead they sought to portray reality as it is. Among the German realists, two stand out: Wilhelm Leibl (1844–1906) and Adolph von Menzel (1815–1905).Leibl's preferred subjects were the farmers and peasant folk in the Bavarian villages to which he had retreated. His "Three Women in Church" (1878–82, Hamburg, Kunsthalle) shows three simple peasant women dressed in traditional dress absorbed in prayer in church. Von Menzel is often considered the chronicler of Prussia, especially the Prussia of Frederick the Great, whose history he illustrated in 400 wood engravings. In addition, he depicted scenes from Frederick's life in a number of magnificent paintings. Famous is his "Flute Concert at Sanssouci" (1850–52, Berlin, Nationalgalerie), in which he recreated, through accurate depiction of the costumes and furniture, one of the famed flute concerts with which the Prussian monarch entertained his guests. After 1860, von Menzel also turned to industrial landscapes in and around Berlin, and some of his later paintings have been called Impressionist.

Impressionism

Impressionism is an essentially French art movement, associated with the names of Renoir, Monet, Degas, and Pisarro. Working mostly outdoors, the Impressionists tried to capture the play of light and shadow on their canvasses. Claude Monet (1840–1926), for instance, the greatest of the French Impressionists, repeatedly painted the same subject matter, be it the cathedral of Rouen, haystacks, or waterlilies, at different times of the day and under different atmospheric conditions. The best known German Impressionists, Max Liebermann (1847–1935), Lovis Corinth (1858–1925), and Max Slevogt (1868–1932), shared with their French colleagues a preference for bright colors, quick brushwork, and inattention to detail. On the other hand, they were never as radical as the French in their concentration on surface appearance. Both Slevogt and Corinth painted literary, religious, and mythological subjects, while Liebermann showed a strong interest in social themes, so that his paintings were initially dismissed at the time by some critics as "ugly and socialist." However, at the beginning of the twentieth century, he was considered the undisputed head of the German painters.

The Twentieth Century—The First Half

Expressionism

Modern art in Germany was born in June 1905. In that month a number of students from the Dresden Polytechnic Institute, including Ernst Ludwig Kirchner (1880–1938), Erich Heckel (1888–1970), and Karl Schmidt-Rotluff (1884–1976), founded a group that they called *Die Brücke* (The Bridge). Later, other painters joined, such as Max Pechstein (1881–1955), Otto Mueller (1874–1930), and, for only a brief time, Emil Nolde (1867–1956). *Die Brücke* was the first and most coherent, but by no means the only, group of a movement that art historians call Expressionism and which constitutes Germany's major contribution to the development of avant-garde art in the twentieth century.

The term Expressionism is an elusive one and covers a wide variety of different artists. To add to the imprecision, the term has also been extended to literature, dance, stage design, film (*The Cabinet of Dr. Caligari*), drama, and architecture (Eric Mendelsohn). In the visual arts it includes such different works as the abstract paintings of Wassily Kandinsky, the lovely animal portraits of Franz Marc, the landscapes painted in vibrant colors of Emil Nolde, the prismatic pictures of Lyonel Feininger, and the playful semi-abstract miniatures of Paul Klee, to name only a few. It thus embraces most of the avant-garde art produced in Germany between 1905 and 1920. Common to all Expressionist artists is a rejection of the traditional art as it was taught at the art academies of the time, as well as a rejection of naturalism and Impressionism that dominated the art scene at the beginning of the twentieth century in Germany. Inspired by the Dutch artist Vincent van Gogh, the French painter Paul Gauguin, and the Norwegian artist Edward Munch, the Expressionists were not interested in a realistic depiction of the world but in the creation of a new "inner" reality of their own making. To achieve that aim, they dispensed, for instance, with the traditional perspective in their pictures but used sharp angles and distortions. Nor did they try to achieve three-dimensionality by using different shades of colors. Instead they applied brilliant, unmixed colors, which they spread as flat surfaces on their paintings. In order to emphasize this flatness, they often surrounded their figures or objects with dark lines.

The *Brücke* artists not only rejected the artistic conventions of the time but also the smug respectability and the staid morality of the Wilhelminian society. Their preferred subjects were outsiders of the bourgeois society: circus artists, gypsy girls, dancers, music hall artists, and prostitutes. Their summers were spent in the countryside near Dresden, where they painted each other and their girlfriends frolicking in the nude in the reeds of the Moritzburg lakes. Their search for earlier societies free from the constraints of German bourgeois society prompted them to explore primitive cultures, first through visits to the Museum of Ethnography in Dresden and later through extended trips to the South Seas. This fascination with primitive cultures is reflected in a deliberately crude craftsmanship.

In 1911 Kirchner moved from Dresden to Berlin. The change from the provincial Dresden to the pulsating life of the German capital is reflected in his style and themes. Distortions and the angular shapes of the city architecture abounded. In 1913 the *Brücke* dissolved itself, and the artists went their own ways.

Emil Nolde's position among the German Expressionists was unique. Although briefly a member of *Die Brücke,* he was basically a loner who in the 1920s even refused to take part in any exhibition. Yet his watercolors, lithographs, and paintings belong to the best work German Expressionists have produced. For Nolde, everything depended on the expressive power of color. The brilliant colors, the spontaneous brushwork which he applied thickly on the canvass, characterize his style. The coastal landscapes painted in his native Schleswig, portraits, pictures of flowers, and, from 1909 onwards, religious motifs dominate his art.

The second major group of German Expressionism was *Der Blaue Reiter* (The Blue Rider) in Munich. In contrast to the *Brücke, Der Blaue Reiter* was a much looser association. The artists in that group neither painted together nor lived together as did the *Brücke* artists, but merely collaborated on joint exhibitions. Their name derived from the almanac that two of its members, Wassily Kandinsky, and Franz Marc, published in 1912, which contained articles on art, music, and theater and was illustrated with woodcuts and reproductions of paintings. As a group, such as it was, they differed from the *Brücke* artists in two important respects: they were more intellectual and they were more international than the Dresden association. Their intellectual interests were reflected not only in their endless discussions they had about art but also in Kandinsky's own seminal essay, "Über das Geistige in der Kunst" (On the Spiritual in Art). Their internationality showed itself in the composition of the group. Two of its most important members were Russian, Kandinsky and Jawlensky; one was Swiss, Paul Klee; and a Finnish and a French artist were also participating in the exhibitions.

The leading artist of *Der Blaue Reiter* was Wassily Kandinsky (1866–1944), a Russian who had come to Munich as early as 1896. He began as a landscape painter. But increasingly his landscapes became merely the basis of pictures in which pure colors and forms dominated, until the link to nature almost disappeared completely. In 1911 Kandinsky painted what is believed to be the first abstract painting in the twentieth century, that is, a painting that did not pretend to be a representation of a concrete object but was a free composition consisting of forms, colors, and lines. Named "Composition IV" (Düsseldorf, Kunstsammlung Nordrhein-Westfalen), it constituted a major break with a century-old European tradition that was to have far-reaching consequences. Abstract, or nonrepresentational, art was to become one of the major art forms of the twentieth century. Kandinsky developed and refined this art throughout the rest of his life, creating canvasses of rich textures of lines, colors, and forms. In his theoretical works, Kandinsky often drew parallels with music, which, he argued, was also abstract in the sense that it did not, generally, attempt to imitate nature.

Kandinsky's countryman, Alexej von Jawlensky (1864–1941), went through a similar development as an artist, although he never went as far as Kandinsky. Even in his most abstract paintings, links to reality can be identified. This development can be seen in his numerous portraits of women. Initially he painted them in a fairly naturalistic manner by striving for three-dimensionality by using different-shaded colors; later he abandoned this realistic approach and created flat surfaces, painted in bright unmixed colors, which he surrounded by black contours. In his final phase, Jawlensky created almost abstract painting in which color and form dominated and the connection to the sitter's face was very tenuous.

Franz Marc (1880–1916) is known as the painter of animals to whom he felt he had an almost religious relationship. But like the other Expressionists, he was not interested in naturalistic depiction but in their "true essence." To express this essence he assigned certain characteristics to colors. For him, yellow, for instance, represented the female principle, gentle and sensual; blue on the other hand, stood for the masculine element, which explains why Marc often used blue for his horses, which he apparently saw as representative of the masculine principle. His career, like that of many young men at the time, was cut short by the First World War. He fell at Verdun in 1916.

August Macke (1887–1914), another founder of *Der Blaue Reiter,* was less interested in theory than Kandinsky. Influenced by Cézanne, Seurat, Matisse, and, above all, Delaunay, with whom he was personally acquainted, he created, in brilliant colors, mostly representational paintings. Some of his favorite motifs were walkers on the banks on a lake, young girls under trees, and women looking at shop windows. He died at age 27 in the first weeks of World War I.

Although Paul Klee (1879–1940) was loosely associated with *Der Blaue Reiter* and participated in the second exhibition of that group, he later went his own way. Like Kandinsky, with whom he was joined in a lifelong friendship, Klee rejected realism. But unlike his Russian colleague, he never committed himself totally to abstract art. Although he painted numerous purely abstract paintings, he also created many works in which figurative elements, although stripped to their essentials, are recognizable. With over 9,000 works, ranging from small whimsical miniatures to the large canvasses in his later period with enigmatic hieroglyphs, pictograms, and stick figures, Klee left a unique work. Expelled from Germany in 1933 as a "degenerate artist" and unappreciated up to his death in 1940 in his native Switzerland, he is today ranked next to Kandinsky and Picasso as one of the most important artists of the twentieth century.

The Weimar Republic

The First World War, the political turmoil following the defeat of the Kaiser's armies, and the birth of the Weimar Republic had a major impact on artists in Germany. They reacted in different ways to these events. Faced with the horror of the war, the Dadaists called into question the whole intellectual, social, and cultural system that had made possible that destructive conflict.

Dadaism—the name Dada was randomly picked from a French-German dictionary and is baby talk for horse—was an international literary and artistic movement. It was born in 1916 in Zürich in neutral Switzerland and lasted up until about 1922. Among the Zürich group were the Germans Hugo Ball, Richard Hülsenbeck, and Hans Arp. The Dadaists were provocative, used shock tactics, and ridiculed conventions. As the German Dadaist George Grosz (1893–1959) said: "We spat upon everything, including ourselves."[5] After the war, Berlin became a center of German Dadaism. Among the Berlin Dadaists were Hannah Höch, Raoul Hausmann, and Wieland Herzfelde and his brother John Heartfield (who had Anglicized his name Helmut Herzfelde in the middle of the war in protest against German chauvinism), as well as George Grosz (who also had changed his first name Georg into the English George). Once in Berlin, Dadaism became radicalized and politicized. In his drawings and paintings, Grosz mercilessly attacked the military establishment, war profiteers, and the bourgeoisie in general, while Heartfield did the same thing with his biting photomontages, a genre he is generally credited with having invented. In Hanover, meanwhile, Kurt Schwitters held high the flag of Dadaism all by himself. He pasted together collages of the most incongruent objects: old tram tickets, wire, buttons, pieces of driftwood, and chocolate and cigarette wrappings in an attempt to show that our life consisted of fragmented, disintegrated parts.

Other artists took a different approach. A "second generation" of Expressionists became politically very active. Shocked by the horrors of the war, they wanted to do their part in shaping the new republic. In order to achieve this goal, they joined together in the *Novembergruppe* (November group), whose manifesto stated: "We stand on the fertile ground of Revolution. Our slogan is liberty, equality and fraternity. We regard it as our noblest task to dedicate our efforts to the moral task of building Germany young and free."[6] Hoping that out of the chaos a better world would emerge, some of them created posters for the new republic, while others, like Otto Dix (1891–1969), wanted to drive home the senselessness and brutality of the war. He produced numerous etchings, drawings, and paintings depicting in unforgettable images mutilated bodies, decaying limbs, and scarred landscapes. "Never again!" was the most heard slogan.

By the middle of the twenties, the political temperature of the Weimar Republic had been considerably lowered. The hyperinflation of 1922–23 had been brought under control, the economy had stablilized, the political parties on the right and left had lost votes, and the international isolation of Germany following the First World War had been ended with the admission of Germany into the League of Nations and treaties with France and Russia.

This new stability was also reflected in the art produced at the time. The artists of *Die Neue Sachlichkeit* (New Sobriety, or Objectivity)—the term was coined in 1925—turned away from what they considered the excessive subjectivity of the Expressionists and the anarchistic nihilism of the Dadaists. But while they executed their paintings with meticulous care, using fine brushwork, the painters of *Die Neue Sachlichkeit* continued in their social criticism, which had characterized the second generation of Expressionists. Otto Dix and George Grosz are among the most prominent representatives of this trend, although their earlier works, as we have seen, were clearly painted in the Expressionist style.

Max Beckmann (1884–1950) stands apart. He can neither be called an Expressionist nor a representative of *Die Neue Sachlichkeit,* although throughout his life he remained a figurative painter. He developed his own unique style and is considered by some art historians Germany's greatest painter of the twentieth century. His initial enthusiasm for the First World War gave way to abhorrence at the slaughter he witnessed as a medical orderly on the Western front. In his painting "Nacht" (Night, 1918–19, Düsseldorf, Kunstsammlung Nordrhein-Westfalen), three criminals have forced their way into a claustrophobic room in which a family of three have gathered for dinner. The husband is being strangled, his left arm brutally twisted, while his wife is tied up, her legs spread apart, and the daughter is about to be thrown out of a window. The painting is generally interpreted as a powerful metaphor for man's inhumanity to man. Beckmann always created complex pictures. From 1932 to his death, he painted, among many other works, nine triptychs modeled on medieval tripartite altarpieces. Blending his own experiences during the Third Reich—he was dismissed from his post as professor in Frankfurt in 1933 and left Germany in 1937—with ancient myths, he composed unforgettable, albeit sometimes hard-to-decipher, paintings.

The Third Reich

With the assumption of power by the National Socialists in 1933, the brilliant flowering of modern art of the Weimar Republic came to an end. The campaign to discredit all avant-garde art began almost immediately. Modern artists were dismissed from their teaching posts and were banned from exhibiting their works. Some left Germany, among them George Grosz, Lyonel Feininger, John Heartfield, Josef Albers, Max Beckmann, Oskar Kokoschka, Kurt Schwitters, and Wassily Kandinsky. Others, like Emil Nolde, Max Pechstein, Otto Dix, Käthe Kollwitz, and Ernst Barlach stayed only to be vilified and persecuted by the new regime.

The campaign against modern art culminated in the "Degenerate Art" exhibition in 1937 in Munich. Instead of an outright ban and the destruction of the works, which would possibly have made martyrs out of the proscribed artists, the Nazis staged this show in the attempt to let the people see for themselves how incomprehensible, in poor taste, and "un-German" modern art allegedly was. Prior to that exhibition, about 16,000 works of modern art had been taken from public museums. Out of these, 730 were selected for the exhibition. The tone was set by Adolf Ziegler, the head of the Chamber of Visual Arts: "You are about to see the products of insanity, of impudence, of ineptitude, and of decadence."[7] In the exhibition itself, paintings, drawings, and sculptures were placed in crowded rooms and commented on with slandering remarks. A catalog accompanying the exhibition provides a clear indication of what the Nazis so virulently objected to: the distortions of form and "misuse of color," the alleged mocking of religious feeling, the ridiculing of the "deep respect Germans had for military virtue and courage," "the depiction of bordellos and pornography," and the modern artists' fascination with "Negro art."[8] The exhibition was immensely popular: within four months it was viewed by two million people. Whether visitors regarded the exhibition as the last chance to see modern art in Nazi Germany, or whether they shared the National Socialists' rejection of it, is not clear.

One day before this exhibition opened, Hitler had inaugurated the "Great German Art Exhibition" (Grosse Deutsche Kunstausstellung) in the newly constructed House of German Art (see chapter on architecture). In line with Hitler's rejection of all modern "-isms," the show was arranged not by movements or artists, but by themes: one hall was devoted to landscapes, another to peasants, a third to family portraits, a fourth to nudes, a fifth to pictures glorifying the Nazis. Both in their technique and in their themes, artists favored by the National Socialists were inspired by nineteenth-century art and Greek and Roman classical art. It ignored the problems and anxieties of our modern age, which the Expressionists and other modern artists had so strikingly captured.

It is one of the ironies of history that the art produced during the Third Reich disappeared after the Second World War into the basements of Germany's art museums, while the defamed "degenerate" artists were gloriously rehabilitated and now fetch high prizes at international art auctions.

CONTEMPORARY GERMAN ART

In 1945 Germany lay in ruins; cities were largely devastated. Cut off from other countries for more than a decade, German artists were eager to catch up with international trends. And the dominant international style at that time happened to be abstract art. It was not only thought to be progressive but also allowed the German artists to distance themselves from the discredited Nazi regime with its state-imposed super-realist mode of painting. But there may have been another reason why West German artists dogmatically adopted abstraction: it freed them from confronting their uncomfortable past.

The two leading representatives of abstract painting in postwar Germany were Ernst Wilhelm Nay (1902–1968) and Willi Baumeister (1889–1955), "Germany's foremost nonconstructive abstract painter."[9] Between 1958 and 1966, the members of the "Zero Group" in Düsseldorf, Otto Piene (born 1928), Heinz Mack (born 1931) and Günter Uecker (born 1930) became West Germany's most important art group. By introducing moving sources of light in their sculptures, they transcended the traditional boundaries of sculptures. They also tried to reach a wider public by staging spectacular happenings.

The Sixties and Seventies

The 1960s and 1970s were a time marked by a number of crises: the building of the Berlin Wall in 1961, the Cuban crisis in 1962, the assassination of U.S. President John F. Kennedy one year later, the civil rights movement, and the anti-Vietnam War protests. This rebelliousness and restlessness of the period also manifested itself in the arts. The concept of traditional art was questioned and expanded to include happenings, performance arts, op art, and pop art. German artists and the public showed great interest and participated in these developments, as is shown by the enormous success of the Documenta in Kassel, an art exhibition that began in 1955 and has taken place ever since. Often referred to as "the Olympics of contemporary art,"[10] the Documenta showcases international trends in art every four to five years, attracting half a million visitors each time.

The best known artist to emerge at that time in Germany was Joseph Beuys (1921–1986). Initially ridiculed as a charlatan and political muddle-head, Beuys was recognized in the seventies and eighties as "the most radical, charismatic and evocative artist of his times."[11] In 1979 he was honored by a large exhibition in New York's Guggenheim Museum. Always dressed in jeans, an old worn felt hat, and a fishing vest, he became a well-known presence on the international scene. His reputation was based on his widely broadened concept of art that included watercolors, sculptures, room installations, and happenings/performances. In his sculptures, for instance, he juxtaposed everyday objects such as copper, batteries, and flashlights with perishable materials such as honey and wax. Beuys was particularly obsessed with felt and fat, two substances that he believed saved his life when he was shot down over Russia during the Second World War. His unorthodox sculptures invariably symbol-

The Greatest World Renown for a Charlatan? Reprinted by permission of *Der Spiegel.*

ize survival. His so-called honey pump became famous. It consisted of a complicated system of transparent plastic pipes through which 300 pounds of honey was continuously pumped. His most memorable performance was probably his "How to Explain Pictures to a Dead Rabbit" (1965), in which the artist, his face covered in honey and gold leaf, walked through a Düsseldorf art gallery, explaining the pictures to a dead rabbit on his arm. With his works, Beuys challenged his viewers to contribute their own associations and to create a meaning for themselves.

The New Savages—Die Neuen Wilden

Dissatisfied with the international styles of Abstract Expressionism, pop art, and minimal art, a new group of German artists emerged in the late sev-

Visitor admiring art in Städtisches Museum Abteiberg,
Mönchengladbach. Photo by Eckhard Bernstein.

enties that returned to a figurative style, that is, they depicted in their paintings recognizable objects but also started to deal with the German past. Critics quickly found convenient labels for these artists: The "New Savages,"
"Neo-Expressionists," "New Expressives." They were, however, never an
organized group, such as *Die Brücke* in the first decade of the twentieth century, but individual artists, each with his distinctive style. The most prominent among them are Anselm Kiefer, Jörg Immendorff, Georg Baselitz, and
A. R. Penck.

Anselm Kiefer (born 1945), a student of Joseph Beuys, has enjoyed the
most success at home and abroad. On his large canvasses, he paints with a
broad brush and includes sand, straw, wire, glass splinters, and other materials. His dark, somber pictures often contain references to Germany's mytho-

logical or historical past. One such painting is, for instance, called "Die Hermannsschlacht" (Hermann's Battle), referring to the defeat of Roman troops in A.D. 9 by Germanic tribes, an exploit that has been become a celebrated event in German history. Other allusions are to the Song of Nibelung or to incidents in the more recent German past. His "Operation Sea Lion" (1975), a reference to Hitler's planned invasion of England in 1940, shows battleships operating in a gigantic bathtub.

While Kiefer is preoccupied with Germany's history as a whole, Jörg Immendorff (born 1945), also a student of Beuys, is concerned, more narrowly with the division of Germany into a capitalist West and a Communist East, a theme he has taken up repeatedly in his cycle of works called "Café Deutschland" (Café Germany). His gloomy pictures are full of symbols of the divided nation: barbed wire, the eagle, the East and West German flags, the Berlin Wall, pictures of politicians and literary figures, and, again and again, Berlin's Brandenburg Gate. This prime emblem of Germany's division is also featured in another of Immendorff's paintings. Called "Naht" (Suture, 1981, Cologne, Private Collection), the painting depicts a starfish, symbolizing Germany, in the middle of which are scars in the shape of the Brandenburg Gate, sutured but still oozing blood. However, on the starfish, an eagle, Germany's heraldic bird throughout the centuries and also during the Nazi era, has marched across, leaving bleeding scars, and possibly reminding the viewer that Germany's painful division is the result of Hitler's aggressive politics.

While Immendorff paints pictures with strong narrative elements crammed with symbols and human figures, Georg Baselitz's (born 1938) concern is the human figure, which totally fills the canvass. Since 1969 he painted his figures upside down, forcing the viewer to look at the picture as a colorful composition, not necessarily as a depiction of a person. In addition to his bold canvasses, Baselitz has also created a number of wooden sculptures. A. R. Penck's (born 1939) paintings remind the viewer of prehistoric wall paintings. Using stick figures, symbols, hieroglyphs, letters, numbers, and symbols, Penck creates pictures that the viewer is challenged to decipher.

One of the quirks of the art market is that the abstract painters of the fifties, who so desperately wanted to be international, were virtually ignored abroad, while the "New Savages," with their German obsessions have been greeted with great enthusiasm at home and abroad.

NOTES

1. Sharon Macdonald, "Museums and Identities: Materializing German Culture," in *Contemporary German Cultural Studies,* edited by Alison Phipps (London: Arnold, 2002), 117.

2. According to Gros and Glaab, *Faktenlexikon Deutschland,* 525.

3. Gros and Glaab, *Faktenlexikon Deutschland,* 526.

4. Hanspeter Landolt, *German Painting. The Late Middle Ages (1350–1500)* (Cleveland: World Publishing, 1968), 81.

5. Quoted in C. W. E. Bigsby, *Dada and Surrealism* (London: Methuen, 1972), 5.

6. Stephanie Barron, ed., *German Expressionism, 1915–1925: The Second Generation* (Munich: Prestel, 1988), 48.

7. Peter-Klaus Schuster, ed., *Die "Kunststadt" München 1937. Nationalsozialismus und "Entartete Kunst."* (Munich: Prestel, 1987), 217.

8. The catalog is reproduced in Schuster, *Die "Kunststadt" München,* 183–216.

9. Franz Roh, *German Painting in the Twentieth Century* (Greenwich, Conn.: New York Graphic Society, 1968), 122.

10. *Newsweek,* 24 July 2002, 84.

11. The *Guardian,* quoted in Ardagh, *Germany and the Germans,* 285.

11

Architecture

THE WEIMAR REPUBLIC, that turbulent period between the end of the First World War and Hitler's assumption of power in 1933, saw the birth of modern architecture. Of the four men who are widely considered as having shaped modern architecture, Walter Gropius, Ludwig Mies van der Rohe, Frank Lloyd Wright, and Le Corbusier, the first two were German architects revolutionizing our concept of architecture. As a British critic observed: "In our late twentieth-century cities, dominated by the clean lines of concrete, glass and steel, the influence of architecture inspired by German modernism is clearly visible."[1] In addition, the *Bauhaus,* that architectural and design school where Gropius and Mies taught, altered the look of everything around us: the tubular steel chair you sit in, the wallpaper in your house, the cups you are sipping your tea from, the coffee grinder and silverware in your kitchen, the lamp in your study, and the typeface in the ads and catalogs you read.

However, Gropius, Mies, and numerous other modern German architects stood on the shoulders of generations of previous builders and designers who have left a magnificent heritage of buildings in Germany. Therefore, before we delve more deeply into the contributions of German architects to modern architecture and design, let us pause for a moment to sketch, however briefly, some of the architectural treasures of the past a visitor will find in Germany (many of which are listed among Unesco World Heritage Sites, see chapter 1). They range from well-preserved Roman monuments from the third century in Germany's oldest city, Trier, and soaring Gothic cathedrals and elaborate Baroque palaces to sleek modern skyscrapers in Germany's most modern city, Frankfurt.

The Romanesque Benedictine Abbey of Maria Laach. Photo by Eckhard Bernstein.

THE PAST

Romanesque architecture prevailed in Germany from around A.D. 950 to 1150. Outstanding examples of that style are the three large cathedrals on the Rhine in Worms, Speyer, and Mainz, as well as St. Michael's Church in Hildesheim and the abbey Maria Laach in the Eifel Mountains. Any visitor will be enchanted when listening to the Benedictine monks singing Gregorian chants in this magnificent building, just as they did 1,000 years ago. Characteristic features of these Romanesque churches are the monumental west facades crowned by one tower, or sometimes two towers, the massive barrel vaults that replaced the flat wooden ceiling of churches in the previous era, the round arches, the solid pillars, and the small windows, which give these churches a somber interior. Unlike Romanesque architecture with its stress on earthbound, heavy masses, *Gothic architecture* (c. 1150–1450) is heavenbound and characterized by lightness and soaring spaces. The best-known example of Gothic church architecture is undoubtedly the Cologne cathedral, which was begun in 1248 but only completed in 1880. Other significant Gothic cathedrals are the Münster in Straßburg, Ulm, and Freiburg. While Ulm's cathedral, with its 526-foot-high tower, can boast of being the tallest church in the world, Freiburg's Münster, with its filigreed tower and intricate sculptures, is said to have "the most beautiful tower in Christendom." Romanesque and Gothic architecture found primarily expression in churches. *Renaissance* architects, on the other hand, were concerned with secular buildings, designing and constructing palaces, castles, and town halls. The castles of Stuttgart and Heidelberg, here especially the so-called Ottheinrichbau, are outstanding examples of Renaissance architecture. *Baroque,* like the previous styles, was a European style, prevailing approximately between the early seventeenth to the middle of the eighteenth century. It was the time when absolutist rulers tried to assert their power by having imposing residences with grand portals, wide staircases, and extended gardens built. Baroque architects like Balthasar Neumann (1687–1753) and the Asam brothers created magnificent buildings incorporating sculpture and painting into a harmonious whole. Outstanding examples of that style are Nymphenburg Castle near Munich, the Residenz in Würzburg, and the Zwinger in Dresden. Southern Germany has numerous Baroque and Rococo (a slightly later, even more ornate, style) churches, among them Neumann's Vierzehnheiligen Church with its sumptuous interior decoration. *Neoclassicism* developed in the late eighteenth century in reaction to the exuberance and overornateness of the Baroque and Rococo. Drawing its inspiration from Greek and Roman architecture, neoclassical architects favored orderliness, balance, clarity, and simplicity. Strict geometry, columns, and pediments are the most striking features of neoclassical buildings. Under the patronage of King Ludwig I of Bavaria, much of Munich's inner city was rebuilt in the early nineteenth century in this style. In Berlin it was Karl Friedrich von Schinkel (1781–1841) who was celebrated as the most famous and prolific classicist, so much so that the rhymed witticism made the rounds "In jedem Winkel ein Schinkel," (in every corner a Schinkel [building]). His Altes Museum (1822–28) and Grosses Schauspielhaus (1818–1821) are only the most famous of the more than 80 buildings he left behind. Much of Old Berlin owes its characteristic look to Schinkel. But the most famous neoclassical structure is likely the Brandenburg Gate, built between 1789 and 1793 by Karl Langhans. Once separating East and West Berlin, it now has become a symbol of German unification.

The later nineteenth century did not develop a characteristic style. Instead, it embraced what, for lack of a better word, has been called "historicism." By that is meant the blind veneration of tradition that expressed itself in the plundering of past styles or stylistic elements of the previous centuries. From around 1850 onwards, neo-Gothic town halls, neo-Renaissance department stores and railroad stations, neo-Romanesque churches, and neo-Baroque government buildings sprung up everywhere in Germany.

THE TWENTIETH CENTURY

The Weimar Republic

It was exactly against this historicism or eclecticism that the avant-garde architecture we now associate with the Weimar Republic's *Bauhaus* reacted.

The *Bauhaus,* called "the most celebrated art school of modern times,"[2] was founded in 1919 out of the merger of an arts academy and an applied arts school; it revolutionized art education, set standards for present-day industrial design, and helped to create modern architecture. The very name *Bauhaus* (literally, building house) revealed its program. It was meant to evoke the medieval term *Bauhütte* (literally, building shack), which referred to the team of architects, sculptors, masons, carpenters, and artists who worked collaboratively on medieval cathedrals. Like the *Bauhütte*, the *Bauhaus* tried to bridge the crafts and arts. This effort was reflected in the organizational structure of the *Bauhaus* itself. Teachers, no longer called professors but *Meister* (masters), would work together with the students on problems. After an initial "foundation course," students could choose between a variety of courses, ranging from furniture design, weaving, pottery, and photography to product design, painting, graphics, typography, advertising, stagecraft, and ballet. The architecture course was only the culmination.

The founder of the *Bauhaus,* and its director between 1919 and 1928, was the architect Walter Gropius (1883–1969). Through his teaching in Germany and later, after 1937, at Harvard University, as well as through his own designs, he became one of the most important creators of modern architecture. Gropius was able to attract a number of artists that today reads like a "Who's Who" of the international avant-garde. At one time or another, the following persons taught in the *Bauhaus:* the German-American painter Lyonel Feininger (1871–1956); the sculptor Gerhard Marcks (1889–1991); the Swiss painter Paul Klee (1879–1940); the Russian painter Wassily Kandinsky (1866–1944); the German painter and designer Oskar Schlemmer (1888–1943); the German painter Josef Albers (1888–1976); the Hungarian sculptor and painter László Moholy-Nagy (1895–1946); the Hungarian furniture designer and architect Marcel Breuer (1900–1981); and the German architect Ludwig Mies van der Rohe (1886–1969).

However, from the very beginning, the *Bauhaus* was controversial. To rightist nationalists, it was too cosmopolitan and too "un-German," a "hotbed of bolshevism"; to the Weimar craftsmen it represented a threat to their various own trades. Cut off from the funding it had received earlier from the city of Weimar, the *Bauhaus* moved to Dessau in 1925 and from there to Berlin in 1932, where it was shut down by the National Socialists a year later.

Gropius's fame as an architectural revolutionary in prewar Germany rests on the buildings he designed and built in 1911 for a factory in Alfeld near Hildesheim. With thousands of similar buildings now dotting industrial parks all over the world, it is hardly possible today to appreciate Gropius's pioneering design. What was startling about this building was not only its simplicity and functionality at a time when other architects were still adorning their factories with decorations of past centuries, but also the construction itself; instead of the conventional load-bearing walls, Gropius used a skeleton of vertical steel supports to which he attached walls of glass and concrete. The lightness and grace of the building is accentuated by the way Gropius handled the corners. Since the steel supports are moved back from their traditional corner position, he could enclose the open corners entirely with glass, giving the effect of an unbroken glass facade. The curtain wall, the system of hanging the walls from a steel skeleton instead of making them load-bearing, pioneered by Gropius in this comparatively modest building, was to become a standard feature of the "international style."

In spite of the heavy administrative burdens placed upon him as the director of the *Bauhaus,* Gropius managed to design a number of buildings during the Weimar years, including a stunning skyscraper for the Chicago Tribune and a "Total Theater" for Max Reinhardt in Berlin. Neither of these designs became buildings. In Chicago, a neo-Gothic tower won the competition, and the theater complex in Berlin was canceled for financial reasons. However, a number of private dwellings he designed, as well as homes for housing projects, such as the Weissenhofsiedlung in Stuttgart, were realized. His most important building in Germany was the *Bauhaus* building in Dessau, a complex consisting of five interconnected structures housing classrooms, an administration building, workshops, social areas, and dormitories. With their flat roofs, use of steel, concrete, and their white surfaces, these buildings became the prototype of countless others all over the world.

Mies van der Rohe

Like Gropius, Mies van der Rohe was associated with the *Bauhaus,* although for only a short time, and like Gropius, he left Hitler's Germany, albeit rather late, realizing that he had no future in Germany as an avantgarde architect, and, finally, like the founder of the *Bauhaus,* Mies had a long and distinguished career in the United States.

Mies burst onto the architectural scene in 1922 with a design for a skyscraper in the Friedrichstrasse, at that time one of Berlin's busiest shopping streets. Sleek and unadorned, the building's exterior was designed totally of glass. Though it was never built, it represented a new kind of architecture.

However, no other building embodied Mies's credo of "less is more" than the German pavilion he designed for the World Exposition in Barcelona in 1929. Demolished after the end of the exhibition because nobody wanted to buy it from the German government, it was recreated in its original form and on the same site in 1981–86 by the Barcelona City Council. Though at the time, the pavilion was known to most critics only from photographs, it had an enormous influence on the emerging "international style." It is impressive through its simplicity and clarity. Since the weight of the flat canopy roof was carried by columns, not load-bearing walls, Mies used the walls only to create spaces. Glass walls from floor to roof break down the distinction between outside and inside.

It is fair to say that his reputation as one of the world's leading architects of the second half of the twentieth century rests on the buildings he created while in the United States. These include, among others, the campus of the Illinois Institute of Technology, two high-rise apartment houses (860 and 880 Lake Shore Drive) on Chicago's North Side (1948–51), the Seagram Building in New York City (1954–58), the Toronto Dominion Center in Toronto (1967), and the New National Gallery in Berlin (1962–68) (see below).

Erich (later Eric) Mendelsohn (1887–1953)

During the Weimar Republic, Erich Mendelsohn's architectural firm in Berlin was one of the largest in Europe. Today, however, Erich Mendelsohn, the third great architect of that period, is chiefly remembered as the creator of the so-called Einstein Tower in Potsdam, near Berlin (1921–24). And it was the design for this observatory and astrophysical laboratory that launched Mendelsohn to prominence.

Unlike the *Bauhaus* architects who favored cubic forms and straight lines, Mendelsohn used dramatic curved shapes in this building of concrete and steel, as if he wanted to exploit the elastic potential of these materials. But unlike the buildings of Gropius and Mies, the steel here is hidden. The walls seem to be bulging out, the windows are set in deep, non-rectangular recesses. Rather than a building, it looks like a gigantic sculpture. When Einstein was asked to comment on it, he is reported to have said, "It's organic." Today, the Einstein Tower, restored in 1978 to its former white beauty, is regarded as a masterpiece of Expressionist architecture. But it has remained a unique structure. That it found no imitators lies in the character of Expressionism, that revolutionary movement in the arts between 1905 and 1924 that stressed the expression of inner feelings. While this subjectivity led to the magnificent flowering of the visual arts in Germany in the first decades of the twentieth century, in architecture, with its dependence on materials and clients, Expressionism did not succeed to the same extent. Thus, whereas a great number of Expressionist buildings were *designed*, few were actually built. As one critic said, "The age of Expressionism is the age of great unbuilt buildings."[3]

It was only natural that Mendelsohn, in the second half of the 1920s, turned away from Expressionism and designed, and more importantly built, a number of structures that are closer to the cubism of the *Bauhaus,* while retaining some of the playfulness of his earlier work. Like the *Bauhaus* architects, he stressed the function of a building, but he never forgot that a building also has to be beautiful, saying "The primary element is function, but function without sensual admixtures remains mere construction."[4] His designs for factories, villas, a cinema, and, above all, department stores are all considered milestones in modern architecture.

When Hitler came to power in 1933, Mendelsohn, as a Jew, saw no future for himself in his native land. He left first for England and later for the United States. In England, Palestine, and the United States he had a successful career, building private homes, community centers, libraries, hospitals, banks, college halls, and synagogues.

The National Socialists had different ideas about art and architecture. Though a majority of the German *Bauhaus*-trained architects remained in Hitler's Germany,[5] "stars" like Gropius, Mies, Mendelsohn, and Marcel Breuer immigrated to the United States. From there the "international style," as it was called since 1932, when it was introduced in an exhibition in New York's Museum of Modern Art to the American public, began its triumphal march all over the world.

The Third Reich

"Never in German history were greater and nobler buildings planned, begun and completed than in our time," declared Hitler in 1937, four years after he had become chancellor of the German Reich.[6] While one can argue over the "greatness" and "nobility" of the buildings built during the Third Reich, it is undeniable that the period following Hitler's assumption of power in 1933 saw an unprecedented building boom.

After the humiliating defeat of World War I, the punitive Treaty of Versailles, and the endless series of ineffectual Weimar governments, the National Socialists had given Germans new pride and self-confidence. Within a few years, unemployment had disappeared and the most severe provisions of the Versailles treaty had been repealed unilaterally by Hitler. The architectural style of the numerous public buildings of the Third Reich, that is, the buildings designed for the Nazi Party, the government, and for the "folk community," was meant to express this "reawakening of Germany," to display the revived power of Germany, and to foster in Germans a new sense of national community and togetherness. Large national buildings were intended to be "words in stone," as Hitler himself put it. Architecture itself was to play an important part in what the National Socialists called the "German Revolution." Rejecting the steel, concrete, and glass construction of the Weimar

Republic's modernists as unsuitable for representational public buildings and as too international and "un-German," Hitler, as in so many other instances, turned to the past, in this case to European neoclassicism, an architectural style widely favored between 1770 and 1850. The irony was, of course, that there was nothing typically German about classicism or neoclassicism; in fact it was as international as the *Bauhaus* architecture. After all, public buildings in this style had been constructed in ancient Greece and Rome, in Renaissance Italy, in eighteenth-century America (The Capitol in Washington), nineteenth-century England (British Museum in London), and in Napoleonic France. So it was not the internationality but its perceived timelessness that attracted Hitler when he said, "These buildings of ours should not be conceived for the year 1942 nor for the year 2000, but like the cathedrals of our past, they should stretch into the millennia of the future."[7]

Neoclassicism, broadly speaking, became the official style of *public* buildings. The first major building constructed in this style during the Third Reich was the House of German Art in Munich. Designed by Paul Ludwig Troost (1878–1934) and built between 1933 and 1937, it recalls Schinkel's famous Old Museum in Berlin: the series of mighty columns placed at regular intervals before the facade, the so-called colonnade, eight steps along the entire length of the facade, and the emphasis on horizontal lines. The House of German Art became the prototype of numerous other buildings.

After the death of Troost in 1934, the young and ambitious Albert Speer (1905–1981) became the Third Reich's leading architect. At age 28, Speer had been appointed commissioner for the technical and artistic organization of the annual party rallies. In 1933 he created for the first time the impressive "cathedral of lights" by directing 150 powerful torch lights 10 miles into the night, a feat that was to become a regular feature of the annual rallies of the Nazi Party in Nuremberg. For the 1937 World Exposition in Paris, Speer built a large and imposing German pavilion in the monumental neoclassical style, a few years later the new chancellery in Berlin. Individual structures like these, to which we also have to add the gigantic Olympic Stadium in Berlin built for the 1936 Olympic Games by Werner March (1894–1976) and designed to accommodate 100,000 spectators, were intended to display not only the revived power of Germany and the authority of the National Socialist Party but also to create in Germans a sense of national community.

But the National Socialists were not content with erecting individual buildings. Hitler's long-term plans called for a complete reshaping of entire cities, such as Berlin, Linz, Weimar, and Augsburg. The most spectacular of these urban renewal projects was to take place in Berlin. Two large boulevards, one running north-south, the other west-east, were to intersect at a large square. No other project demonstrates more clearly how Hitler had lost all sense of proportion than the plans developed by Speer, at Hitler's request, for two colossal structures in the middle of Berlin: a gigantic triumphal arch, measuring 386 feet high, 550 feet wide, and 329 feet deep, celebrating Germany's expected military victories, and an equally enormous domed Great Hall that would rise over 1,000 feet, dwarfing St. Peter's Basilica in Rome and holding 180,000 people. Because of the outbreak of the war, neither of these structures was ever built.

Although very few of these megalomaniac projects were realized, the very existence of the plans have determined our image of the Third Reich's architecture. These buildings, it is claimed, epitomize the official and only style permitted during the Third Reich. This view is unhistorical. Critics, it seems, have uncritically swallowed Hitler's propaganda, which focused on these monumental structures. Not only did these public buildings represent a mere fraction of the construction going on, but contrary to what often has been asserted, there was no one unique architectural style during the Third Reich. There was of course the monumental, neoclassical style favored by Hitler for public and representational buildings. Many factories, however, were built in the sober functionalism of the *Bauhaus,* and there was the so-called vernacular style for housing developments and youth hostels. Given the totalitarian nature of the Third Reich, this diversity might be surprising but is easily explained by Hitler's lack of interest in anything but the representative, prestigious structures meant to immortalize his regime. This resulted in a relative freedom in other areas of design, such as in industrial architecture and the design of the superhighways (*Autobahnen*).

The stark, geometrical style of modernist architecture in the *Bauhaus* style was permitted and even encouraged for some types of buildings with the result that buildings in this modernist style would outnumber all other buildings in the Third Reich.[8] What was rejected emphatically by the Nazis was the modernists' claim that their style was suitable for *all* buildings, no matter what their function.

That the Nazis wholeheartedly embraced modern technology is also evident in the construction of the *Autobahnen* . Built to provide work for hundreds of thousands of unemployed workers, but also to allow easy and quick travel between major urban centers (and of course for military reasons), these superhighways not only were remarkable engineering feats but were also built with respect for the beauty of the landscape. This appreciation of the German countryside can be seen, for instance, in the stunning bridge constructions that were made necessary by the hilly topography of central and southern Germany. Rejecting one particular style, the architects adapted their bridge designs to local and regional architectural traditions. In some cases, bridges were built in stone from local quarries, in others functional steel constructions were used to fit into an urban industrial environment. At the time, the *Autobahnen* were much admired by foreigners; at home they contributed to Hitler's myth as the Third Reich's forward-looking master builder. Each section was dedicated with great fanfare by Nazi officials.

If neoclassical monumentalism was the style of the official buildings, and an undogmatic modernist functionalism prevailed in the construction of factories and the *Autobahnen,* the preferred architectural style for houses was what is called the "vernacular style," meaning the use of traditional local or regional styles. The flat roof of *Bauhaus*-style housing developments was denounced as "un-German," while developments of single-family, detached houses with gabled roofs were encouraged.

POSTWAR

In 1945 Germany lay in ruins. Major cities like Hamburg, Frankfurt, Hanover, Berlin, and Cologne were devastated. Millions of Germans had lost their homes. Another 12 million, who had either fled from the Red Army or had been expelled from their homelands in Silesia, East and West Prussia, and the Sudetenland, were pushing into overcrowded West Germany with the result that in 1948 there was a shortfall of 6.5 million housing units. Finding shelter for these millions of homeless people presented a major challenge to politicians and architects alike. The resulting architecture was of course in many cases unremarkable and mediocre. Pragmatism or practicality won out over aesthetics. However, to criticize the time as a "chronicle of missed opportunities," as some critics have done, seems unfair. Given the huge demand for housing and the limited resources available, providing rapid remedies was the first priority. Little time was left for attention to architectural quality. In addition, for a family who had been living in a basement or in a single room, an apartment with a kitchen and bath was "beautiful," no matter how unappealing the exterior apartment complex looked.

The Marshall Plan, the currency reform, and the economic miracle of the fifties triggered an unprecedented building boom in West Germany, resulting in millions of new apartments, thousands of new schools, hospitals, and theaters, and a number of remarkable and widely acclaimed buildings that have become landmarks in a country that is unusually rich in modern architecture. A few examples must suffice.

The leading architect of the 1950s was Egon Eiermann (1904–1970), who designed the German Embassy in Washington, D.C., a modernist, glass-enclosed building that is embedded into the hilly topography of northwestern Washington. In West Berlin he created a remarkable architectural ensemble consisting of an old bombed-out church and a modern one. He preserved the ruin of the neo-Romanesque *Gedächtniskirche* (Memorial Church) as a memorial to the folly of war, but confronted it with an ultra-modern church built of a steel framework structure filled with honeycomb concrete fillings. It consists of a hexagonal freestanding tower and an octagonal nave. Thousands of small blue stained-glass windows give the interior a mystic quality, providing a quiet place for prayer and meditation amidst the hectic traffic at the intersection of two of the busiest streets in Berlin.

West Berlin, situated like an island in the midst of East Germany, became the site of numerous other remarkable buildings, two of which should be mentioned here. In the early sixties, Hans Scharoun attracted international attention with a striking building, the Philharmonie, the home of the Berlin Philharmonic Orchestra, one of the world's most renowned orchestras. Rejecting the conventions of the *Bauhaus* and international styles, with its stark geometrical forms, clear lines, and spartan functionality, Scharoun designed the building from the inside out, or in his own words: "The hall is conceived as a well with the orchestra at the bottom surrounded by rising vineyards."[9] By having the orchestra surrounded on all sides by the audience, Scharoun not only created an intimate atmosphere for the 2,000 listeners but also the superb acoustics the hall has become famous for. The novel interior also determined the unusual exterior; it is shaped like a tent with its convex curvature of the roof and the odd, polygonal outside walls.

In marked contrast to Scharoun's Philharmonie stands Ludwig Mies van der Rohe's Neue Nationalgalerie (New National Gallery, 1962–68). Following his alleged aphorism "less is more," Mies designed a building that consists of a glass-encased, square-shaped structure with a large, flat overhanging roof that seems to float lightly over the building and which is supported by a mere eight slender steel columns. The classical symmetry of the museum gives the impression of weightlessness and lightness. In spite of its simple beauty, the museum is not a practical building. The huge aboveground exhibition hall is not really suited for hanging pictures. The main exhibition hall is underground.

Scharoun's Philharmonie and Mies van der Rohe's Neue Nationalgalerie reflected a new vitality in German architecture. But no other building complex attracted more attention than the structures built for the 1972 Olympic Games in Munich by Günther Behnisch and Partners (1965–72).

The games, the first held in Germany after the end of World War II, were intended as a showcase for the new democratic Germany. Billed as the "cheerful games" (*heitere Spiele*), they were conceived as a deliberate antithesis to the 1936 Berlin Olympic Games, which the National Socialists had exploited for their propagandistic purposes. Behnisch found a perfect architectural expression in his design. Shunning the discredited monumentality of Nazi architecture, he designed an informal ensemble of tent-like structures that linked the stadium, the Olympic Hall, and the swimming pool. The tent roofing not only suggested the provisional nature of these structures—in contrast to the architecture of the "Thousand Year Reich"—but also evoked the playful and happy atmosphere of a circus. The whole complex was integrated into an artificially created landscape complete with a small lake and a hill created out of the rubble of the Second World War. Today, more than 30 years after the games, the Olympia-Park has retained its value as a leisure center for Munich's citizens and visitors.

In the mid-1980s, Günter Behnisch was commissioned to design a new building for the German parliament in Bonn, at that time the capital of West Germany. The architect created a glass-enclosed building, symbolic of the transparency of West German democracy. To encourage dialogue rather than confrontation, the parliamentarians sit in a circle. Large balconies on three sides allow visitors to watch the proceedings of their representatives. Located on the left bank of the Rhine, the building provides a view of the mighty river flowing by. However, parliamentarians had only a few years to enjoy the new building. After the reunification of Germany in 1990, the German parliament decided to move the government to Berlin. Today, the building in Bonn is therefore used for other purposes.

The 1980s: The Decade of Museum Building in the West

The 1980s were marked by the construction of a large number of museums in the Federal Republic. Each city seemed to vie with the other in the building of new museums or renovating existing ones. But not only the number of museums is impressive but also their architectural quality. That is due to the fact that the best and most innovative architects of the world are invited to architectural competitions. Germany has become the playground of the international architectural elite. Again, a few selected examples must suffice.

One of the most spectacular museums, the Neue Staatsgalerie in Stuttgart (1977–83), was designed by the Scotsman James Stirling. Rejecting the cold functionality of the international style, Stirling and his partner Michael Wilford created a museum complex that is broken up by courtyards, stairs, and alleys. The exterior of the main hall consists of an undulating and skewed glass facade. The large blocks of yellow and brown stone are juxtaposed by brightly colored technical elements such as pipes and girders. The whole building is overflowing with playful allusions to other historical styles. No wonder that this example of postmodernist architecture has become one of the most popular museums in Germany. Wandering about in the building complex has become an experience in itself.

Kunstmuseum in Bonn,
designed by Axel Schultes.
Photo by Eckhard Bernstein.

The city, however, that during the 1980s embarked on the most ambitious museum-building program was Frankfurt am Main. Dubbed "Mainhattan" because of its numerous skyscrapers—the only German city that has such a concentration of high-rise buildings—Frankfurt commissioned internationally renowned architects to design a number of museums on the left bank of the Main River, and in the process created a fascinating "Museum Mile." Günter Behnisch, the architect of Munich's Olympic Complex and Bonn's parliamentary building, designed the German Postal Museum (1984–90); Oswald Mathias Ungers was responsible for the German Architecture Museum (1979–84); the American Richard Meyer created the Arts and Crafts Museum (1979–85); and Helge Bofinger built the German Film Museum. Across the river, in the midst of the old city, the Austrian Hans Hollein designed the stunning Museum of Modern Art (1987–89). A Museum Mile was also built by the city of Bonn, for 40 years the capital of West Germany and therefore financially well provided for by the parliamentarians. It includes the Haus der Geschichte (Home of [German] History), with its fascinating and engaging exhibits of postwar Germany; the Exhibition Hall of the Federal Republic, designed by the Viennese architect Gustav

Peichl; and, next to it, the *Kunstmuseum Bonn,* designed by Axel Schultes, with its stress on Rhenish expressionists and modernists like Joseph Beuys, Anselm Kiefer, and Georg Baselitz.

Architecture in East Germany

In the immediate postwar period, East Germany faced the same problems of acute housing shortages as West Germany. But the solutions that were found were often quite different, reflecting the different ideological orientations of the two states.

Divided Berlin offers an instructive example. Here the confrontation between the two hostile blocks and ideologies, the Communist East and the democratic West, was sharper than elsewhere. This difference expressed itself also in architecture. While in West Berlin, a group of international artists, including Gropius and LeCorbusier, created a loose ensemble of high-rise apartment blocks in the park-like Hansa Viertel (Hansa Quarter), the Communists followed Soviet models in their sector. The showcase for their architecture became the Stalinallee (later Karl-Marx-Allee; today Frankfurter Allee). On the rubble of the destroyed city, a wide boulevard was created, lined on both sides with new apartment buildings for the workers. These houses were designed in a pseudo neoclassical style favored in the Soviet Union under Stalin. The simplicity and functionality of the *Bauhaus* style was rejected by the Communists as "nothing more than a genuine style of American cosmopolitanism," as Walter Ulbricht, the chairman of the East German Communist party, declared.[10]

Hardly was Stalin dead, however, when his successor, Nikita Khrushchev, at the end of the fifties, prescribed a new functionality and simplicity. The result was an industrialized architecture for the masses. Henceforth, the wall-sized, reinforced concrete slab became the basic unit of almost all building in the GDR. *Plattenbauten* (buildings made out of these prefabricated concrete slabs) became the hallmark of East German buildings. With their unsightly homogeneity and unfortunate tendency to fall apart after a mere 10 years, the *Plattenbauten* became an eyesore and, after the German unification, an ugly legacy of the Communist regime. Today, they are either thoroughly renovated or torn down.

As the vast majority of the resources were poured into these standardized apartment buildings, scant money was left for individual public buildings. Only a handful of buildings are architecturally noteworthy, including the new home of the world-famous Gewandhaus Orchestra in Leipzig and the modernistic Palast der Republik (Palace of the Republic) in East Berlin. The latter was erected on the site of old historical Hohenzollernschloß (the castle of the Hohenzollern kings), which the East German authorities had blown up as a remnant of a feudal society in the 1950s.

Architecture after Reunification

On November 9, 1989, the East German authorities were forced to open the Berlin Wall. Within less than a year, the two German states, which had been separated by the Iron Curtain, were united. An enormous building boom began in the "five new states," as the former GDR is now called; billions of deutsche marks were poured into the reconstruction of roads, the restoration of historical city centers, long neglected by the Communists, and the construction of housing and cultural projects.

After the German parliament had decided in 1991 to move the government from Bonn to Berlin, Berlin became the largest construction site in Europe. Everywhere, but especially in the old eastern part, offices, government buildings, and new department stores were built and old ones refurbished.

Again, in keeping with modern Germany's cosmopolitan outlook, the best international architects were invited to create the new Berlin. What other country would have commissioned a foreign architect to redesign its parliament building? But that is exactly what the German Bundestag did when it entrusted the British architect Sir Norman Foster with the redesign

The New Chancellery in Berlin, designed by Axel Schultes and Charlotte Frank. Photo by Eckhard Bernstein.

The Glass Dome of the Renovated Reichstag, designed by
Norman Foster. Photo by Eckhard Bernstein.

of the old Reichstag building. Originally constructed in 1894 in a neo-
Renaissance style, burnt out in 1933, and shot to pieces by the Red Army in
1945, the Reichstag was renovated provisionally in the sixties. Foster completely gutted the building, leaving only the 3-foot-thick exterior walls. He
transformed the inside into a clear, beautiful, functional building and
crowned it with a huge glass dome. Since its completion in 1999, the dome
has become a major tourist attraction. Every day thousands of visitors are
climbing to the top of the glass dome on an interior ramp to enjoy a magnificent view of the city.

Next to the Reichstag, Axel Schultes and Charlotte Frank have built the stunning new chancellery, the official residence of the federal chancellor. Within walking distance of the Reichstag and the chancellery, a completely new city quarter has sprung up around the old Potsdamer Platz. In the twenties the Potsdamer Platz (Potsdam Square) was one of Europe's busiest road junctions. Its very name stood for night life, amusement, and lively urban activity. Devastated by Allied bombs and further destroyed by the wrecking balls of the East Germans who wanted to give their border guards a free field of vision and fire—the site lay between East and West Berlin—the Potsdamer Platz became a barren wasteland and an oasis for rabbits. After reunification of the two German states, the area presented Berlin's urban planners with a unique opportunity to reconnect the artificially separated parts of the capital with a new center. Again, architects from all over the word were invited. Heated debates followed—and construction began—and within a few years, a new city center arose. The area comprises office blocks, apartment houses, cinemas, a theater, a huge shopping gallery, a luxury hotel, restaurants, and bars. The Potsdamer Platz consists of two sections: the Debis (Daimler Benz) area designed by the Italian architect Renzo Piano and the Sony Center, the European headquarters of the Japanese electronics giant Sony, designed by the German-American Helmut Jahn. Jahn's design centers around a large plaza covered with a huge roof-tent made out of glass and surrounded by glass-enclosed buildings. It also features a 24-story glass high-rise building. Piano's design, on the other hand, has a more homey feel, in spite of the two high-rise buildings at its entrance. The traditional street paved of cobblestones, old trees, small alleys, a piazza, numerous street cafés, and fountains are more reminiscent of a medieval city than a newly created urban center. Next to the Reichstag's glass dome, the Potsdamer Platz has become one of new Berlin's favorite tourist attractions.

Within walking distance of the gleaming buildings of the Potsdamer Platz lies Berlin's new Jewish Museum. Designed by Daniel Libeskind and completed in 1998, the zinc-clad building has the form of a zigzag, which has been alternately interpreted as a lightning bolt or a broken star of David. Before it was used as a museum, the empty building, with its jagged windows, architectural voids, and slanting corridors had become an attraction by itself, with its very emptiness symbolizing the disappearance of Jewish life from German culture. Since September 2001, the building, with its many artifacts, serves as a museum documenting centuries of German-Jewish history. On the occasion of its opening, *Newsweek* magazine wrote: "In spirit the Jewish Museum is the new Berlin: a reconciliation of past and present, looking to the future, not as a rebuke or warning, but as an exhortation, a reminder of what Berlin once was and could be again."[11]

Notes

1. Gillian Pye, "Constructing Germany: Architecture and Cultural Identity," in *Contemporary German Cultural Studies*, edited by Alison Phipps (London: Arnold, 2002), 90.

2. Frank Whitford, *Bauhaus* (London: Thames and Hudson, 1984), 9.

3. Julius Posener, *Hans Poelzig. Reflections on His Life and Work*, edited by Kristin Feireiss (Cambridge, Mass.: MIT Press, 1992), 11.

4. Quoted in Peter Gay, *Weimar Culture. The Outsider as Insider* (New York: Harper & Row, 1968), 97.

5. Elaine S. Hochmann, *Architects of Fortune: Mies van der Rohe and the Third Reich* (New York: Weidenfeld and Nicolson, 1989), 277: "Of the 37 German nationals associated with the Bauhaus...23 remained in Germany, 2 were jailed, 12 left. 1 left before 1930."

6. Quoted in Berthold Hinz, *Art in the Third Reich* (New York: Pantheon Books, 1979), 189.

7. Quoted in Peter Adam, *Art of the Third Reich* (New York: Harry N. Abrams, 1992), 225.

8. Hochmann, *Architects of Fortune*, 236.

9. Quoted in Wolfgang Pehnt, *German Architecture, 1960–1970* (New York: Prager Publishers, 1970), 199.

10. Quoted in Gerhard G. Feldmeyer, *New German Architecture* (New York: Rizzoli, 1993), 35.

11. *Newsweek,* 10 September 10 2001.

Glossary

Abitur   A graduation diploma awarded after passing a set of exams at the end of the academic high school education.

Anschluss   Joining. The accession of Austria into the German Reich in March 1938.

ARD   Arbeitsgemeinschaft der Rundfunkanstalten Deutschlands (Association of broadcasting stations in Germany). Usually referred to as the First German Television Program.

Autobahn   German superhighways.

Bauhaus   German design and architecture school in Weimar (1919–1926), later Dessau (1926–1932) and Berlin. Closed by National Socialists in 1933.

BDM   Bund deutscher Mädel (League of German Girls). Part of the Hitler-jugend. Consisted of 14-to-17-year-old girls.

Bekennende Kirche   Confessing Church. Protestant anti-Hitler church.

Bildungsroman   Literally "novel of education." Work in which the development of an individual is the central issue.

Blitzkrieg   Lightning war. Coined in 1940 by the Germans, the term was taken over by other countries. It refers to a quick war.

Bundesrat   Voice of the state governments. Second chamber of German parliament.

Bundestag   German parliament.

Burg   A castle.

Christkindlmarkt   Christmas market. Also called **Weihnachtsmarkt.**

DDR   Deutsche Demokratische Republik (German Democratic Republic). Official name of the East German state (1949–1990).

Dirndl   Traditional women's dress.

DM   Deutsche mark. Official West German currency unit between 1948 and 2001.

Drittes Reich   Third Reich. Name of the Hitler-dictatorship. The Nazis avoided the title from 1939 on.

Entartete Kunst   Degenerate Art. Disparaging name of modern art used by Nazis.

Fasching   Boisterous pre-Lent celebration, used especially in southern Germany.

Führer   Leader. Official name of Adolf Hitler between 1934 and 1945.

Gastarbeiter   Guest workers. Mostly from Italy, Spain, Greece, the former Yugoslavia, and Turkey working in Germany.

Gebrauchslyrik   Functional lyric poetry. A name that can be applied to all topical poetry.

Gemütlichkeit   Coziness, warmth, and convivial atmosphere.

Gesamtkunstwerk   Total work of art, applied especially to Richard Wagner's music dramas in which the various arts (libretto, music, staging, choreography, etc.) are integrated in a whole.

Gestapo   Geheime Staatspolizei (Secret State Police). Name of Secret Police in the Third Reich.

Grundgesetz   Basic law. Name of the West German Constitution, from 1990 the all-German constitution.

Grundschule   The basic elementary school.

Gymnasium   Academic high school, the most challenging of the tracks. Ends with **Abitur.**

Hauptschule   The least demanding track of secondary education in Germany. Hauptschule ends after a total of nine years of formal education, when students are fifteen and sixteen years old.

"Heil Hitler"   Greeting, customary in NSDAP since 1925, introduced in 1933 in Germany as German greeting. Hitler was to be greeted with "Heil, mein Führer!"

HJ (Hitlerjugend) Official name of the youth organization during the Third Reich (1933–45). Existing since 1926, since 1933 official. Mandatory since 1940.

Hochdeutsch High German, standard German.

Imbiss or Imbissstube A snack or a snack stall.

Jugendstil Art noveau.

Jugendweihe Youth initiation. Established in the 1950s by the East German government, this coming of age ritual was meant to take the place of the Protestant confirmation and Catholic communion. Still popular in former East Germany.

Kabarett Show in which actors lampoon, with songs and political skits, politicians, and social problems.

Kaffee und Kuchen Coffee and cake. German tradition of having coffee and cake in the afternoon.

Karneval Pre-Lenten festivities, especially in Rhineland.

Kiosk A small stall where you can buy newspapers, cigarettes, snacks.

Kneipe A German pub.

Konditorei A pastry shop cum café.

Kristallnacht The night of the broken glass. Nationwide, state-organized pogrom against Jewish stores and synagogues on November 9, 1938; 7,500 Jewish stores and 171 synagogues were destroyed, 91 people were murdered, 26,000 were deported into concentration camps.

KZ Konzentrationslager (Concentration Camps). First meant for political opponents, the KZs were later used to incarcerate homosexuals, Jews, and gypsies.

Lederhosen Traditional leather trousers with attached suspenders. Bavaria only.

Leitmotif A recurring motif in literature (Thomas Mann) or music (Wagner).

Lied Song.

Neudeutsch Literally, New German, a term to describe the many changes currently taking place in the German language, especially the wide use of English.

Neue Sachlichkeit New Objectivity. Movement in literature and music between 1925 and 1933 emphasizing new sobriety.

NSDAP   Nationalsozialistische deutsche Arbeiterpartei (National Socialist German Workers' Party). Official name of the Nazi party between 1920 and 1945.

Ossis   Colloquial, slightly derogatory nickname for the East Germans since reunification. See also **Wessis.**

Ostalgie   A yearning for a return to the GDR era, derived from *Nostalgie*.

Ostpolitik   Policies initiated in the late 1960s and early 1970s by Willy Brandt to effect the reconciliation with the countries of Eastern Europe.

PDS   Partei des demokratischen Sozialismus (Party of the democratic Socialism). Successor party of the East German SED.

Plattenbau   Reinforced concrete slab building method favored by the East Germans.

Ratskeller   Town hall restaurant.

Realschule   Middle track of secondary education in Germany.

Regietheater   Director's theater. Refers to the increasing role of directors in producing plays and operas.

Reich   Empire.

Reichsparteitag   Annual party rally of the NSDAP held in Nuremberg from1927 until 1938.

SA   Sturmabteilung. Paramilitary troops during the Third Reich.

Schlager   A popular tune. Especially popular in the 1950s and 1960s.

SED   Sozialistische Einheitspartei Deutschlands (Socialist German Unity Party). Official name of the East German Communist Party.

Sekt   Sparkling wine.

SPD   Sozialdemokratische Partei Deutschlands (Social Democratic Party of Germany).

SS   Schutzstaffel. Organization within the Nazi Party that supplied Hitler's bodyguard as well as concentration camp guards and the Waffen-SS in WWII.

Stasi   Staatssicherheit (State Security). East German Secret Police.

Stehcafé   Stand-up café; a small café where you imbibe the coffee and eat your cake while standing. Less expensive than a real café.

Straussenwirtschaft   A seasonal wine pub indicated by a wreath (strauss) above the doorway.

Stunde Null   Zero Hour. End of the Second World War.

Sturm und Drang Storm and Stress. Refers to a period in German literature and philosophy between 1770 and 1785.

Vergangenheitsbewältigung Literally, dealing with the past. Refers to the attempt of Germans to come to terms with the Nazi past.

Vormärz Pre-March. The time between the Congress of Vienna in 1815 and the revolutions of (March) 1848.

Wanderlust The joy of hiking.

Wannsee-Konferenz Top secret conference held on January 20, 1942, in a villa on the Wannsee in Berlin in which the "final solution of the Jewish question" was decided.

Wende The turning point. Refers to the events in 1989–90 (revolution in East Germany and the reunification of Germany).

Werkbund Loose organization to promote closer cooperation between the arts and industry. Founded in 1907; dissolved during the Third Reich.

Wehrmacht Name of the German armed forces between 1935 and 1945.

Wessis Slightly derogatory term used by East Germans to describe the West Germans. Used after unification.

Wunderkind Child prodigy.

ZDF Zweites Deutsches Fernsehen. Second German Television. Second public television program in Germany.

Zollverein Customs Union of 1834, first step towards German unification.

Bibliography

Ackermann, Irmgard, ed. *Foreign View Points; Multicultural Literature in Germany.* Bonn: Inter Nationes, 1999.

Adam, Peter. *Art of the Third Reich.* New York: Harry N. Abrams, 1992.

Appignanesi, Lisa. *Cabaret: The First Hundred Years.* London: Methuen, 1984.

Ardagh, John. *Germany and the Germans.* 3rd ed. Harmondsworth, England: Penguin Books, 1999.

———. *Germany and the Germans. An Anatomy of Society Today.* New York: Harper & Row, 1987.

Balfour, Michael. *Withstanding Hitler in Germany, 1933–1945.* New York: Routledge, 1988.

Barlow, John D. *German Expressionist Film.* Boston: Twayne Publishers, 1982.

Barron, Stephanie, ed. *German Expressionism, 1915–1925: The Second Generation.* Munich: Prestel, 1988.

Bergfelder, Tim, Erica Carter, and Deniz Göktürk. *The German Cinema Book.* London: bfi Publishing, 2002.

Bigsby, C. W. E. *Dada and Surrealism.* London: Methuen, 1972.

Bridenthal, Renate, and Claudia Koonz. "Beyond *Kinder, Küche, Kirche:* Weimar Women in Politics and Work." In *Liberating Women's History. Theoretical and Critical Essays,* edited by Berenice A. Carroll, 301–329. Urbana: University of Illinois, 1976.

Briel, Holger. "Media of Mass Communication: The Press, Radio and Television." In *The Cambridge Companion to Modern German Culture,* edited by Eva Kolinsky and Wilfried van der Will, 322–37. Cambridge: Cambridge University Press, 1999.

———. "Mediascapes." In *Contemporary German Cultural Studies,* edited by Alison Phipps, 263–85. London: Arnold, 2002.

Burns, Rob, ed. *German Cultural Studies. An Introduction.* New York: Oxford University Press, 1995.

Childs, David, ed. *Honecker's Germany.* London: Allen and Unwin, 1985.

Cook, Susan C. *Opera for a New Republic. The Zeitopern of Krenek, Weill, and Hindemith.* Ann Arbor, Mich.: UMI Research Press, 1988.

Copsey, Dickon. "Scene Change: Pluralized Identities in Contemporary German Cinema." In *Contemporary German Cultural Studies,* edited by Alison Phipps, 241–62. London: Arnold, 2002.

Corrigan, Timothy, ed. *The Films of Werner Herzog. Between Mirage and History.* New York and London: Methuen, 1986.

Cowart, Jack. *Expressions. New Art from Germany. Georg Baselitz, Jörg Immendorff, Anselm Kiefer, Markus Lüperts, A. R. Penck.* Munich: Prestel, 1983.

Craig, Gordon A. *The Germans.* New York: Putnam Books, 1991.

———. *Germany, 1866–1945.* New York: Oxford University Press, 1978.

Cultural Life in the Federal Republic of Germany. A Survey. Bonn: Inter Nationes, 1981.

Davidson, J. "Overcoming Germany Past(s) in Films Since the 'Wende.'" *Seminar* 33, no. 4 (1997): 356–73.

Demetz, Peter. *After the Fires. Recent Writings in the Germanies, Austria, and Switzerland.* New York: Harcourt Brace Jovanovich, 1986.

———. *Postwar German Literature. A Critical Introduction.* New York: Western Publishing Company, 1970.

Dube, Wolf-Dieter. *Expressionism.* New York and Toronto: Oxford University Press, 1972.

Durrani, Osman. "Popular Music in the German-Speaking World." In *Contemporary German Cultural Studies,* edited by Alison Phipps, 197–218. London: Arnold, 2002.

Eckardt, Wolf von, and Sander L. Gilman. *Bertolt Brecht's Berlin. A Scrapbook of the Twenties.* Garden City, N.J.: Anchor Press; New York: Doubleday, 1974.

Eisner, Lotte. *The Haunted Screen: Expressionism in the German Cinema and the Influence of Max Reinhardt.* Berkeley: University of California Press, 1973.

Elger, Dietmar. *Expressionism. A Revolution in German Art.* Translated by Hugh Beyer. Cologne: Taschen, 1994.

Elsaesser, Thomas. *New German Cinema: A History.* Piscataway, N.J.: Rutgers University Press, 1989.

Eyewitness Travel Guides. Germany. London: Dorling Kindersley, 2001.

The Federal Government of Germany. *Facts about Germany.* Frankfurt am Main: Societäts-Verlag, 2000.

Feldmeyer, Gerhard G. *New German Architecture.* New York: Rizzoli, 1993.

Fest, Joachim. *Hitler.* Translated by Richard Winston and Clara Winston. New York: Harcourt Brace Jovanovich, 1974.

———. *Plotting Hitler's Death. The Story of the German Resistance.* Translated by Bruce Little. New York: Henry Holt & Co., 1996.

Fischer, Robert, and Joe Hembus. *Der Neue Deutsche Film, 1960–1980.* Munich: Goldmann, 1981.

Fitch, James Marston. *Walter Gropius.* New York: George Braziller, 1960.

Flippo, Hyde. *The German Way. Aspects of Behaviour, Attitudes and Customs in the German-Speaking World.* Lincolnwood, Ill.: Passport Books, 1997.

————. *When in Germany, Do as the Germans Do.* Chicago: McGraw Hill, 2002.

Franklin, James. *New German Cinema: From Oberhausen to Hamburg.* Boston: Twayne Publishers, 1983.

Frevert, Ute. *Women in German History. From Bourgeois Emancipation to Sexual Liberation.* Translated by Stuart McKinnon-Evans. Washington, D.C.: Berg, 1990.

Fulbrook, Mary. *A Concise History of Germany.* Cambridge and New York: Cambridge University Press, 1990.

————. *The Divided Nation. A History of Germany, 1918–1990.* New York: Oxford University Press, 1992.

Garland, H. B. *A Concise Survey of German Literature.* Coral Gables, Florida: University of Miami Press, 1971.

Garland, Henry, and Mary Garland. *The Oxford Companion to German Literature.* New York: Oxford University Press, 1986.

Gay, Ruth. *Safe among the Germans. Liberated Jews After World War II.* New Haven: Yale University Press, 2002.

Goldberg, Andreas. "Islam in Germany." In *Islam, Europe's Second Religion,* edited by Shireen Hunter, 29–50. Westport, Conn., and London: Praeger, 2002.

Grant, Sue. "A History of Advent Calendars." *German Life* (December 2001/January 2002): 29–30.

Gros, Jürgen, and Manuela Glaab. *Faktenlexikon Deutschland. Geschichte, Gesellschaft, Politik, Wirtschaft, Kultur.* Munich: Heyne, 1999.

Hallek, Georg. *Presse, Hörfunk und Fernsehen in der Bundesrepublik Deutschland.* Bonn: Inter Nationes, 1999.

Helmer, Stephen D. *Hitler's Berlin: The Speer Plans for Reshaping the Central City.* Ann Arbor, Mich.: UMI Research Press, 1985.

Hinz, Berthold. *Art in the Third Reich.* Translated by Robert Kimber and Rita Kimber. New York: Pantheon Books, 1979.

Hinze, Klaus Michael. *New Developments in Contemporary Music.* Basel: Harwood, 1995.

Hochman, Elaine S. *Architects of Fortune: Mies van der Rohe and the Third Reich.* New York: Weidenfeld and Nicolson, 1989.

Hoffmeister, Gerhart, and Frederic C. Tubach. *Germany: 2000 Years. From the Nazi Era to German Unification.* Vol. 3. New York: Continuum, 1992.

Horak, Jan-Christopher. "German Film Comedy." In *The German Cinema Book,* edited by Tim Bergfelder, Erica Carter, and Deniz Göktürk, 29–38. London: bfi Publishing, 2002.

Hudgins, Sharon. "Our Daily Bread." *German Life* (February/March 2003): 33.

Humphreys, J. P. *Media and Media Policy in Germany: The Press and Broadcasting since 1945.* Oxford: Berg, 1994.

Hunter, Shireen, ed. *Islam, Europe's Second Religion.* Westport, Conn., and London: Praeger, 2002.

Jacobsen, Wolfgang, Anton Kaes, and Hans Helmut Prinzler, eds. *Geschichte des deutschen Films*. Stuttgart: Metzler, 1993.

Jensen, Lamar. *Reformation Europe. Age of Reform and Revolution*. Lexington, Mass.: D.C. Heath & Co., 1992.

Joachimides, Christo M., Norman Rosenthal, and Wieland Schmied. *German Art in the Twentieth Century: Painting and Sculpture, 1905–1985*. Munich: Prestel, 1985.

Kaes, Anton. *From Hitler to Heimat: The Return of History as Film*. Cambridge, Mass.: Harvard University Press, 1989.

Kaufmann, Uri. *Jewish Life in Germany Today*. Bonn: Inter Nationes, 1994.

Kettenacker, Lothar. *Germany since 1945*. Oxford and New York: Oxford University Press, 1997.

Klotz, Heinrich, and Waltraud Krase. *New Museum Buildings in the Federal Republic of Germany. Neue Museumsbauten in der Bundesrepublik Deutschland*. English and German. New York: Rizzoli, 1985.

Kolinsky, Eva, and Wilfried van der Will, eds. *The Cambridge Companion to Modern German Culture*. Cambridge: Cambridge University Press, 1998.

Konold, Wulf. *German Opera—Then and Now. Reflections and Investigations on the History and Present State of the German Musical Theater*. Kassel, Basel, and London: Bärenreiter, 1980.

Kramer, Dieter. *German Holidays and Folk Customs*. Berlin: Atlantik-Brücke Publications, 1987.

Krens, Thomas, Michael Govan, and Joseph Thompson. *Refigured Painting. The German Image, 1960–1988*. Munich: Prestel, 1989.

Kulturelles Leben in der Bundesrepublik Deutschland. Bonn: Inter Nationes, 1992.

Lang, Paul Henry. *Music in Western Civilization*. New York: W. W. Norton & Co., 1997.

Larkin, Leah. "Brot from the Backhaus." *German Life* (February/March 2003): 29–32.

Levi, Erik. "Music." In *The Cambridge Companion to Modern German Culture*, edited by Eva Kolinsky and Wilfred van der Will. Cambridge: Cambridge University Press, 1998.

Levi, Erik. *Music in the Third Reich*. Basingstoke, England: Macmillan, 1994.

Lewis, Derek. *Contemporary Germany: A Handbook*. London: Arnold; New York: Oxford, 2001.

Lewis, Derek, and John R. P. McKenzie, eds. *The New Germany. Social, Political and Cultural Challenges of Unification*. Exeter: Exeter University Press, 1995.

Lord, Richard. *Culture Shock. A Guide to Customs and Etiquette. Germany*. Portland, Ore.: Graphic Arts, 1999.

Macdonald, Sharon. "Museums and Identities: Materializing German Culture." In *Contemporary German Cultural Studies*, edited by Alison Phipps, 117–31. London: Arnold, 2002.

Manvell, Roger, and Heinrich Fraenkel. *The German Cinema*. New York and Washington, D.C.: Praeger Publishers, 1971.

Markovits, Andrei, Beth Simone Noveck, and Carolyn Höfig. "Jews in German Society." In *The Cambrige Companion to Modern German Culture,* edited by Eva Kolinsky and Wilfried van der Will, 86–109. Cambridge: Cambridge University Press, 1998.

Marsh, David. *The Germans. A People at the Crossroads.* New York: St. Martin's Press, 1989.

Metzger, Christine, ed. *Culinaria Germany.* Cologne: Könemann, 2000.

Nachama, Andreas, et al., eds. *Jews in Berlin.* Translated by Michael S. Cullen and Allison Brown. Berlin: Henschel, 2002.

Nees, Greg. *Germany: Unraveling an Enigma.* Yarmouth, Maine: Intercultural Press, 2001.

Nerdinger, Winfried, and Cornelius Tafel. *Architectural Guide to Germany: Twentieth Century.* Basel: Birkhäuser, 1996.

Orth, Martin. "German-Language Broadcasters Abroad." *Deutschland* 3 (June/July 2002): 18–21.

Patterson, Michael. *The First German Theatre. Schiller, Goethe, Kleist and Büchner in Performance.* London and New York: Routledge, 1990.

———. *German Theatre Today. Postwar Theatre in West and East Germany.* London: Pitman, 1976.

———. "The German Theatre." In *The New Germany. Social, Political and Cultural Challenges of Unification,* edited by Derek Lewis and John R. P. McKenzie. Excter: Exeter University Press, 1995.

———. *The Revolution in German Theatre, 1900–1933.* Boston: Routledge and Kegan Paul, 1981.

Patterson, Michael, and Michael Huxley. "German Drama, Theatre and Dance." In *The Cambridge Companion to Modern German Culture,* edited by Eva Kolinsky and Wilfried van der Will, 213–232. Cambridge: Cambridge University Press, 1998.

Pehnt, Wolfgang. *Expressionist Architecture.* London: Thames and Hudson, 1973.

———. *German Architecture, 1960–1970.* New York: Praeger Publishers, 1970.

Pflaum, Hans Günther, and Hans Helmut Prinzler. *Cinema in the Federal Republic of Germany.* Bonn: Inter Nationes, 1993.

Phipps, Alison, ed. *Contemporary German Cultural Studies.* New York: Oxford University Press, 2002.

Pond, Elizabeth. *Beyond the Wall. Germany's Road to Unification.* Washington, D.C.: The Brookings Institute, 1992.

Pye, Gillian. "Constructing Germany: Architecture and Cultural Identity." In *Contemporary German Cultural Studies,* edited by Alison Phipps, 82–101. London: Arnold, 2002.

Rabinbach, Anson, and Jack Zipes, eds. *Germans and Jews Since the Holocaust.* New York: Holms & Meier, 1986.

Rentschler, Eric. *The Ministry of Illusion: Nazi Cinema and Its Afterlife.* Cambridge, Mass.: Harvard University Press, 1996.

———. *West German Film in the Course of Time.* Bedford Hills, N.Y.: Redgrave Publishing Co., 1984.

Rias-Bucher, Barbara. *Feste und Bräuche. Eine Einladung zum Feiern.* Munich: Deutscher Taschenbuch Verlag, 1999.

Richter, Hans. *Dada. Art and Anti-Art.* London: Thames and Hudson, 1966.

Richter, Simon. "Food and Drink: Hegelian Encounters with the Culinary Other." In *Contemporary German Cultural Studies,* edited by Alison Phipps, 179–91. London: Arnold, 2002.

Rogoff, Irit. "Modern German Art." In *The Cambridge Companion to Modern German Culture,* edited by Eva Kolinsky and Wilfried van der Will. Cambridge: Cambridge University Press, 1998.

Roh, Franz. *German Painting in the Twentieth Century.* Greenwich, Conn.: New York Graphic Society, 1968.

Rubinson, Vicki. "Profil/Profile: Claudia Schiffer." *German Life* (February/March 2003): 12–13.

Ruland, Josef. *Weihnachten in Deutschland.* Bonn: Hohwacht, 1978.

Sanford, John. *The New German Cinema.* London: Oswald Wolff, 1980.

Sasse-Schulte, Linda. *Entertaining the Third Reich: Illusions of Wholeness in Nazi Cinema.* Durham,N.C.: Duke University Press, 1996.

Sax, Benjamin C., and Dieter Kuntz. *Inside Hitler's Germany. A Documentary History of Life in the Third Reich.* Lexington, Mass., and Toronto: D.C. Heath, 1992.

Schiff, Gert. "An Epoch of Longing: An Introduction to German Painting of the Nineteenth Century." In *German Masters of the Nineteenth Century,* edited by John P. O'Neill, 9–39. New York: Harry N. Abrams, 1981.

Schmied, Wieland. "Points of Departure and Transformations in German Art, 1905–1985." In *German Art in the Twentieth Century: Painting and Sculpture, 1905–1985,* edited by Christo M. Joachimides, Norman Rosenthal, and Wieland Schmied. 21–74. Munich: Prestel, 1985.

Schulte-Peevers, Andrea, et al. *Lonely Planet. Germany.* Oakland: Lonely Planet Publications, 2002.

Schulze, Hagen. *Germany. A New History.* Translated by Deborah Lucas Schneider. Cambridge: Harvard University Press, 1998.

Schulze-Reimpell, Werner. *Development and Structure of Theatre in Germany.* Bonn: Inter Nationes, 1992.

Sebald, W.G., ed. *A Radical Stage: Theatre in Germany in the 1970s and 1980s.* Oxford: Berg, 1988.

Selz, Peter. *German Expressionist Painting.* Berkeley: University of California Press, 1957.

Sheraton, Mimi. *The German Cookbook. A Complete Guide to Mastering Authentic German Cooking.* New York: Random House, 1968.

Smith, Gregg. *The Beer Enthusiast's Guide.* Pownal, Vt.: Storey Publications, Inc., 1994.

Solsten, Eric, ed. *Germany. A Country Guide.* Washington, D.C.: Library of Congress, 1996.

Spaeth, David. *Mies van der Rohe.* New York: Rizzoli, 1985.

Stern, Susan. *Jews in Germany, 2001.* Bonn: Inter Nationes, 2001 .

————. *These Strange German Ways and the Whys of the Ways. A Cultural Guide to the Germans and Their Customs.* Berlin: Atlantik-Brücke e.V., 2000.

————, ed. *Meet United Germany. Perspectives.* Frankfurt am Maim: Frankfurter Allgemeine Zeitung, 1991.

Stödter, Helga. "Women—Where Are They?" In *Meet United Germany. Perspectives,* edited by Susan Stern, 219–228. Frankfurt am Maim: Frankfurter Allgemeine Zeitung, 1991.

Stoehr, Ingo R. *German Literature of the Twentieth Century. From Aestheticism to Postmodernism.* Vol. 10, *Camden House History of German Literature.* Rochester and New York: Camden House, 2001.

Taylor, Robert R. *The Word in Stone. The Role of Architecture in the National Socialist Ideology.* Berkeley: University of California Press, 1974.

Thorlby, Anthony, ed. *The Penguin Companion to Literature. European Literature.* London: Penguin Books, 1969.

Turner, Henry Ashby, Jr. *Germany from Partition to Reunification.* Rev. ed. of *The Two Germanies since 1945.* New Haven, London: Yale University Press, 1992.

Von Eckhardt, Wolf. *Eric Mendelsohn.* New York: George Braziller, 1960.

Von Rauch, Yamin, and Jochen Visscher, eds. *Der Potsdamer Platz: urbane Architektur für das neue Berlin. Urban Architecture for a New Berlin.* Berlin: Jovis, 2000.

Watanabe-O'Kelly, Helen, ed. *The Cambridge History of German Literature.* Cambridge: Cambridge University Press, 1997.

Watson, Alan. *The Germans. Who Are They Now?* Chicago: cdition q, 1992.

Watson, Wallace Steadman. *Understanding Rainer Werner Fassbinder.* Columbia: University of South Carolina Press, 1996.

Welch, David. *The Third Reich: Politics and Propaganda.* London: Routledge, 1993.

Whitford, Frank. *Bauhaus.* London: Thames and Hudson, 1984.

Whyte, Iain Boyd. "Modern German Architecture." In *The Cambridge Companion to Modern German Culture,* edited by Eva Kolinsky and Wilfried van der Will. Cambridge: Cambridge University Press, 1998.

Wiessmann, Hans. *From Horror to Hope. Germany, the Jews and Israel.* New York: German Information Center, n.d.

Willett, John. *The Theatre of the Weimar Republic.* New York: Holmes and Meier, 1988.

Zevi, Bruno. *Erich Mendelsohn.* New York: Rizzoli, 1985.

WEB RESOURCES

Arte. Http://www.arte-tv.com.

Bunche Verlagsgesellichaft mbh. Http://www.schlemmer-atlas.de.

Bundesrepublik Deutschland. Http://www.kulturportal-deutschland.de.

Catholic Church. Http://dbk.de.

Deutsche Welle. Http://www.dw-world.de.

Deutsche Zeintrale für Tourismus. Http://www.deutschland-tourismus.de.

Die Prinzen. Http://www.dieprinzen.de.

Facets Video, email: sales@facets.org.

German Cinema Inc. Http://www.german-cinema.de.

German Historical Museum in Berlin. Http://www.dhm.de/lemo.

German Information Center, Washington, D.C. Http://www.germany-info.org.

German Language Video Center. Http://www.germanvideo.com.

German Wine Information Bureay, N.Y. Http://www.Germanwineusa.org (in English).

Goethe Institute. Http://www.goethe.de/gr/dub/project/deipess0.htm.

Groenemeyer, Herbert. Http://www.groenemeyer.de.

Hagalil onLine. Http://www.hagalil.com/brd/berlin/jewish.htm (in English and German).

Hagalil onLine. Http://www.hagalil.com/juedisches-museum (in English and German).

Icestorm International, Inc. Http://www.icestorm-video.com.

Institute for German History at Tel Aviv University. Http://www.tau.ac.il/German History/links.html.

International Historic Films. Http://ihffilm.com.

itm Ideas to Market Gmbh. Http://www.theater.de (in German).

Kraftwerk. Http://www.kraftwerk.com.

Kühn, Mario. Http://www.nena.de.

Laut AG. Http://www.laut.de.

Möhlmann, Ole. Http://www.fashion-base.de.

Pahlke-Grygier, Sabine. "Mode in Deutschland-Zwischen Avantgarde und Konfektion."Goethe Institute. Http://www.goethe.de/kug/kue/des/ein/de22412_pr.htm.

Protestant Church. Http://ekd.de.

Rink, Steffen. "Under the banner of dialogue and transparency: Mosques in Germany." Goethe Institute. Http://www.goethe.de/kug/ges/pur/thm/en30158.htm.

Sokolsky, Harold. Http://www.operaphile.com.

SPIEGEL OnLine. Http://www.spiegel.de.

Stadt Nürnberg and Nordbayern Infonet. Http://www.christkindlesmarkt.de.

Tanztheater Wuppertal Pina Bausch. Http://www.pina-bausch.de.

Theaterparadies Deutschland. Http://www.theaterparadies-deutschland.de.Kate Heyhoe. Http://www.globalgourmet.com/destinations.

Universität Leipzig. Http://www.uni-leipzig.de/~religion/remid.htm.

Wilhelm Hermann. Http://www.silvestergruesse.de.

Zeitbild Verlag. Http://www.zeitbild.de/germany.

Index

About the Author

ECKHARD BERNSTEIN is Professor of German and Coordinator of the German Program at the College of the Holy Cross, Worcester, Massachusetts.